CHAPLIN AND AGEE

CHAPLIN AND AGEE

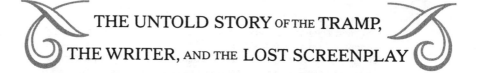

THE UNTOLD STORY OF THE TRAMP, THE WRITER, AND THE LOST SCREENPLAY

JOHN WRANOVICS

First published 2005 by
PALGRAVE MACMILLAN™
175 Fifth Avenue, New York, N.Y. 10010 and
Houndmills, Basingstoke, Hampshire, England RG21 6XS.
Companies and representatives throughout the world.

PALGRAVE MACMILLAN is the global academic imprint of the Palgrave
Macmillan division of St. Martin's Press, LLC and of Palgrave Macmillan Ltd.
Macmillan® is a registered trademark in the United States, United Kingdom
and other countries. Palgrave is a registered trademark in the European Union
and other countries.

ISBN 1-4039-6866-7 hardback

Library of Congress Cataloging-in-Publication Data
Wranovics, John.
　　Chaplin and Agee the untold sotry of the tramp, the writer, and the lost
screenplay / John Wranovics.
　　　　p.　　cm.
Includes bibliographical references and index.
ISBN 1-4039-6866-7 (alk. Paper)
　　1. Agee, James, 1909–1955—Motion picture plays.　2. Authors,
American—20th century—Biography.　3. Motion picture authorship—United
States.　4. Chaplin, Charlie, 1889–1977.　I. Title.
PS3501.G35Z95　2005
818'.5209—dc22
[B]
　　　　　　　　　　　　　　　　　　　　　　　　　　　　　2004062807

A catalogue record for this book is available from the British Library.

Design by Letra Libre, Inc.

First edition: May 2005
10　9　8　7　6　5　4　3　2　1
Printed in the United States of America

FOR
CHRISTINE, JACK,
AND MATTHEW

$\mathcal{P}$ERMISSION $\mathcal{A}$CKNOWLEDGMENTS

$\mathscr{A}$CKNOWLEDGMENTS

This book is the direct result of the generosity, patience, and kindness of many people. I wish first to thank Paul Sprecher and Deedee Agee for the gift of their support and encouragement. It would not be possible to exaggerate the contribution of Kate Guyonvarch at the Association Chaplin, who at my request searched for and found the lost manuscript for *The Tramp's New World* and in the process also found previously unknown correspondence between Agee and Chaplin. Much appreciation to everybody at Palgrave Macmillan, including Gabriella Pearce, Lynn Vande Stouwe, and Amanda Fernández. Thanks also to Sydney Chaplin, Josephine Chaplin, Dr. Robert Coles, Hugh Davis, Mary Evans, Manny Farber, Laurence Homolka, Vincent Homolka, Mayor Bill Levitt, Helen Levitt, Norman Lloyd, Janice Loeb, Michael Lofaro, Pancho Kohner, Charles Maland, Judith Malina, Patricia Patterson, Lillian Ross, William Schallert, Marje Scheutze-Coburn, Kevin Smith, Ross Spears, Curtice Taylor, Theoharis C. Theoharis, Peter Viertel, and Michael Wreszin, each of whom, through their help and encouragement made the research and writing of this book one of the pleasures of my life.

$\mathcal{C}$ONTENTS

PART ONE

The Legend of James Agee

*I*n 1962 the critic Dwight MacDonald, writing in the British magazine *Encounter*, contemplated the star-like popularity his friend the writer James Agee had recently begun to attract, seven years after his death from a heart attack at the age of forty-five: "In some literary circles, James Agee has come to excite the kind of emotion James Dean did in some non-literary circles. There is an Agee Cult that has come into existence partly because of the power of his writing and his lack of recognition while he was alive, but chiefly because it is felt that Agee's life and personality, like Dean's, are at once an expression of our time and a protest against it."[1]

Helping to fuel the Agee cult was the increasing availability of Agee's writing, beginning with the posthumously published novel *A Death in the Family*. A year after its publication in 1957, this novel garnered wide attention by winning the Pulitzer Prize for Fiction, the first awarded to a deceased author. That same year also saw the publication of *Agee on Film*, a collection of Agee's influential film criticism and essays written for the *Nation*, *Time*, and *Life*. Its sequel, *Agee on Film, Volume II*, which followed two years later, collected examples of his screen-writing, including scripts for *The African Queen*, *The Bride Comes to Yellow Sky*, and *The Night of the Hunter* as well as several unproduced projects. But perhaps most importantly, in 1960, Agee's *Let Us Now Praise Famous Men*, was re-issued for the first time since its original publication nineteen years before. Considered

Agee's masterpiece by many, the book, a collaboration with the photographer Walker Evans, is a nonfictional, poetically intense exploration of the lives of dirt-poor tenant farmers in Alabama during the height of the Great Depression.

A financial disaster when it was first published, *Let Us Now Praise Famous Men* found a receptive new audience in the early days of the civil rights movement. Robert Coles recalled the power that the book held then: "*Let Us Now Praise Famous Men* was reissued in 1960, a generation's time after its first publication in 1941 . . . I remember not only buying *Let Us Now Praise Famous Men* at that time but seeing many others do so. I remember finding copies of the book, in hard cover no less, all over the South . . . read by white, well-to-do students from Ivy League colleges but read as well by black students from the North and from the South—it was a bible of sorts, at least for a while, a sign, a symbol, a reminder, an eloquent testimony that others had cared, had gone forth to look and hear, and had come back to stand up and address their friends and neighbors and those beyond personal knowing."[2]

For a time, Agee embodied—in truth defined—the hard-drinking, Greenwich Village bohemian poet. Winthrop Sargeant, *Time*'s music critic and Agee's friend, remembered him as "a sort of hippie a generation prior to the hippie era. . . . He used to save up his paychecks without cashing them. He disliked the idea of income tax, and was often behind in his payments. On the other hand, Agee had an almost Christlike sympathy for all people. He could talk to a ditch digger with the same open, innocent camaraderie that he maintained with his fellow writers."[3] Sargeant also had a close-up view of Agee's self-mortifying work habits: "For several years Agee occupied the office next to mine. On one side of his desk stood a bottle of whiskey; on the other a bottle of Benzedrine tablets (then a newly discovered stimulant). He would tank up on whiskey while he was writing until the point was reached where he could no longer concentrate. Then he would take Benzedrine to sober up, reach the point of concentration again, and remain there until he felt he needed more whiskey—and so on back and forth."[4] In 1942 Agee somewhat corroborated this anecdote when he sketched himself in a satiric self-portrait, "He breakfasts on the better-publicized dry cereals, dusted with benzedrine sulphate."[5] It's certainly likely that, though impossible to know to what extent, the recreational use of stimulants combined with his heavy drinking and cigarette smoking exacerbated Agee's chronic insomnia and contributed to the weakening of his heart.

After his death, *Life* magazine published a series of photographs of Agee's hometown, Knoxville, Tennessee, made to accompany excerpted text from *A Death in the Family*. Along with this tribute, the issue featured a portrait of Agee's tenure at *Time*, in which the writer Richard Oulahan compared Agee's office to the headline-grabbing, trash-filled home of the reclusive Collyer brothers. He described Agee's office as "cluttered with old playbills, newspaper clippings, magazines, handouts, scraps of paper. The mass flowed across the desk, drifted onto the floor and piled in the corners up to the height of a man's shoulders . . . among the flotsam were many uncashed checks and other valuable papers. . . . The messy office was typical of Agee, a big, untidy man who frequently looked like a tramp and who cared not a bit for material things."[6] But Oulahan recognized that Agee's lack of concern with external appearances was irrelevant to his deeper values: "[S]ome of his critics have said that he was a poseur who delighted in the role of the careless poet rejecting all things material and inconsequential. This was not true. Agee was extremely fastidious about many things—about people, about humanity, about music, movies and, above all about writing."

Few who knew Agee wrote about him without commenting on his unique physical presence. In the years after his death, many of Agee's friends and colleagues, veteran observers of humanity trained as journalists, photographers, poets, painters, and filmmakers, attempted to capture his unique persona in prose. His way of talking with his hands was particularly impressive. Oulahan recalled that at *Time*, "Some imitated his mannerisms—the stern-wheel gestures he used with his hands when talking. . . ." The photographer Walker Evans wrote, "[Agee's] gestures were one of the memorable things about him. He seemed to model, fight and stroke his phrases as he talked."[7]

Almost fifty years after Agee's death, the painter and film critic Manny Farber, while being honored at the 2003 San Francisco Film Festival, related how Agee "did a funny thing with his hands when he was talking. He would get his hands up to his lips and lean toward you." Farber recollected how Agee's memorable gestures attended their frequent conversations about movies: "He would do strange things with his fingers like he was directing the movie. It was a beautiful thing to watch."[8]

Robert Fitzgerald, the poet and renowned translator of Homer, wrote a moving portrait of Agee. The two men had been close friends while students at Harvard and later as colleagues at *Time*. Fitzgerald attempted to capture the memorable sight of Agee's hands in mid-conversation: "The hands and fingers long and light and blunt and expressive, shaping his thought in the air, conveying stresses direct or splay, drawing razor-edged lines with thumb and forefinger: termini, perspectives, tones."[9] Movie director John Huston, in his portrait of Agee, remembered the writer's "slab-like hands" and, during conversation, his fingers "working as if they were trying to untie a knot."[10]

For many who knew him, the memory of Agee's physical appearance is nearly inseparable from his deep-welled eloquence and literary talent. In one humorous essay, Agee sketched a self-portrait: "Mr. Agee is tall, faintly rustic in appearance, with slightly walled eyes. He is gentle when not aroused, and always kind to animals. Thanks to an inexcusable bit of carelessness he has lost several teeth, but still retains a legal sufficiency to bite the God of War, should their paths cross."[11] Robert Fitzgerald, wrote, "Of the physical make and being of James Agee and his aspect at that time, you must imagine: a tall frame, long-boned but not massive; lean flesh, muscular with some awkwardness; pelt on his chest; a long stride with loose knee-joints, head up, with toes angled a bit outward. A complexion rather dark or sallow in pigment, easily tanned. The head rough-hewn, with a rugged brow and cheekbones, a strong nose irregular in profile, a large mouth firmly closing in folds, working a little around the gaps of lost teeth. The shape of the face tapered to a sensitive chin, cleft. Hair thick and very dark, a shock uncared for, and best uncared for. Eyes deep-set and rather closely set, a dull-gray-blue or feral blue gray or radiantly lit with amusement. Strong stained teeth. On the right middle finger a callous as big as a boil: one of his stigmata as a writer."[12]

To John Huston's eye, Agee had a "mountaineer's body," "neither muscular nor fat," with a "mouth from which a number of teeth were missing. I remember that every time he laughed he would put his hand up furtively to cover his mouth."[13] Walker Evans saw an awkward strength in the writer, "Physically, Agee was quite powerful, in the deceptive way of uninsistent large men. In movement, he was rather graceless."[14]

Agee famously clothed his memorable frame with careless disregard. He was notorious for his appearance, or rather his complete indifference to it. Although his hero, the great film comedian Charles Chaplin, took on the raiments of a tramp in performance, in private life the comedian was fastidious and well tailored. Agee, on the other hand, was completely uninterested in how he looked, and on several occasions his mode of dress created friction with fellow workers. Fitzgerald remembered, "He wore blue or khaki work shirts and under the armpits there would be stains, salt-edged, from sweat." Huston observed, "[Agee's] clothes were dark and shiny. I can't imagine him in a new suit. Black shoes scuffed grey, wrinkled collar, a button off his shirt and a raveled tie—he wore clothes to be warm and decent."[15] It struck Walker Evans that Agee "got more delight out of factory-seconds sweaters and a sleazy cap than a straight dandy does from waxed calf Peal shoes and a brushed Lock & Co. bowler."[16]

Like a spy among strangers, Agee was an outsider almost everywhere he went. In elementary school his erudition and seriousness earned him the nickname "Socrates." His southern background, discernible from his accent and his gentle manners, set him apart at Phillips Exeter, at Harvard, and in New York. His passions embraced a hybrid of cultures and empathies. As fixated by Beethoven as he was by Louis Armstrong's jazz and by Mitchell's Christian Singers gospel music, Agee's sensibilities ranged from popular culture to classical. And while he could readily affect through mimicry his familiarity with rural southern speech and manners, his upbringing had been cultivated and upper-middle class. Father James Harold Flye, an Episcopalian priest, had been a friend and mentor of Agee since his days at St. Andrews, a school for boys near Sewanee, Tennessee, where Flye taught. Flye and Agee maintained a lifelong correspondence. While Flye is reputed to have destroyed many of Agee's most personal letters, the surviving letters were published in 1962 as *Letters of James Agee to Father Flye*. Flye was protective of Agee's legacy. On January 7, 1965, the *Village Voice* published a bristling letter from Father Flye in which he took issue with a writer's attribution of a "hillbilly" background to Agee. Flye complained that, in addition to being derogatory, the term also belied the true character of Agee's ancestry. He noted that Agee's mother's parents were "both university graduates, intellectual, well-read, with interests and good tastes in literature and music." What's more, Flye argued, although Agee's father's family hailed from the countryside and small towns they were "not yokels." As evidence, Flye wrote, "James Agee's father was a great reader, with

eagerness for knowledge, who had taught school and then held positions in the Postal Service in Knoxville and in Panama. A brother of
his was a lawyer. Their father (James Agee's grandfather) was a doctor,
a man held in high regard."[17]

Agee's early death in 1955 was interpreted by many of his admirers as a parable of talent unfulfilled. In the popular view he personified
the artist of great potential squandered, a poet ruined by pitiless days
churning out prose for the masses at *Fortune*, *Time*, and *Life*, the three
pillars of Henry Luce's temple of popular journalism. A price was
paid, too, it was perceived, for endless nights and sleepless hours of
bar talk and whiskey poetry inevitably bleeding into morning light,
with finely wrought words squandered in the smoky air.

Little understood in the Agee legend is how much important writing he had actually produced in his short time. Helping to obscure the
scope of Agee's accomplishment is the sheer breadth of his efforts.
Agee was a truly modern artist: He explored and made enduring contributions to almost every significant literary form available to a writer
in the first half of the twentieth century. He wrote poetry, a novel, a
novella, experimental journalism, essays for *Fortune*, *Time*, the *Nation*
and *Life*, and numerous small press publications. He wrote screenplays for film and for television. He was hired by Leonard Bernstein
to try his hand at a libretto for *Candide*. During his life and after, his
lyrical prose and poetry were adapted and set to music by some of the
era's most important American composers: David Diamond put Agee's
poetry to music and Samuel Barber turned his prose poem "Knoxville:
Summer 1915" into an oratorio. The latter compelled Aaron Copland
to tell Barber that he regretted not having discovered the Agee text
first. Copland found his own inspiration in *Let Us Now Praise Famous
Men*, which served as the starting point for his first opera, *This Tender
Land*.[18]

In the field of film criticism, Agee represents a milestone. Agee,
along with his peers Robert Warshow and Manny Farber, brought
film criticism to a new level of intellectual discourse that enlarged the
public's conception and expectation of what film could and should
strive to be. His writing provided a model for successive generations
of film reviewers, from Pauline Kael forward, who never shirked
from acknowledging their debt. For Kael, "There were movie critics
that I liked a lot—James Agee more than anyone else . . . I disagreed
with him a lot, but I loved the passion of his language."[19] Richard

Schickel, in his recent memoir, recalled how as a boy, when reading *Time*, he would first turn to Agee's unsigned reviews in the Cinema section, and through the writings of his "sainted predecessor" discovered the love for criticism that inspired his own career.[20] David Thomson, in his 700-word essay on Agee in his indispensable *New Biographical Dictionary of Film*, quibbles with Agee's opinion that "Chaplin and Huston were without equal in America," but observes that Agee "wrote like someone who had not just viewed the movie but been in it—out with it, as if it were a girl; drinking with it; driving in the night with it. That direct physical response was new, it was done with terrific dash and insight."[21] For armies of film scholars, amateur and salaried, a full assessment of a film is not complete until Agee's opinion has been consulted.

In 1952, Agee was prodded by his agent Ilse Lahn to write a brief autobiography to help publicize Huntington Hartford's film of Stephen Crane's *The Bride Comes to Yellow Sky*, for which Agee had written the screenplay. Agee replied with a brusque summary of his career:

Born Knoxville, Tenn., November 27, 1909. Public & private schools in Tennessee; Exeter; Harvard (1932). Staff writer for *Fortune*, 1932–35, and later free-lance contributor. Staff writer for *Time*, 1939–48; movie editor there roughly 6 years. Movie review column for *Nation*, 1943–48.

Have published a book of verse (*Permit Me Voyage*, Yale Press, 1934); a book of anti-sociology about cotton tenant farmers (*Let Us Now Praise Famous Men*; with Walker Evans photographs; Houghton Mifflin, 1941); and a short book of fiction (*The Morning Watch*; Houghton Mifflin, 1951). Also short stories, articles, verse, in *Life, Partisan Review, Botteghe Oscure, Harper's Bazaar, Politics*, etc.

First excited by moving pictures at age of four, by gyrations of Charlie Chaplin on steps of a public building. Interest soon intensified by moment when Annette Kellerman changed from mermaid to fully qualified human being. Interest made rabid by failure to steal admission fee to Von Stroheim's *Foolish Wives*, which was under parental ban. Interest has remained pretty steady ever since. For many years wrote, rather than did movie work (or even tried to get it), governed by reflection that pencil and paper cost less than a feature-length motion picture, with corresponding increase in independence in execution. So far, however, have mainly enjoyed interdependence of movie work. Wrote commentary and dialogue for *The Quiet One* (nominated for documentary Academy Award 1948); screenplay for *African Queen*, with John Huston (nominated for Academy Award for screenplay 1951); *The Bride Comes to Yellow Sky*; commentary and dialogue paraphrase for the Filipino film *Genghis Khan* [*sic*] (not yet released); screenplay for Stephen Crane's *The Blue Hotel* (not yet produced). Am at present writing television plays about Abraham Lincoln for the Ford Foundation.

Politics: independent. Special interests: playing slow movements on piano; researcher, since a normally early age, in the psychology (and allied fields) of sex. Vital statistics: married; three children; upper dentures.[22]

This account provides perspective on the wide range of Agee's literary efforts; even better, it pinpoints the origin of his lifelong interest in Charles Chaplin. Today, Agee is much beloved by those who have come to know him through his writing, but few are aware of the extent to which he found his inspiration, throughout his entire life, in the art of the great film comedian. It is no exaggeration to say that Agee idolized Chaplin. Agee wrote continually, both for publication and in his personal notes and letters, about how Chaplin's Little Tramp character stood for him as a modern, secular Jesus figure.

During the 1940s and '50s, Chaplin the private man, increasingly under siege for his politics and personal life, represented for Agee the artist at odds with society. In *Let Us Now Praise Famous Men*, Agee wrote, "A good artist is a deadly enemy of society; and the most dangerous thing that can happen to an enemy, no matter how cynical, is to become a beneficiary. No society, no matter how good, could be mature enough to support a real artist without mortal danger to that artist. Only no one need worry: for this same good artist is about the one sort of human being alive who can be trusted to take care of himself."[23] For Agee, Chaplin embodied such an artist, and the comedian's victimization during the "Red Scare" of the late 1940s only served to strengthen this view. Agee later wrote, "Charlie Chaplin is, I believe the greatest artist of our time, in any medium."[24]

Agee's love of film and his love for Chaplin were inseparable. These loves were symbiotic, each encouraging the other. He came to see Chaplin's Little Tramp as a new spiritual hero for the capitalist era, speaking to the masses through film, its most promising and popular new art form. In 1938, after he first saw Chaplin's film *Modern Times*, Agee wrote in a private journal that Chaplin "shares with Blake and Christ this: that he indicates what is obviously the good way to live: to live that way would mean complete 'withdrawal from the world' for each individual; would mean the destruction of the world as is." Contemplating Chaplin the private man, Agee wrote, "I understand he is a good and careful business man: and that certainly he is good and rich. This is a good contradiction, and a sad one. The man who understands both sides of poverty and of vagabondage, as much as Jesus, of Francis of Assisi, in his mind and spirit, is very careful in his physical life." [25] Agee would later take his conception of Chaplin's Tramp to its ultimate height when he developed an idea for a film in which he imagined the Little Tramp as the apparent sole survivor of an atomic war. In the screenplay for this film, Agee wrote, "The Tramp, besides being himself, is at various stages of the film Pan, Adam, Jesus, and the Scapegoat."[26]

That Agee eventually turned away from a career in journalism and literary fiction to pursue a career as a screen writer was, in a sense, inevitable. After his death, many who knew his work reacted with regret that Agee had "sold out" to Hollywood instead of dedicating himself solely to fiction or poetry. But for Agee, film promised more than large paychecks and a mass audience. He believed sincerely that film had the potential to replace and supersede literature as the dominant art form of his time. By 1945 he was writing, "If you compare the moving pictures released during a given period with the books published during the same period . . . you may or may not be surprised to find that they stand up rather well. I can think of very few contemporary books that are worth the jackets they are wrapped in . . ."[27] He recognized, though, an emerging threat from the new medium of television and warned, "how few years remain before the grandest prospect for a major popular art since Shakespeare's time dissolves into the ghastly gelatinous nirvana of television . . . if moving pictures are ever going to realize their potentialities, they are going to have to do it very soon indeed."[28]

Agee's cinematic dreams began in his youth. As early as 1927, when he was seventeen years old, he had already begun to articulate his faith in film as the new art form poised to supplant literature. The evidence lies in numerous letters written between Agee and the future critic Dwight MacDonald, then twenty years old. After leaving Exeter for Yale, MacDonald discussed with Dinsmore Wheeler, a friend still at Exeter, his idea of starting an intellectual community on a farm in Ohio.[29] Wheeler suggested that his classmate Agee would make a good candidate for their imagined utopia and encouraged MacDonald to contact him. Agee already knew of MacDonald from short stories published in the school magazine, and the two began a correspondence. It was the beginning of a dialogue, friendship, and rivalry that lasted throughout Agee's life. From the first, the two shared all they knew and thought about movies and what they could become:

> *June 16th, 1927*
> *Dear Mr. Macdonald,*
> *For the last two years I've been reading your contributions, both in the Yale List and in old numbers of the [Exeter] "Monthly." A year ago last fall you wrote me—Agee is my name—an extremely nice letter saying about the same sort of things I want to say. . . . One interest I know positively we have in common—interest in moving pictures, especially from the director's point of view. For next year, as president of The Lantern Club, I'm doing my best to get* Variety, Potemkin *and such films up here.*[30]

It was in film that Agee believed he would make his mark. In late July, a month after his introductory letter, he wrote again to MacDonald:

> *To me, the great thing about the movies is that it's a brand new field. I don't see how much more can be done with writing or with the stage. In fact, every kind of recognized "art" has been worked pretty nearly to the limit. Of course great things will undoubtedly be done in all of them, but, possibly excepting music, I don't see how they can avoid being at least in part imitations. As for the movies, however, their possibilities are infinite— that is, in so far as the possibilities of any art CAN be so. So far as I can see, all that's been done so far is to show that art is really possible on the screen. We've barely begun to stir the fringes of their possibilities, though. . . . Can writing or drama hope to rub your nose in realism as the movies do! Could POTEMKIN have been staged or described to even approximate the realism of the movie itself? I don't see how.*[31]

The youthful Agee grasped the power of realism blended with the lyrical. He argued to MacDonald that "the screen needn't stop at realism. The moving camera can catch the beauty of swaying, blending lights and shadows, and by its own movement impart to it as definite a rhythm as poetry or music ever had."[32] Agee's early letters to MacDonald are filled with his own ambition to partake in the shaping of the future of film. After he graduated from Yale, MacDonald joined the writing staff of *Fortune*. Afterward, Agee wrote to MacDonald from Cambridge about an early plan to try his hand at filmmaking: "A fellow in my dormitory owns a movie camera . . . at present it's possible we'll make two movies: one a sort of '$24 Island'[33] of Boston . . . I'll devise shots, angles, camera work, etc., and stories; he'll take care of the photography and lighting."[34]

Agee graduated from Harvard in 1932, in the middle of the Depression. Needing a job, he looked for help from Dwight MacDonald. MacDonald's recommendation of Agee to his bosses at *Fortune* was bolstered by attention Agee had earned for directing a scathingly accurate parody of *Time* during his tenure as president of Harvard's campus magazine, the *Advocate*. Armed with an offer to join MacDonald as an editor at *Fortune*, Agee hitchhiked from Cambridge to Manhattan. MacDonald recalled, "He desperately needed a job, and I got him a job."[35] It was a favor that MacDonald lived to regret: Agee continued to work for Henry Luce, barring occasional sabbaticals, for the next sixteen years. After Agee's death, MacDonald reflected on Agee's tenure as a journalist: "I do think that it was great mistake that he kept on so long [at *Time*]. He should have stayed there much less time."[36]

Robert Fitzgerald described Agee's years under Luce in an extended essay:

> The office building where we worked . . . had been erected in the late 20's as a monument to the car, the engineer and the [Chrysler] company and for a time it held the altitude record until the Empire State Building went higher. It terminated aloft in a glittering spearpoint of metal sheathing. From the fifty-second and fiftieth floors where Agee and I respectively had offices, you looked down on the narrow cleft of Lexington Avenue and across at the Grand Central Building, or you looked north or south over the city or across the East River toward Queens. . . . In our relationship to this building there were moments of great simplicity, moments when we felt like tearing it down with our bare hands.[37]

Agee revisited this fantasy and featured the Chrysler Building's destruction in the screenplay he later wrote for Chaplin. According to Fitzgerald, he also liked to fantasize the murder of Luce: "[Agee] was visited at least on one occasion by a fantasy of shooting our employer . . . Jim imagined himself laying the barrel of the pistol at chest level on the Founder's desk and making a great bang."[38]

Agee's skill with words soon made him stand out at *Fortune* and brought him a new mentor, the poet Archibald MacLeish. MacLeish arranged to have Agee's poetry published in the Yale Young Poets series. The resulting volume of poems, *Permit Me Voyage*, was Agee's first published book. Agee took its title from a line in Hart Crane's poem "The Bridge." Crane, too, had worked for a while as an editor at *Fortune*. *Permit Me Voyage* includes a poem entitled "Dedication," purposely placed third by Agee to keep readers from confusing it with an actual dedication to the book. An extended prose poem, it features what would become Agee's habitual listing of his heroes and idols; it honors "Those who in all times have sought truth and who have told it in their art or in their living" and includes in its lists Christ, Dante, Mozart, Shakspere [*sic*], his own family ancestors, his wife, and his mother. In another list, of "those living and soon to die who tell truth or tell of truth, or who honorably seek to tell, or who tell the truths of others,"[39] Agee includes the names of James Joyce, Charles Spencer Chaplin, and his friends Walker Evans and Robert Fitzgerald.

A rebel in the corridors of *Fortune*, Agee never took to the chore of grinding out the business stories that were the core of Luce's ornate monthly chronicle of American capitalism. He thrived on working late in the emptied offices and was known to throw open the high-altitude windows, prop a phonograph on the ledge, and pour Beethoven's Ninth Symphony at full volume out into the Manhattan sky. In one anecdote from this time, a colleague, Wilder Hobson, entered Agee's office to find the writer dangling by his fingers from the window sill. Agee pulled himself back into the office, brushed his clothes off, and proceeded as though nothing out of the ordinary had occurred.[40]

As a business journalist, Agee made his mark in highly descriptive essays on a variety of arcane topics ranging from medieval manuscripts to cockfighting. Luce made a personal attempt to encourage Agee's interest in the everyday facts of business and industry journalism, going so far as to consider sending him to business school. But by

March 1935 Agee's work was beginning to deteriorate. Writing to a friend about Agee's condition, MacDonald observed, Agee "is in poor shape psychologically. No interest in his work here, and small ability at faking. He spends three times as long on his pieces as he should, and has a devil of a time with them. I've advised him, and I think he's going to do it, to ask for a six- or ten-month leave in which to collect himself and get back into decent condition again."[41] Agee took Mac-Donald's advice and with his first wife, Olivia, took a break of several months in Florida. From Florida Agee wrote to Father Flye, "Saw the new Charlie Chaplin a while back. If it comes and if it doesn't conflict with Lenten rule, it's a wonderful thing to see—a lot, to me, as if Beethoven were living now and had completed another symphony."[42]

Shortly after he returned, Agee was offered the assignment of a lifetime—a perfect match for his southern background and his politically progressive interest in the travails of the working class. The job was to travel to the poorest rural section of Alabama at the lowest ebb of the Great Depression and report on the conditions of white tenant farmers. Agee took Walker Evans with him and the two lived for almost two months among three impoverished families. The assignment took on a life of its own, and though rejected by *Fortune*, the article became the basis of *Let Us Now Praise Famous Men*. The book, now considered by many as a true American classic of twentieth-century writing, took Agee almost five years to complete. Agee was then a devout disciple of James Joyce, and his self-revealing documentary experiment embraced numerous literary and journalistic styles and forms, from surrealism to straight economic reportage. Agee reprinted in *Let Us Now Praise Famous Men* his response to a questionnaire entitled "Some Questions which Face American Writers Today," to which he had been asked to respond by Dwight MacDonald (then editing the magazine *Partisan Review*). Included in his answer to the question "Are you conscious, in your own writing, of the existence of a usable past?" was this list of "usable" ancestors: "Christ: Blake: Dostoyesvky: Brady's photographs: everybody's letters: family albums: postcards: Whitman: Crane: Melville: Cummings: Kafka: Joyce: Malraux: Gide: Mann: Beethoven: Eisenstein: Dovschenko: Chaplin: Griffith: Von Stroheim: Miller: Evans: Cartier: Levitt: Van Gogh: race records: Swift: Celine . . ."[43] Later, near the book's fevered conclusion, Agee unreeled an extended Molly Bloom soliloquy of automatic writing in which he reveals another list of artists and heroes:

" . . . early-chaplin, late-beethoven, early-steinbeck, orson welles, tom wolfe . . ."[44]

In some ways *Let Us Now Praise Famous Men* was Agee's first film, a film with covers. Agee envisioned the book as a literary analogue to a documentary film, its images provided by Evans. Agee even included an intermission with a section entitled "Intermission: Conversation in the Lobby." When the book was finally released, it met a disinterested public and sold only 500 copies. Since its republication though, it has attained a growing stature as a landmark of mid-twentieth century literature. Dwight MacDonald liked to compare its initial public response to that which *Moby-Dick* first received: "*Moby-Dick* sold five hundred, which was six times as good a showing taking into account the increase of population."[45]

Having failed to find success with *Let Us Now Praise Famous Men*, Agee hoped to return to his old job at *Fortune*. In the meantime though, Robert Fitzgerald had joined *Time*'s growing roster of poet-journalists recruited by its managing editor, T. S. Matthews. Agee joined Fitzgerald in the magazine's book review section. Again Agee's talents set him apart. T. S. Matthews wrote of Agee, "there is one soloist among us whom I think all can applaud and none envy, for his best passages . . . do us honor as his fellow workers."[46] After Agee's death, Louis Kronenberger, *Time*'s drama critic, was quoted in a memorial written for the magazine's in-house publication, *f.y.i.*:

> You did not need to know Jim Agee personally to grasp how marvelously special he was. . . . In his creative writing there are passages that—quite simply—it took genius to write, but that not even genius could have written without an accompanying largeness of heart and mind. . . . He was one of the very few—they are really painfully few—men of great gifts who are even more distinguished as human beings. . . . As for his place here, he was *Time*'s finest writer, and will remain one of its most beautiful memories.[47]

During his years in journalism, Agee made several attempts at film writing, but these efforts were mostly literary rather than seriously intended for the screen. In 1937 he wrote a short surrealistic treatment, more of a prose experiment than a serious film project, called *The House*. He also wrote a scenario for a scene from André Malraux's novel *Man's Fate*, which was published in *Films*, a journal of film essays, by Jay Leyda in 1939. Leyda, a friend of Walker Evans, served for four years, beginning in 1936, as the assistant curator of films for the Museum of Modern Art. In that position, he provided Agee invaluable access to rare and obscure films. After Agee and Evans returned from their Alabama trip, Leyda made an unsuccessful effort to encourage to them to make a film about tenant farmers based on their experiences. In 1940, Leyda was forced to resign his post at the museum after he was publicly accused of being a communist.

One early, and more serious, attempt to write a screenplay was undertaken by Agee in 1945. He and his fellow film critic Manny Farber arranged to meet numerous times at a park bench during their lunchtime to hash out a screenplay they called *Furlough*, about the adventures of a soldier on leave in New York City. The script, never developed beyond a hundred pages of spiral notebook outlines and sketches, was abandoned after the director Vincent Minnelli released his film *The Clock*. Manny Farber remembered, "I thought up an idea, very original, about a soldier on furlough—like *The Clock*. Jim, for some reason, thought it was a great idea for a movie. We had it all plotted out. We'd meet in the Waverly Diner, or in the park on Sixth Avenue near the subway, and try to write some of the script. He was so fecund; he had so many Eisenstein-type Russian shots, he scared me to death."[48]

At *Time*, T. S. Matthews attempted to put Agee's talents to their best use by teaming him with the writer Whittaker Chambers to create a two-man special features department tasked with developing cover stories. It was Agee who was assigned the awful responsibility of writing *Time*'s cover-story reaction to the bombing of Hiroshima. Agee became obsessed with the fate of mankind in the new world of atomic threat and he channeled his worst fears into a screenplay in which he imagined Chaplin's Little Tramp as the apparent sole survivor in a New York City destroyed by atomic war. The manuscript for this unknown screenplay was written directly to Chaplin in an effort to convince him of the importance of the piece. It is a tour de force of Agee's poetic imagination informed by his deep love and appreciation for Chaplin, his life's greatest hero.

This book is the story of how Agee came to write this remarkable, unnamed screenplay that will, for practical reasons, be referred to here as *The Tramp's New World*. It also recounts Agee's efforts to interest Chaplin in his film idea, and how following these attempts, Chaplin became a dear friend and a profound influence in both his life and art. Previously, only a fragmented, misordered holograph manuscript of *The Tramp's New World* screenplay was known to exist. But through the generous efforts of the Association Chaplin in Paris, France, the complete typed manuscript that Agee delivered to Chaplin in 1948 has recently been discovered. This manuscript is published here for the first time, in its entirety. Agee's amazing screenplay is a great but unknown work of the twentieth century, the dream of one of its finest writers, written for its greatest performer, in response to one of its most horrendous events. It is, without exaggeration, a sermon and warning from one of America's most profoundly sensitive and spiritual writers. Sadly, it is no less timely now than when it was written, fifty-eight years ago.

One

L'AFFAIRE VERDOUX

On his 58th birthday, Charlie Chaplin, driven to the wall by this column and trying to salvage his $2,000,000 flop picture, tells 103 newspapermen he is not a Communist . . . tell that to the Marines who died at Tarawa.
—Ed Sullivan, "The Talk of the Town," *New York Daily News*, April 16, 1947

*E*d Sullivan wanted to destroy Charlie Chaplin. Sullivan, fueled with an obsessive hatred for communism and an unquenchable animus for Chaplin, never missed a chance to skewer or sully the comedian's image. Best known as the host of a long-running television variety show, Sullivan earned his tabloid pedigree at the source, writing for the *Graphic*, a New York newspaper he would later describe as "one step removed from pornography." Long before he had moved into the television set in the middle of America's living room, the dour-looking man on whom detractors bestowed Buster Keaton's famous moniker "The Great Stone Face" began his career as a sportswriter at a local paper in his hometown of Port Chester, New York. In 1922, when he was twenty years old, Sullivan moved to the *New York Evening Mail*. He spent the next five years covering sports at the *Philadelphia Ledger*, the *World*, the *New York Bulletin*, and the *Morning Telegraph*. In 1927 he joined the staff of the *Graphic*, then New York's most popular scandal sheet. His big break came in 1931, when he was given the chance to abandon sportswriting to join the chroniclers of "the Stem," as Broadway was then known. The *Graphic*'s editor assigned Sullivan to replace the departing Louis Sobol, who had replaced the legendary Walter Winchell, the paper's chief rumormonger who had jumped ship in 1929 to join the *Mirror*, William Randolph Hearst's tabloid. The *Graphic* holds a particular place in the history of American journalism as a prototabloid renowned for its innovative, if ethically despicable, use of photomontage (called "composographs") to fake images of contemporary scandals. It was here that Sullivan perfected his imitation of Winchell's trademark three-dot journalism, an endless river of gossip and plugs separated by an equally endless supply of ellipses.

Sullivan learned to attack his enemies with ink, but contrary to the image he later cultivated on television, he was no stranger to physical violence. In his grandstanding inaugural column, Sullivan demeaned his rivals and puffed that "To get into this column will be a badge of merit and a citation—divorces will not be propagated in this column"[1] Louis Sobol responded to this holier-than-thou debut with a column entitled "The Ennui of His Contempt-oraries." Soon after, Sullivan saw Sobol at a theater premiere and rushed toward him. Sobol had to run away to escape while bystanders held Sullivan back. Sobol recalled: "I saw him charging me. . . . He was really angry. 'I'll rip your cock off, you little bastard,' he said."[2]

The man who in several years would later bring America the little mouse puppet Topo Gigio, the chart-topping Singing Nun ("Dominique"), and the Beatles later landed a gossip column called "Little Old New York," published in the *New York Daily News*. Until his unquestioned success in television, beginning in the late 1940s, Sullivan unhappily measured his own career by how much his arch rival Winchell was besting him. While Sullivan's column was syndicated in over thirty newspapers nationwide, Winchell's was carried in close to a thousand. Years later, in the summer of 1952, having suffered for years in Winchell's shadow, Sullivan trailed his rival into the men's room at the popular watering hole The Stork Club. Sullivan's assistant, aware that Winchell was known to carry a gun, followed him only to find Sullivan dunking Winchell's head in a urinal while continuously pulling the flush handle.[3]

A devout Catholic, Sullivan was strongly influenced in his conservative politics by the virulently anticommunist Bishop Fulton J. Sheen and Francis Cardinal Spellman, and staked out a position as a super-patriot on the constant hunt for communist influence in the entertainment arena. A motivation for his career as a red baiter is suggested by his biographer, Jerry Bowles, who points out that "Sullivan had been too young for World War I and too old for World War II. Like many men who have not served in the military during war periods, Sullivan was sensitive about it and insecure about his 'patriotism.'"[4]

As a gossip columnist, Sullivan knew as well as anyone that the greatest damage to a man's life could be effected through the destruction of his reputation. Reputation was, after all, his stock in trade. And the reputation of Chaplin, arguably the most famous man in the world, made one hell of a target. In April of 1947 Chaplin was still recovering from the damage done to his public image three years earlier by the media scandals resulting from his disastrous affair with a young, emotionally unstable woman named Joan Barry. The public had feasted for months on gossip and innuendo as the private life of the world's most famous man was revealed in two paternity suits and an unsuccessful effort by the federal government to convict the comedian on charges under the Mann Act. Chaplin was not the first controversial celebrity to be targeted by the law, which banned the transportation of women across state lines for "prostitution or debauchery or for any other immoral purpose." In 1913, three years after the law was passed, the Mann Act had been used to send the African American boxing champion Jack Johnson to jail for one year—its first application in a case involving consenting adults. Chaplin's trials featured their own first: the second of the paternity suits brought against him was the first in which blood test evidence was admitted in the state of California to establish paternity, and though the chemistry proved Chaplin innocent, the jury ignored the new science and found him liable for child support. In the years following the three trials, the comedian suffered additional blows from political conservatives who viewed his support for the Soviet Union during World War II, an ally of America at the time, and his continued high-profile interest in progressive causes through a much narrower postwar lens.

It was time for Chaplin to regain his audience. He was coming to New York City to premiere a film, his first new release in the seven years since the critical and financial triumph of *The Great Dictator*. His new movie, *Monsieur Verdoux*, was a black comedy, a critique of the human toll of capitalism's periodic downswings told through the various guises of an entrepreneurial Bluebeard. It was a risky film on numerous counts, not least because it jettisoned Chaplin's popular Tramp character. Even chancier, Chaplin played the villain—a serial killer, no less. While it proved to be Chaplin's most controversial work and a financial disappointment, he steadfastly defended it, describing it in his memoir nearly twenty years later, as the "cleverest and most brilliant film I have yet made."[5] He was buoyed before the film's launch by the support of close friends who, having seen advance screenings, encouraged his hopes. The novelist Lion Feuchtwanger, for example, wrote to Chaplin on March 11, 1947, that *Monsieur Verdoux* "is a great ethical lecture, and makes the relationship between crime and the general economic situation clearer than a thousand essays. In your own way you have put into practice the principle that many a philosopher and writer adhered to: 'By laughter we improve the world.'"[6]

Against the wishes of his own public relations experts at United Artists, the film distribution company that he co-owned with Mary Pickford, Chaplin insisted on holding a press conference following the film's debut. The UA staff feared that Chaplin was opening himself up to an uncontrolled situation where he would undoubtedly be assailed for his personal controversies. Ed Sullivan, having received notice of the event, recognized just such an opportunity and alerted the troops, including representatives of the Catholic War Veterans and the American Legion, by dropping the following item into his column: " . . . Charlie Chaplin to have meeting with the N.Y. press, no holds barred."[7] A couple of days later, Sullivan kicked off his column with the announcement that Chaplin would hold a press conference at the Gotham Hotel, and would make himself available to answer any question posed, "political, social and cinematic." Sullivan proposed a list of questions for the press to grill the comedian with: "Why didn't Chaplin entertain U.S. troops or visit our wounded in military hospitals during the war? Does Chaplin prefer democracy, as defined by Russian Communism, to democracy as it defined in the United States?" Lastly, Sullivan challenged the press to demand that Chaplin explain why, after "abandoning" England and enriching himself in the United States for thirty years, the comedian had declined to obtain American citizenship.[8]

Sullivan was by no means the only gossip columnist to go after Chaplin. Like Sullivan and Walter Winchell, Hedda Hopper served as a regular bidirectional channel of secrets and favors for J. Edgar Hoover. Natalie Robins in her investigation into the FBI's surveillance of writers, *Alien Ink*, cites a 1947 letter that Hopper wrote to Hoover, congratulating him on his book *The Story of the FBI:* "I loved what you said about the Commies in the motion picture industry . . . I'd like to run every one of those rats out of the country, starting with Charlie Chaplin."[9] Hopper was easily Sullivan's equal in vituperation: In her own column the week before the *Monsieur Verdoux* premiere, she wrote, "Pardon me! The Charlie Chaplins ain't campin' out at the Waldorf—they couldn't get reservations. I always get a kick out of Jim Tully's line on Chaplin—'He pities the poor in the parlors of the rich.'"[10]

Hopper had it right: Chaplin and his young wife, Oona, the daughter of the playwright Eugene O'Neill, were not staying at the Waldorf but at the Gotham Hotel. They had come to New York City from their estate perched on the top of Summit Drive, overlooking Beverly Hills, and needed a hotel that would allow extended stays. Chaplin's first task was to launch *Monsieur Verdoux*. The second was to sit as defendant in a lawsuit brought by a former friend and collaborator Konrad Bercovici, who claimed he had given Chaplin the idea for *The Great Dictator* without receiving fair compensation. The Bercovici suit was only the latest in a string of claims against Chaplin's integrity. He had also recently been sued for plagiarism by a European film company that claimed he had lifted the famous assembly line scene in *Modern Times* from René Clair's film *A Nous La Liberté*. That case had been settled out of court. Meanwhile, another broadside was launched on Chaplin's integrity. Before *Monsieur Verdoux* had even opened, Orson Welles was feeling slighted for not having received the screen credit he thought he had been promised by Chaplin for having inspired the new film when he suggested, six years earlier, that the two collaborate on a story based on the real-life wife murderer Henri Landru. Although Chaplin had paid him $5,000 for the story idea, Welles was spreading the word that he had been wronged.

Shortly after arriving at the Gotham Hotel, Oona began writing a letter describing her impressions of New York City to Lou Eisler, wife of the composer Hanns Eisler. The Eislers were two of the Chaplin's closest friends back home in Southern California:

Lou Darling—Well New York is horrible! Charlie & I are longing to return to Beverly Hills—really! The picture opens April 11th and that is

exciting, of course—Charlie is very busy rushing around getting every-
thing arranged—and he is nervous—I am not—Then after the opening
he has the Bercovici case—which he hasn't even thought much about—and
then we are returning to California (end of April)—and then to England
probably.

    New York is full of Hollywood. The day we arrived we saw Garbo on
Fifth Ave.—and Gene Tierney that evening—and since then have seen
Gary Cooper, Joe Cotton—Selznick—Jennifer Jones—Milestone—Nor-
man Lloyd—and even Louella Parsons—And Mary Pickford is coming the
end of the week to really make our life "HELL." It is terribly crowded—we
are in an awful hotel—unbelievably dirty!—which depresses us naturally.
Other hotels won't allow you to stay for more than a week—The autograph
children (they are absolute gangsters!) make it almost impossible to walk
anywhere—They even try to force open the doors of your taxi and jump in
with you—Charlie curses & swears at them & finally nearly kicked one
horrible boy in the face! Just like the "Pilgrim."[11] *We have been out every*
night seeing people and doing everything—and it's so boring—I can't even
tell you—we keep saying—"If only we were home & going down to Malibu
to see the Eislers." We've seen my friends the Saroyans—and met Artie
Shaw there—Charlie thinks his wife is very attractive. Went to a party at
Lillian Hellman's last night for Henry Wallace—and ended up at the
Stork Club with Elliott Roosevelt & Jo Davidson . . . [12]

Monsieur Verdoux was scheduled to open on April 11, 1947 at the
Broadway Theater, a legitimate theater house refitted especially for
the occasion with a motion picture screen. To the consternation of his
public relations advisors, Chaplin, on the day before the premiere,
met with members of the foreign press, some of whom were primed
by Sullivan's suggested line of questioning. The next day the Associated Press wire carried an account of the news conference in which
"Chaplin answered questions asked by Ed Sullivan in his *New York
Daily News* column Wednesday and raised today by one of the foreign
reporters." Chaplin was questioned on why he had declined to take
American citizenship and responded, "I haven't become an American
citizen, because I am not a nationalist. Seventy percent of my income
is derived from Europe, and 30 percent from the United States. The
United States takes 100 percent of that income for taxation
purposes . . . I'm a very good paying guest." When he was asked
which brand of democracy he preferred, Russian communism or the
American version, Chaplin responded by "raising his hands in the

flutteringly futile gesture so well known in his baggy pants picture era" and said, "I'm not touting for any ideology. I'm for the progress of the human race. I'm for the little man. I won't enter into any political discussions. I'll leave that to the men in Washington."[13]

Recognizing an opportunity to score points against Chaplin, Hedda Hopper knocked Chaplin a few days later for having his attorney, Jerry Giesler—who had been his counsel during the Joan Barry trials—by his side while meeting with the foreign press: "Charlie Chaplin, at his press interview in New York, needed his former mouthpiece, Jerry Giesler, to supply his answers. Chaplin's didn't seem good enough. He was always better in silent pictures than in talkies. The same thing is true in real life . . ."[14]

On April 11 the film was premiered to mixed results. A portion of the audience even hissed in displeasure. Chaplin, stunned, left the theater to wait in the lobby. At an awkward postpremiere party, friends attempted fake cheer and Chaplin drank too much. Afterward, the comedian was accompanied back to his hotel room by the screen writer Donald Ogden Stewart. Stewart recognized Chaplin's suite as the site of a notorious media tragedy that had taken place nine years before. "Jesus! Do you realize what room this is? The one where the boy stepped out on the ledge and stood for twelve hours before plunging off and killing himself!" Stewart's memory was fairly accurate. On July 26, 1938, a cadre of cameramen, many lying on their backs on the cement sidewalk, waited for hours to play their part in a dubious milestone in modern journalism: a suicide recorded on film. Thousands of spectators filled Fifth Avenue while the cameramen trained their lenses on the seventeenth floor of the Gotham Hotel where a distraught young man named John W. Ward paced the ledge. Late in the evening, just as some fireman had succeeded in raising a cargo net as far as the fourteenth floor, Ward jumped to his death. The event was captured by the newsreel cameramen and an army of newspaper photographers. A couple of years later, the event was turned into a film, called *Fourteen Hours*, starring a young Richard Basehart. Chaplin accepted Stewart's news as "a fitting climax to the evening."[15]

It was difficult to imagine how things could get much worse, but Chaplin didn't have to wait long to find out. The next day, Chaplin met nearly one hundred members of the American press in the Gotham Hotel's Grand Ballroom. Chaplin wrote his own account of the press conference in his autobiography, without the luxury of a

Against the advice of his public relations advisors, Charles Chaplin hosted a press conference in the Grand Ballroom of the Gotham Hotel in New York City following the premiere of *Monsieur Verdoux* on April 12, 1947. Agee, from the balcony, rose to protest the hostile behavior of right-wing journalists, who, encouraged by Ed Sullivan, then a gossip columnist, peppered Chaplin with attacks on the comedian's personal life and politics. (Collection of Jeffrey Vance)

verbatim transcript that was published three years later in *Film Comment.*[16] Chaplin recalled, "The publicity staff of United Artists deliberated whether it was advisable for me to meet the American press. I was indignant, because I had already met the foreign press the morning before, and they had given me a warm, enthusiastic welcome. Besides, I am not one to be browbeaten." Chaplin's public relations staff acquiesced and arranged for drinks to be served before the conference, perhaps hoping to encourage a friendly reception. But it was clear to Chaplin from the onset that he was in for rough going, "After cocktails were served I made my appearance, but I could smell mischief. I spoke from a rostrum at the back of a small table . . ."[17]

Chaplin began the press conference by saying "Thank you, ladies and gentlemen of the press. I am not going to waste your time. I should say—proceed with the butchery. If there's any question anybody wants to ask, I'm here, fire ahead at this old gray head." The very first question from the floor was about Orson Welles's dispute over the story credit and it went downhill from there. (Welles later called the press conference "the worst lynching by critics you ever heard."[18]) Radio producer George Wallach, using a borrowed film recorder, captured the exchange between Chaplin and the press. According to Wallach, "The ballroom was filled literally to the rafters. Every seat on the floor was taken. People were standing in the doorways and on the seats encircling the balcony."[19] He recalled what followed as "more like an inquisition than a press conference." Two assistants carried hand microphones from questioner to questioner to "answer any and all questions that may be asked." Chaplin soon found himself under attack for his politics and his personal friendships. He recalled the following exchange:

"Do you know Hanns Eisler?" said another reporter.
"Yes, he's a very dear friend of mine, and a great musician."
"Do you know that he's a Communist?"
"I don't care what he is; my friendship is not based on politics."
"You seem to like the Communists, though," said another.
"Nobody is going to tell me whom to like or dislike. We haven't come to that yet."

Amidst the accusatory voices, Chaplin heard one friendly voice attempt to end the cycle of attacks: "a voice out of the belligerence said,"

"How does it feel to be an artist who has enriched the world with so much happiness and understanding of the little people, and to be derided and held up to hate and scorn by the so-called representatives of the American press?" I was so deaf to any expression of sympathy that I answered abruptly: "I'm sorry, I didn't follow you, you'll have to repeat that question again." My publicity man nudged me and whispered: "this fellow's for you, he said a very fine thing.' It was Jim Agee, the American poet and novelist, at that time working as a special feature writer and critic for *Time* magazine. I was thrown off my guard and confused. "I'm sorry," I said, "I didn't hear you—Would you kindly repeat that again?"

"I don't know if I can," he said, slightly embarrassed, then he repeated approximately the same words. I could think of no answer, so I shook my head and said: "No comment . . . but thank you." I was no good after that. His kind words had left me without any more fight. "I'm sorry ladies and gentlemen," I said, "I thought this conference was to be an interview about my film; instead it has turned into a political brawl, so I have nothing further to say." After the interview I was inwardly sick at heart, for I knew that a virulent hostility was against me.[20]

As a press conference intended to help promote a newly launched film, the event was an unmitigated disaster. Charles Maland, in *Chaplin and American Culture*, calculated that, barring restatement and elaboration, 60 percent of the questions asked at the press conference "dealt with political issues, with no reference to films at all." Of the remaining questions, Maland figured that only "about half asked Chaplin specifically about *Monsieur Verdoux* and the other half asked him about films in general."[21]

That night, Oona sat down to finish her forgotten half-written letter to Lou Eisler:

Lou darling—I started this letter, as you can see, a week ago at least—& found it in my drawer today—reading it over it's so boring! Since then the picture opened—& got a lot of bad—really bad—reviews—even the good ones were not very good—this was a great blow to Charlie—and to me—naturally—Also there has been a lot of trash in the papers about Charlie's not being a citizen—& being a communist and not helping "our boys" in the war—He had a mass interview of about seventy-five reporters this afternoon—It was broadcast over the radio—And they really all came to slaughter him—And I must tell you that one of the questions they asked was "Are you a friend of Hanns Eisler?" Charlie said that you were close friends & then they asked if Hanns was a communist & Charlie said he didn't think so—that Hanns was a great musician & not in politics. Then of course they said—"well if he were a communist, would you still be friends with him?" and Charlie said "Of course." Then they said "Well if he were a spy would you be friends?" So Charlie said they were being absurd & that ended that—But they seemed to be mixing up Hanns & Gerhart [Gerhart and Hanns Eisler were brothers]—The press here is worse—or at least as bad—as Los Angeles.

To get back to the picture—people are not going to see it as they should—business is "all right" but not wonderful. We only hope that it hasn't been advertised enough & perhaps people don't know it's playing. Maybe it will pick up this week. Poor Charlie is so depressed & low—This has never happened to him before—It is really a horrible strain—He feels that the press may have turned the public against him—You see, it isn't that people don't like it—the audience loves it—but there haven't been any great crowds coming to the theater—The Chaplin name has always attracted them before—However it's only been playing three days so we shall see what happens. . . . We saw something very small in a paper about Hanns being investigated by the Un-American committee—Also different things about Gerhart which we don't quite understand—I hope the news is not too bad—And that you & Hanns are well and not letting it all get you down— When we return we will all get drunk together—and forget everything for one evening!"[22]

Things were not going well for Chaplin's friend Hanns Eisler, either. On April 14, two days after Chaplin's press conference, Hanns's brother Gerhart was indicted on charges of making "fraudulent and fictitious"[23] statements while seeking a permit to leave the United States in 1945. The *New York Times* reported "Eisler is in custody on Ellis Island. The German alien has been described as a top man in the communist movement in this country by witnesses before the House Committee on Un-American Activities [HUAC]." On April 16 Gerhart was released on $20,000 bail and publicly announced that "he planned to explain to the American people in articles and lectures that he was not 'the right hand man of Stalin' in the United States."[24] Chaplin lent his name to a campaign to postpone the upcoming trial in order to provide more time to allow Gerhart to prepare a defense and "to avoid undue prejudice . . . at a time when red-baiting hysteria is so violent." When Chaplin was himself later interrogated by the Immigration and Naturalization Service, he was asked about his support for Gerhart. He responded, "it was the humane thing to do."[25] Less than a week later, the U.S. government set its sights on Gerhart's musician brother. On April 20, 1947, the *Los Angeles Times* reported "Political activities and labor union connections of Han[n]s Eisler, Hollywood song writer, will be the subject of a closed-door inquiry in Los Angeles in May, the *Times* learned today. A special unit of the House Un-Americanism Committee is planning to interview witnesses . . . Han[n]s Eisler recently was named by his sister, a Mrs. Fischer, as just as dangerous to the safety of the United States as their brother Gerhart, who has been described by the F.B.I. as the supreme director of Communist activities here."[26]

Over the previous six months, the strange tale of the Eisler brothers and their sister had become a major news story. Gerhart had been arrested on February 4 for passport fraud and was imprisoned on Ellis Island. "He was indicted for contempt of Congress in February after he refused to take the oath on being called to testify before the committee."[27] His supporters responded by issuing pamphlets, "Gerhart Eisler: My Side of the Story: The Story the Newspapers Refused to Print" and "Eisler Hits Back"; readers were requested to wire and write their congressmen and the State Department to demand that Gerhart be allowed to return to Germany where "a man of Eisler's knowledge and experience in the struggle against fascism is urgently needed to help in the denazification, demilitarization and democratization of Germany."[28]

In its February 17, 1947 issue, *Life* magazine ran a ten-page profile of Gerhart. "The career of Gerhart Eisler as a Comintern Agent,"[29] began with an account of the previous week's HUAC hearing at which Gerhart, described in the article as "the pudgy little Austrian-German," was brought from his cell on Ellis Island to angrily deny (he was "a picture of outraged innocence") that he was "the boss of all the Reds." Earlier, Louis Budenz, the former editor of the communist newspaper the *Daily Worker*, while testifying in front of HUAC, had fingered Gerhart as the Kremlin's top man in the United States. Even worse, the Eislers' sister Ruth Fischer, formerly Elfreide Eisler, had published a notorious series of columns in the Hearst newspapers denouncing both of her brothers as spies and potential murderers. Fischer herself had served in leadership positions in the German Communist Party, before being thrown out of the party. Reflecting on their complex family politics, Chaplin told Hanns Eisler, "In your family things happen as in Shakespeare."[30]

HUAC's predecessor, the Special Committee on Un-American Activities, began in 1938 and continued operations until 1944, chaired by Congressman Martin Dies. In 1945 the Mississippi Democrat moved to make the committee permanent. By 1947 the committee had recognized the potential value of holding hearings into communist influence in Hollywood. In the spring of that year the ground was being prepared for open hearings that would be held in Washington, D.C. later that autumn. When these hearings commenced, nineteen Hollywood writers and directors were subpoenaed. Eleven of the writers announced that they would not cooperate with the committee's investigation and were called to Washington to testify. The first of the eleven so-called un-friendlies to testify was Bertolt Brecht. Under questioning Brecht disingenuously denied having ever been a member of the communist party, and as soon as his testimony was completed, he and his wife got on a plane and escaped to Europe. The remaining ten writers became known as the Hollywood Ten, and after refusing to cooperate when called to testify, each was cited for contempt of Congress. The Supreme Court refused to hear their case, and each of the ten was later sentenced to jail for up to one year.

But before HUAC turned its focus on the film industry, its star target had been Gerhart Eisler. On February 18, a newly minted congressman from California, Richard M. Nixon, gave his first speech in the House of Representatives. Nixon, a junior member of HUAC, spoke on the threat that Gerhart Eisler posed to the United States: "Mr. Speaker, on February 6, when the Committee on Un-American Activities opened its session at 10 o'clock, it had, by previous investigation, tied together the loose end of one chapter of a foreign directed conspiracy whose aim and purpose was to undermine and destroy the government of the United States. The principal character of this conspiracy was Gerbert Eisler, alias Berger, alias Brown, alias Gerhart, alias Edwards, alias Liptkin, alias Elsman, a seasoned agent of the Communist International."[31] Nixon asserted that Gerhart Eisler had been sent by Moscow "to direct and mastermind the political and espionage activities of the Communist Party in the United States." Gerhart ultimately avoided prison time; he jumped bail and stowed away to Europe on a Polish freighter.

All the attention paid to Gerhart put enormous pressure on his brother Hanns, who had been quietly living in Southern California and working as a film composer. He had first come to the United States in the spring of 1935 on a concert tour to raise money for the children of victims of fascism. After Hanns Eisler moved to New York, the American composer Marc Blitzstein helped organize a benefit concert featuring Eisler's music at the New School for Social Research. Eisler received a grant from the American Guild for German Cultural Freedom, led in part by the novelist Thomas Mann, and he landed a teaching position at the New School, giving lectures on the social history of music.

In early 1946, after moving to California, Eisler began teaching at the University of Southern California and rented a small bungalow on the beach in Malibu, next door to the actor and director Norman Lloyd. Eisler was soon introduced to Chaplin through their mutual friends, the Feuchtwangers and Salka and Berthold Viertel; the composer's wit and the comedian's love of music soon made them close friends. Eisler witnessed the production of *Monsieur Verdoux*, and wrote to playwright Clifford Odets to describe the experience. Eisler told Odets that he was impressed with Chaplin's skill at direction and acknowledged the comedian's ability to write good scenes, but he found fault with his "naïve pseudophilosophical observations." Eisler, having repeatedly failed in his own attempts to influence Chaplin, proposed that Odets, if present, might have better luck in influencing the "amiable and pig-headed" comedian. Even so, Eisler told Odets, the faults were trivial and Chaplin's *Monsieur Verdoux*, he predicted, would be a masterpiece.[32]

Though Eisler complained that he was frustrated by Chaplin's refusal to listen to advice, he claimed credit, years later, for helping to politicize the comedian by laughing more enthusiastically at his jokes that had "a strong political thrust." James K. Lyon, in his biography of Bertolt Brecht, *Brecht in America*, relates this telling anecdote: Eisler and Brecht were invited to a private preview screening of *Monsieur Verdoux* and "In the presence of 200 Hollywood celebrities including the bankers who had financed the film, Brecht and Eisler laughed in the wrong places, e.g., when bankers jumped out of skyscraper windows during the depression."[33] Chaplin recalled showing a copy of the *Monsieur Verdoux* script to Brecht, but was confounded by his cryptic response; "At the Hanns Eislers' we used to meet Bertolt Brecht . . . I showed him the script of *Monsieur Verdoux*, which he thumbed through. His only comment: 'Oh, you write a script Chinese fashion.'"[34]

There are, in fact, strong echoes of Brecht to be found in *Monsieur Verdoux*. Brecht's updating of John Gay's *Beggar's Opera*, renamed *The Three Penny Opera* (*Die Dreigroschenoper*) at the suggestion of Lion Feuchtwanger, tells the tale of a criminal antihero, MacHeath ("Mackie the Knife"), the murderer of several women, who tends to see his own criminal activities in business terms. He admonishes lesser criminals with the insult, "You'll never make businessmen. Cannibals, but never businessmen!" He scrupulously keeps account books and "a list of the staff." Under pressure, MacHeath declares, "Between ourselves, it's only a question of weeks before I switch to banking exclusively." As MacHeath faces imminent hanging he reflects, "We bour-geois artisans, who work with honest jimmies on the cash boxes of small shopkeepers, are being swallowed up by large concerns backed by banks. What is a picklock to a bank share? What is the burgling of a bank to the founding of a bank? What is the murder of a man to the employment of a man?"[35]

While MacHeath may have aspired to a banking career, Chaplin's Verdoux had worked as a bank clerk, but after losing his position dur-ing the Depression following World War I, becomes a serial killer, a Bluebeard, for purely economic reasons. Sentenced to the guillotine for murdering numerous wealthy, lonely women, Verdoux declares, "For 35 years I used my brains honestly. After that, no one wanted them. So I was forced into business for myself. As for being a mass killer, doesn't the world encourage it? Is it not building weapons of destruction for the sole purpose of mass killing? Has it not blown un-suspecting women and little children to pieces? And done it very sci-entifically? As a mass killer I'm an amateur by comparison . . ."[36] Interviewed in his jail cell shortly before his execution, Verdoux tells a friendly reporter, in words reminiscent of Brecht's MacHeath, that his crimes were just business, "that's the history of many a big business. One murder makes you a villain, millions a hero. Numbers sanctify." The film ends, not with the traditional ending of a Chaplin film, with the Tramp disappearing down the road into the distance, alone and free, but with its exact opposite. Verdoux walks into the middle dis-tance toward his death, flanked by uniformed guards. Bosley Crowther, in his mixed review of *Monsieur Verdoux*, accepted that many of the film's "notions are sophomoric, as some of the critics have observed. . . . The point is that they are considerable in this dangerous day and age and that the man who is still the most adroit and subtle comic on the screen has tackled them. More power to him and to his talent! For the fade on philosophic Verdoux, walking alone to the guillotine, has more meaning for us today than the sentimental sight of the baggy-trousered little Tramp going on his humble way."[37]

During this period, the writer Christopher Isherwood was living in a small apartment above the garage in the back of the screenwriter Salka Viertel's home. He recorded in his diaries how one day he was taken by Salka's husband, Berthold, to visit Brecht, and there met Hanns Eisler: "Eisler, the Red composer, is a little moon-faced man with peg teeth, short fat legs, and a flat-backed head, who talks very rapidly in a loud unharmonious voice, with whirring wittiness."[38] Though he failed to make much of an impression on Isherwood, many of the people who met Eisler in Hollywood were taken by his charm and sense of humor. Parties at Eisler's Malibu home would typically include a wide variety of artists, including Chaplin, Clifford Odets, Harold Clurman, Artie Shaw, Ava Gardner, Arnold Schoenberg, Theodor Adorno, and Greta Garbo. According to Eisler's biographer Albrecht Betz, many of the composer's casual friends "knew about Eisler's serious music only from hearsay; for them he was a social attraction as a brilliant and witty conversationalist."[39]

Chaplin's friendship with Eisler, the brother of a reputed "atom bomb spy,"[40] was certainly hurting his image, but the comedian steadfastly refused to denounce him. Ed Sullivan, in the wake of the disastrous press conference, sensed that Chaplin had been weakened. To keep the fires stoked, Sullivan printed a statement purportedly written by his secretary: "Dear Boss—The Marines who died at Iwo Jima, the World War II paraplegics, amputees and the blinded must writhe at Charlie Chaplin's smug explanation that 'I'm a very good paying guest in the United States.'" Underlining Sullivan's contribution to the grilling Chaplin received from the press, the column noted that "Chaplin's answers to your three questions demonstrate he believes the purpose of language is to conceal ideas rather than convey ideas," and pointedly asked "Charlie, is you is or is you ain't our baby? Are you with Uncle Sam or against him?"[41] For Chaplin, the one-two punch of the press conference and premiere were proof that the postwar rightward shift in American politics was having a measurable effect on his previously dependable public. As Oona had pointed out in her letter, Chaplin's name was no longer enough to pull in the crowds. On April 18, a week after the press conference and premiere, Hedda Hopper reported in her column under the heading "Chaplin's Last Chapter": "After seeing the opening of Charlie Chaplin's new film in New York, a prominent motion picture executive wired me: 'I've witnessed a historic occasion. I've just seen Chaplin's last picture.'"[42] Making matters worse, Chaplin's close friends were being interrogated and he was under constant threat of subpoena by HUAC. But his next problem was the Bercovici suit. On April 18 the *New York Times* ran a brief article entitled "Suit Against Chaplin for $6,450,000 Opens."[43] The article described how on the previous day a jury of nine men and three women had been selected to hear Bercovici's attorney, the legendary Louis Nizer, argue that Chaplin had "contracted with his client to collaborate in the production of a series of pictures for which Mr. Bercovici was to receive 15 percent of the gross profits." The suit also argued that Chaplin had based *The Great Dictator* on a satirical scenario based on Hitler and dictatorship that Bercovici claimed to have written in 1938. Underlining how poorly the week had gone for Chaplin, the article noted that one prospective juror had been rejected when "he said that his reaction to the stories on a recent press conference was 'unfavorable to Mr. Chaplin.'"

Without question, the launch of *Monsieur Verdoux* had been near catastrophic for Chaplin, but for Agee, the opportunity provided by the press conference was both a dream come true and the hand of God at work. Chaplin was a touchstone for Agee throughout his life, serving him as an artistic idol and as an emotional connection to his father, who was killed in a car accident when Agee was only six years old. Agee would later write a moving account of his childhood memories of accompanying his father to the local movie theater in Knoxville to watch Chaplin's Little Tramp cavort. While the press conference provided him the thrill of meeting one of his life's greatest heroes, Agee actually had a bigger, more pressing reason for wanting to meet Chaplin. In his spare and stolen hours Agee had been secretly working on a screenplay, a film idea written specifically for Chaplin. Earlier in the spring, just months before the press conference, Agee had attempted and failed to get the actor's attention by writing a pitch letter to the Chaplin Studios. But now, here was Chaplin, in New York, in the flesh, as though it had all been ordained by fate.

Agee's third wife, Mia, recollected, "Jim had met Chaplin at a press interview after *Monsieur Verdoux* in New York, where Chaplin was very much attacked. Jim came to his defense at the meeting because he was outraged at the way Chaplin was treated and the kinds of questions he was asked. So he came up with some perfunctory questions of his own which stopped the show." Mia recalled that after the press conference ended, Agee was given the opportunity to meet the man who had held such a prominent place in his imagination since childhood: "He met Chaplin at that meeting at least to talk to him for five minutes."[44]

Immediately after the press conference, Agee redoubled his efforts to get *The Tramp's New World* in front of Chaplin, this time with the sure knowledge that Chaplin would know his name and would be more likely inclined to give his idea a hearing. In a letter dated April 13, 1947, written the day after the press event and their brief introduction, Agee wrote:

> *Dear Mr. Chaplin: A couple of months ago I wrote to ask you whether I might submit some ideas I have for a new movie, for the tramp character. I should not intrude on you again, or risk further embarrassment for myself; I do so only because I am all the more sure, after seeing your new film, that these ideas would really interest you. Please let me assure you that I am not trying to gain money or reputation. I am anxious that you consider these ideas because they mean a great deal to me, and belong essentially to you, and could, I believe become a very great film as you would use and develop them. This letter, if you should so care to use it, would sign the ideas over to you, free of charge or of screen credit or any other strings. But meanwhile I can only hope you will be willing to give the ideas a hearing. I realize that my persistency must offend you. I regret that, and my own embarrassment. But under the circumstances that cannot be helped. I dislike saying here, what under the circumstances must be suspected of insincerity, but it is important to me to tell you particularly after reading some stupid things in the press—how greatly I like and esteem your new film and your courage.*
>
> *I will be very grateful if you will let me know whether or not I may discuss these ideas for an hour or so, and if so, when that would be convenient for you.*
>
> *My deep apologies for bothering you again.*

Agee was now on a path that would eventually lead him away from journalism and deliver him to Hollywood. He would succeed beyond his dreams in his effort to connect with Chaplin. But his time in Hollywood would also bring bitter disappointment and failure.

Two

AGEE AND THE ATOM BOMB

The screenplay for Chaplin was directly inspired by Agee's reaction to America's use of the atomic bomb in Japan. Today, almost sixty years since the bomb was dropped on Hiroshima, it is nearly impossible to imagine the effect that the event had at the time on the national psyche. It was in many ways a science-fiction nightmare come to life. The experience profoundly affected Agee. When the bomb was dropped, Father Flye was in New York, serving his annual summer residence at St. Luke's Chapel in Greenwich Village. He remembered Agee's reaction to the bomb: "Early one evening Jim Agee came over and said at once, 'Have you heard any news today?' And I said, 'No, I haven't. I didn't get a paper, and I haven't had the radio on today, so I haven't.' And he said, 'You'd better get a good, stiff drink. They have discovered the secret of atomic power and have made a bomb of tremendously destructive power and have dropped it on Japan.' And he was deeply moved."[1] Agee was compelled to meditate deeply on the meaning of the atom bomb and implications of its use when he was assigned by his editor, T. S. Matthews, to write *Time*'s interpretation of the event for the American public.

In his article "The Bomb," *Time*'s cover story on August, 20, 1945, Agee turned the story of America's decision to use the barely tested technology on a populated city into a terrible prediction of man's fate. He saw immediately that mankind would be for all time forward at the mercy of unleashed unknown forces:

When the bomb split open the universe and revealed the prospect of the infinitely extraordinary, it also revealed the oldest, simplest, commonest, most neglected and most important of facts: that each man is eternally and above all else responsible for his own soul, and in the terrible words of the Psalmist, that no man may deliver his brother, nor make agreement unto God for him. Man's fate has forever been shaped between the hands of reason and spirit, now in collaboration, again in conflict. Now reason and spirit meet on final ground. If either or anything is to survive, they must find a way to create an indissoluble partnership.

In T. S. Matthews opinion, Agee's atom bomb article set the high-water mark of *Time*'s prose. He later wrote, "When people tell me about 'Time style' or assert that *Time* was always written in some form of pidgin English, I remember Agee—and this piece in particular."[2]

Concern about the bomb began to affect Agee's work. He found himself too distracted and troubled to concentrate and write well. In the first film review Agee published in the *Nation* following his Hiroshima article, he wrote, "I must apologize for postponing even the attempt to review *The Story of G.I. Joe*; the secondary radiations of the atomic bomb render me unfit to consider a piece of work I so deeply admire." A couple of weeks later he again turned his attention to the delayed review, but he was unable to do so without again invoking the destruction of Hiroshima and Nagasaki and the danger it represented for the fate of mankind: "It seems to me a tragic and eternal work of art, concerned with matters which I know are tragic and which I suspect are as eternal, anyhow, as our use of recent scientific triumphs will permit."[3]

Agee was convinced that the advent of atomic weapons would inevitably lead to the end of civilization. In the weeks that followed the bombing of Hiroshima and Nagasaki, the social and historical implications of the atom bomb weighed heavily on his mind. On September 19 he wrote to Father Flye to express his sense of the inevitability of atomic war and the prospects for his own personal survival: "We write at least the first words of our death-sentence; and prove ourselves once more, hopelessly inadequate morally, and so in every other way, to survive the atomic bomb. Of course we and/or others would be inadequate for that survival anyhow; but in that case there is everything to be said for dying as near in a state of grace as possible."[4]

Taking a second job, Agee began writing a movie review column for the *Nation* in December of 1942. From the very beginning he used the column as a platform for challenging the expectations of his readers. In his first *Nation* piece he wrote a statement of purpose, reminiscent of Charles Foster Kane's "Declaration of Principles," in which he promised to devote his film criticism "to honor and discriminate the subject through interesting and serving you who are reading it." In the familiar self-effacing manner that was a characteristic mode of much of his private and public writing, Agee confessed his lack of experience but contended that an amateur had his own compensating virtues. One advantage of an amateur, he argued, is that an amateur is free from the professional's bad habits and "preoccupation with technique." As an amateur critic he could, though cognizant of his ignorance, "feel no apology for what my eyes tell me as I watch any given screen, where the proof is caught irrelevant to excuse, and available in proportion to the eye which sees it, and the mind which uses it." His pledge made, he began to discuss current movies and almost immediately took a swipe at all the new films released that year when he declared that "the best picture I saw this year was *The Gold Rush*," Chaplin's seventeen-year-old film, which had been reissued for the first time in April of that year.[5]

Agee's new column succeeded with the *Nation*'s readers by presenting a fresh intelligence that took film seriously. His writing never shied from comparing Hollywood product with classic literature and theater. He mixed erudition with sharp wit and a constant hope that films could and should aspire to greatness. After Agee died, his friend and fellow critic Manny Farber wrote in a classic essay, "Nearer My Agee to Thee," that "Agee's deep-dish criticism in *The Nation* was motivated by a need to bridge Hollywood with the highest mounts of art."[6] To Dwight MacDonald, whose own career as a film critic included six years at *Esquire*, Agee was able, unlike himself, to ignore predominating dross for the bit of rare jewel it surrounded: "[Agee's] a romantic critic and I'm a classic critic. The classicist looks at the thing as a whole; the romantic has no sense of the structure as a whole but looks at details. Agee would see one thing in an hour-and-a-half movie and would magnify it and that would color his whole view of the movie."[7]

Agee's unique approach to film criticism was both serious and idiosyncratic enough to gain a loyal following of readers who hungered for a passionate, literate discussion of movie art. Two years into his tenure at the *Nation*, where he was paid $25 for each column, a fan letter arrived from the poet W. H. Auden, who, without solicitation, had written an unqualified mash-note, grateful for Agee's "astonishing excellence." Auden declared that he cared little for movies, saw few of them, and even worse, had especial doubts about the value of film criticism, but found himself "all the more surprised, therefore, to find myself not only reading Mr. Agee before I read anyone else in *The Nation* but also consciously looking forward all week to reading him again. . . . In my opinion, his column is the most remarkable regular event in journalism today."[8] This sort of enthusiastic reader support strengthened Agee's confidence to use his column in the *Nation* as a free zone of self-expression.

On October 15, 1945, Agee again grappled with the bomb in the pages of *Time*. In an assessment of the global reaction to the bomb in the months following Hiroshima, Agee condemned the world community's failure to respond appropriately. Agee was in part inspired by a recent article, "The Bomb," written by Dwight MacDonald in the magazine *Politics*. The title of Agee's *Time* article, "Godless Gotterdammerung," a reference to Richard Wagner's *Twilight of the Gods*, was borrowed from MacDonald's text. MacDonald had observed that the atom bomb "was not developed by any of the totalitarian powers" whose political atmosphere "at first glance seem to be more suited to it," but rather, by the United States and England. He noted that the politicians who made the decision to drop the bomb weren't "figures of certain historical and personal stature," such as Roosevelt and Churchill, but their bland successors, Truman and Attlee, "both colourless mediocrities, Average Men elevated to their positions by the mechanics of the system." MacDonald concluded: "The more commonplace the personalities and senseless the institutions, the more grandiose the destruction. It is Gotterdammerung without the gods."[9]

Agee wrote in *Time* of his urgent concern that the true significance of the bomb was being ignored: "When they got news of the atomic bomb, intelligent men were filled with awe. Yet the most portentous news since that date has been the abundant evidence that mankind in general remains insufficiently aware of his predicament. There has been much talk about how to get the new monster into an unbreakable cage—and few admissions that the real monster is the human race." As evidence of the world's failure, he cited a Gallup poll in which "85% approved the use of the bomb against Japanese cities: and of the 49% who were against using poison gas, most explained that this was through their fear of retaliation—a possibility which, in the case of the bomb, they strangely overlooked."[10]

Agee's article listed numerous examples of what he took as evidence that the world had failed to understand the bomb: "The 34 U.S. clergymen . . . who sent a protest and appeal to President Truman, while vigorously condemning the way in which the bomb was used, seemed to imply that its use might have been excusable to 'save ourselves in an extremity of desperation.' They were 'grateful for the scientific achievement' behind the bomb and wanted to see its power reserved 'for constructive civilian uses.'" He saw initial shock and horror slowly but surely being replaced with acceptance and reinterpretation: "The *Christian Century* after flatly calling the use of the bomb 'an American atrocity,' explained that this was because the editor did not believe that the impetuous manner of using it was 'a military necessity.' The writer went on to say that military necessities are 'beyond moral condemnation,' and that whatever is necessary is mandatory."

In his article for *Time*, Agee directly quoted his friend, referring to MacDonald as a nonreligious American: "'Nobody knew just how deadly or prolonged [the] radioactive poisons would be'"; yet they went ahead and made and used the bomb. "'Perhaps only among men like soldiers and scientists, trained to think "objectively"—i.e., in terms of means, not ends—could such irresponsibility and moral callousness be found. . . . There is something askew in a society in which vast numbers of citizens can be organized to create a horror like The Bomb without even knowing they are doing it.'"

Agee was especially concerned by the fact that hundreds of scientists, many of whom had no idea what they were working on, had mundanely worked together to fashion the most destructive force known to man, and that this product of society would ultimately produce its self-destruction: "This emphasizes that perfect automatism, that absolute lack of human consciousness or aim, which our society is rapidly achieving. As a uranium pile, once the elements have been brought together, runs through a series of 'chain reactions' until the final explosion takes place, so the elements of our society act and react, regardless of ideologies or personalities, until The Bomb explodes over Hiroshima . . ." Agee agreed with MacDonald that the scientists' actions reflected a pervasive dehumanizing trend in modern

society: "'It is fair to expect such men . . . to be aware of the consequences of their actions. And they seem to have been so. . . . Yet they
all accepted the "assignment" . . . because they thought of themselves
as specialists . . . not as complete men . . .' Of the scientists—still unnamed—who refused: 'They reacted as whole men. . . . Today the tendency is to think of peoples as responsible and individuals as
irresponsible. The reversal of both these conceptions is the first condition of escaping the present decline to barbarism.'"

Agee channeled this sense of fated doom and the complicity of the
scientific community into the screenplay he wrote for Chaplin a year
and a half later. Before he began writing the screenplay, themes similar
to those raised by MacDonald were already evident in Agee's writing.
One month after "Godless Gotterdammerung" appeared in *Time*, the
first indication that Agee had embraced the bomb as a literary subject is
found in a letter to Father Flye. On November 19, 1945, Agee expressed to Flye his terrible concerns about the likelihood of an ap-
proaching atomic war, and also revealed the first elements of the story
that would become his Chaplin screenplay: "I've done just a draft of a
story which might with enough work be good, about the atomic
bomb." In the letter, Agee also writes that he has begun work on "a
short novel about adolescence." Suffering from the shock and psychological fallout of Hiroshima, Agee described his struggle with the
problem of doing good work in a world doomed to destruction: "With
so little time from work and so very little time left for anything faintly
recognizable as civilization, it seems rather too obligatory to work only
on the best things possible. But those are even hard to hold to—for
anyone of my weak will. I started a book about the atomic bomb—so
far as an amateur could see the consequences . . . I ought to go crazy
but probably won't. It seems possible to 'adjust' to anything short of
atomic liquefaction, and I'll probably keep right on adjusting."[11]

Agee's November 19 letter continued, describing his struggle with
competing impulses: the will to survive and a growing resignation to
doom. "Supposing 2 to 25 years to go, what is worth doing and what is
worth writing?" As he would later ask in *The Tramp's New World*, Agee
contemplated the chances for survival after an atom war: "But from
there on, what? At the end of the next war we either survive or don't
survive almost total annihilation (i.e., of everyone, everywhere) or: we
survive either as 'victors' or vanquished under a world tyranny." In anticipation of his film idea, Agee began to consider likely survival sce-

narios in a postatomic world: "Even if annihilation is really total, I presume there will be gestures towards a tyranny, likely successful. But more likely one great power will survive nearly untouched. In that case all good and consciousness on either side will be equally defeated and will have equal responsibilities." The responsibilities, Agee calculates, will be survival and the preservation and integrity of "one's consciousness," which he predicts will ultimately compete, "for they will be at each other's throat, far more than now."

Briefly, Agee argued that this end-of-the-world scenario "seems the only thing much worth writing or thinking about." He then swung to the opposite approach to consider that a better response might be to "act as if the house weren't on fire; to use one's consciousness as broadly and leisurely as if this were a time of peace (as indeed it is, or should be, in each individual mind and soul)." Agee's letter to Father Flye ends with the writer resigned to the darkness of man's fate: "As for averting the next war, I see no use even to try. Everything should be rather preparations for the aftermath, if any."

The atomic bomb story that Agee mentioned in his letter to Father Flye was a wild, satiric, and surrealistic piece titled "Dedication Day," which was first published in Dwight MacDonald's *Politics* in April 1946. In this piece Agee's meditation on the complicity of the atom scientists is given full range. Agee's satiric story describes the dedication of a new monument, an arch designed by Frank Lloyd Wright and built of fused uranium. The arch, whose dedication is broadcast on "television's first major hookup," features an Eternal Fuse, burning at the rate of one inch a second, fed from an underground workshop staffed in alternating twelve-hour shifts by disabled war heroes and Japanese, wryly described as "surviving collaborators in the experiment at Hiroshima and Nagasaki." These workers are joined by an American physicist, "one of the more elderly of those scientists who contributed their genius towards the perfecting of the bomb." Driven by "atonement, guilt and individual responsibility" and after first turning to Christianity, Mahatma Gandhi and Tibetan Buddhism, the elderly scientist volunteers to be one of the arch's Keepers of the Flame, and insists on joining the shift staffed by the Japanese.

The physicist is fired after his incessant tears and self-mortifying behavior ("he tore at his thin hair and beat his bruised face with clenched fists and tore at it with his nails") becomes too disturbing to tourists visiting the Arch prior to its formal dedication. He is, though, granted the privilege of throwing the switch that will "start the fuse on its eternal journey." Immediately after he ignites the fuse, the physicist commits suicide; a note pinned to his lab coat explains his act as "a kind of religious or ethical 'sacrifice,' through which he hoped to endow the triumphal monument with a new and special significance, once more (as he thought) to assist the human race."[12]

A few months after Agee's story was published, the *New Yorker* devoted its entire August 31, 1946 issue to John Hersey's landmark piece on the atomic bombing of Japan, later published as the book *Hiroshima*. Details in Hersey's story are echoed in Agee's screenplay for Chaplin. In *The Tramp's New World*, plants, growing at incredible rates, sprout threatening tendrils and wrap around any convenient body like an anaconda. Hersey had reported how plant life was strangely stimulated by the atomic blast:

> . . . there was something she noticed about it that particularly gave her the creeps. Over everything—up through the wreckage of the city, in gutters, along the riverbanks, tangled among tiles and tin roofing, climbing on charred tree trunks—was a blanket of fresh, vivid, lush, optimistic green; the verdancy rose even from the foundations of ruined houses.
>
> The high levels of radiation had apparently sped the vegetative growth in an unexpected and unsettling manner, rapidly overgrowing the burnt city's ashes with an abundance of weeds and wild flowers
>
> The bomb had not only left the underground organs of plants intact; it had stimulated them. Everywhere were bluets and Spanish bayonets, goosefoot, morning glories and day lilies, the hairy-fruited bean, purslane and clotbur and sesame and panic grass and feverfew. Especially in a circle at the center, sickle senna grew in extraordinary regeneration, not only standing among the charred remnants of the same plant but pushing up in new places, among bricks and through cracks in the asphalt. It actually seemed as if a load of sickle-senna seed had been dropped along with the bomb.[13]

Hersey also described how the intense heat and light of the atomic explosion had burned shadows into solid material—a disturbing image that many readers never forgot. He wrote, "the bomb had, in some places, left prints of the shadows that had been cast by its light. The experts found, for instance, a permanent shadow thrown on the roof of the Chamber of Commerce Building (220 yards from the rough center) by the structure's rectangular tower; several others in the lookout post on top of the Hypothec Bank (2,050 yards); another in the tower of the Chugoku Electric Supply Building (800 yards); another projected by the handle of a gas pump (2,630 yards); and several on granite tombstones in the Gokoku Shrine (385 yards)."

Even more disturbing were the shadows of human forms left by the bomb. Like some perverted new variation on the ashen molds of victims left by the eruption of Mt. Vesuvius in 79 A.D., these atomic photographs left nightmarish reminders of the devastation: "A few vague human silhouettes were found, and these gave rise to stories that eventually included fancy and precise details. One story told how a painter on a ladder was monumentalized in a kind of bas-relief on the stone facade of a bank building on which he was at work, in the act of dipping his brush into his paint can; another, how a man and his cart on the bridge near the Museum of Science and Industry, almost under the center of the explosion, were cast down in an embossed shadow which made it clear that the man was about to whip his horse."[14] Agee put this same strange visual effect to powerful use in his screenplay for Chaplin, when he populated Manhattan's sidewalks with the two-dimensional images of the bomb's victims caught midstride.

Key elements of Agee's postatomic screenplay were now in place. He had decided that the black humor of "Dedication Day" was a workable way to approach the unfathomable horror of atomic war. He had also decided that the bland community of order-following scientists was the true enemy of the fully realized human life. Hersey provided the terribly true, science fiction horror story imagery upon which to tell his story. News accounts around this time, which reported that Chaplin's next film, initially called *Bluebeard*, or *The Lady Killer*, might also have encouraged Agee to consider combining Chaplin's Tramp character and the ultimate tale of mass murder.

Three

*D*ESPERATELY *S*EEKING *C*HAPLIN

*S*hortly after Agee began working on his Chaplin screenplay, on February 19, 1947, *The Beginning or the End*, a new film that mixed fiction and fact about the building of the atom bomb, was released in theaters. This film provided a sort of reverse-image of Agee's own subject matter, a negative inspiration, one not to emulate but to counter. *The Beginning or the End* is now recognized as the first post-Hiroshima atomic bomb movie. The film's production was put into motion, according to its press book ("The warm human story behind the world's most vital subject. How it became a film entertainment for the millions"),[1] through the instigation of the actress Donna Reed. Reed had discovered that her high school chemistry teacher, Dr. Edward Tompkins, was one of the scientists who worked on the atomic bomb in Oak Ridge, Tennessee. Reed wrote to Tompkins in October 1945 and he responded, "Do you think a movie could be planned and produced to impress, upon the public, the horrors of atomic warfare, the fact that other countries can produce atomic explosives and the vulnerability of civilization to attack by these explosives?" After she received Tompkins's response, Reed's husband Tony Owen, a former agent, contacted MGM and got the ball rolling. The film's producers met with President Harry Truman, who encouraged the filmmakers and purportedly provided them with the film's title, when he told them "Make a good picture. One that will tell the people that the decision is theirs to make . . . this is the beginning or the end!" The movie was directed by Norman Taurog of *Boys Town* fame, who would later direct many of Elvis Presley's Hollywood films, including *Girls! Girls! Girls!* and *Tickle Me*.

MGM's publicity department claimed that the producers of *The Beginning or the End* had assembled the largest "corps of technical advisors . . . ever employed on a motion picture." The film's depiction of the atom bomb's blast was simulated with a hundred spot lamps and huge skylights that used "over two-and-half million watts of light . . . the equivalent of 42,000 average house bulbs." Norman Lloyd, Hanns Eisler's neighbor, who would later direct Agee's Lincoln television series for *Omnibus*, played a small role as Dr. Troyanski.

The film begins with two doors marked Science Laboratory swinging open to reveal a young Hume Cronyn. Cronyn looks directly into the camera and says, "How do you do, whoever you are? My name is J. Robert Oppenheimer. I'm an American Scientist working in the year of our Lord, nineteen hundred and forty-six. I'm addressing you people of the twenty-fifth century in English, now, and I hope in your time, one of the leading languages of the world. . . . The people of my era unleashed the power, which for all we know will destroy human life on this earth. . . . For you of the twenty-fifth century we have recorded our search to unlock the atom. . . . We know the beginning. Only you of tomorrow, if there is a tomorrow, can know the end."

Later in the film, after they've dropped the bomb on Hiroshima, the bomber's crew turns around to assess the results. Viewing the burning city below, the fictional Col. Jeff Nixon announces, "If there ever is another war it won't be cities burning themselves one at a time, but the whole world on fire, eating itself to ashes." In an earlier scene, Matt Cochran, a guilt-ridden atom scientist played by Tom Drake, is killed by radiation poisoning as he sacrifices himself to prevent the bomb from prematurely detonating. Returning to Washington, D.C., Nixon and his girlfriend inform Cochran's pregnant wife of her husband's heroic death. In the shadow of the Lincoln Memorial, Cochran's ghost is heard reading the letter Nixon has come to deliver, "If . . . primitives learned to use fire, we of an enlightened century can learn to use [atomic energy] . . . God has not shown us a way to destroy ourselves . . . atomic energy is the hand he has extended." After expounding on the marvels of atomic energy to come (a locomotive engine powered by the atoms in a pasteboard ticket), the ghost of

Cochran gushes "we have found a path so full of promise that . . . what we have unleashed is not the end. . . . Human beings are made in the image of God."[2]

Agee reacted to *The Beginning or the End* with dismay. Reviewing the film in the *Nation* on March 1, 1947, he complained:

> You learn less about atomic fission from this film than I would assume is taught by now in the more progressive nursery schools; you learn even less than that about the problems of atomic control; and you learn least of all about morals. There is to be sure a young scientist, played with sincerity by Tom Drake, who suffers from scruples; but his conscience is neatly canceled by the posthumous letter in which it is he and he alone who realizes, discarding his worries like last summer's sand fleas, that in God's own time transcontinental commuting, better complexions, and the millennium itself will be achieved on the power generated from an old hat check.
>
> Oh, yes, the movie. Well, there is very little to say. The bombing and the Alamagordo test are effectively staged, though hardly adequate to one's information, let alone one's imagination of how to handle that information creatively. For the rest it seemed to me surprisingly bad even though I rather expected it to be bad, for a good reason: only people of first-rate talent stand even a chance of not being paralyzed, for a long time, by a new subject; *Wake Island*, the first American movie about the last war, was hardly better than this. The film is also a horrifying sample of what American movies will be like if the state interferes with them much; it gives me unexpected respect for those who, under such circumstances, do so much better even with the worst of the Russian movies which get over here. Barring the two bits of staging I mentioned, which are to the credit of light technicians, the whole show could as well be called *Tom Swift and His Giant Ego*—which, for that matter, could go for practically everything to do with the development of the bomb in fact.[3]

By the time his review of *The Beginning or the End* was published, Agee had developed his postatomic Tramp story idea and sent off his first pitch letter to Chaplin's studio. Taurog's film, which Agee saw as a sanitized piece of government-approved propaganda, could only have encouraged him in his efforts to reach Chaplin to interest him in his screenplay. A month after the review of *The Beginning or the End*, Chaplin had come to New York for his *Monsieur Verdoux* press conference, and one month after that, on May 9, 1947, Agee finally received a reply from the Charles Chaplin Studios. The response was brief, to the point, and anything but encouraging:

> *Dear Sir,*
> *Your letter dated April 13, 1947 was forwarded to this office from New York. In accordance with the rule of this studio we must decline the offer of your ideas for the tramp character as neither Mr. Chaplin nor this company is in the market for material for photoplays. Thanking you for your courtesy, we are*
> *Sincerely yours.*"[4]

This terse rejection letter might have been the end of the story, but Agee believed in the importance of his idea. Beyond the personal and professional benefits that the film could provide, Agee believed that the idea was both of potential interest and value to Chaplin and could serve as a crucial and useful message to mankind. Through the agency of Chaplin's beloved Tramp character, the film could, he believed, deliver a dire message about the threat of science and technology and the fate of civilization, a message that, if handled correctly, might divert society from sure destruction or at worst illuminate the causes of its own doom. While Agee must have been disappointed with the impasse he had reached with Chaplin's studio, he didn't react idly. As both the writer of *Time* magazine's Cinema section and the contributor to a revered and influential weekly film column in the *Nation*, Agee had a bully pulpit, a high-profile vantage that he could use to try to communicate directly to Chaplin.

In fact, before the rejection letter had arrived from the Chaplin Studios, Agee had already published his first review of *Monsieur Verdoux* in the May 5 issue of *Time*. In prose that would prove more balanced and less adulatory than the controversial series of reviews he later published in the *Nation*, Agee, after a concise synopsis of the movie's plot, broached the political aspect of the already notorious comedy with a restrained subjectivity: "[Verdoux] is firmly convinced that good and evil are inextricably mingled—and has come to believe that he is not more essentially evil than good. Chaplin has remarked that Verdoux paraphrases Clausewitz's idea that the logical extension of diplomacy is war. Verdoux's version: 'The logical extension of business is murder.' War, he tells the court which condemns him, is merely a grandiose multiplication of the crime he is dying for. But wholesale murder is condoned by the state."[5] Treading with measured caution, Agee acknowledged in his *Time* review of Chaplin's new film that *Monsieur Verdoux* was less than perfect, that it had "serious shortcomings both as popular entertainment and as a work of art," but he sided with the filmmaker and laid much of the blame on the audience's limitations: "It has its blurs and failures. Finely cut and paced as it is, the picture goes on so long, and under such darkness and chill, that the lazier-minded type of cinemagoers will probably get tired." Having accepted the film's faults, Agee quickly tacked and turned-about: "Whatever its shortcomings, it is one of the most notable films in years. It is not the finest picture Chaplin ever made, but it is certainly the most fascinating." Echoing Bosley Crowther, Agee declared *Monsieur Verdoux* "a daring individual gesture, dared in an era when such acts are rare." He recognized that one of the film's great hurdles was that Chaplin had denied his audience its beloved Little Tramp. "Many will detest the product and despise Chaplin for producing it. He has replaced his beloved, sure-fire tramp with an equally original, but far less engaging character—a man whose grace and arrogance alone would render him suspect with the bulk of the non-Latin world. He has gone light on pure slapstick and warm laughter, and has borne down on moral complexity, terror and irony with an intensity never before attempted in films."

To champion an unpopular film, a critic must consider questioning the audience's own critical capability. Agee argued in *Time* that Chaplin's success was in part due to his heroic refusal to pander to the audience: "In Chaplin's last minutes . . . he opens up with his heaviest guns, and sticks by them to the bitter end. In the whole two hours of the film, there is not one instant of bidding in any shabby way for the audience's sympathy. Morally alone, this is a remarkable thing to have done." Agee admits too that he is in the minority, that "a majority of Manhattan critics found the film baffling, disappointing, offensive, and, in stretches, plain boring." While navigating past the film's more dangerous shoals, Agee, in between hazards, enjoys the view, wasting no opportunity to honor the comedian: "The set pieces of pure slapstick are as skilled and delightful, and as psychologically penetrating, as any Chaplin has ever contrived. . . . The casting is excellent . . . Chaplin still has his sure virtuosity; his is one of the most beautiful single performances ever put on film."

Compared to his writing in the *Nation*, Agee's criticism at *Time* was somewhat constrained, both in argument and the amount of space available. In his regular column for the politically progressive *Nation*, he was able to write more expansively—and to write about *Monsieur Verdoux* with a freer rein, buoyed by the knowledge that *Nation*'s liberal readers would be more sympathetic both to Chaplin the man and to his art. But this freedom was a mixed blessing for Agee. Free to say almost anything, he found he had too much to say. Agee's column for the May 10 *Nation* issue began with an apology and a bit of a tease, "With deep regret I must postpone my attempt to review Chaplin's *Monsieur Verdoux*. I cannot hope to do it justice, but I do prefer to discuss it a little more coherently than I have been able to, to date. In case this leaves any doubt of my opinion of the film, let me say that I think it is one of the best movies ever made, easily the most exciting and most beautiful since *Modern Times*."

Next he simultaneously admitted the film's poor reception while separating himself from the critical herd; "I will add that I think most of the press on the picture, and on Chaplin, is beyond disgrace. I urge everyone to see *Monsieur Verdoux* who can get to it." Agee then proceeded to review other recent films, but they simply became fodder for comparison to Chaplin's latest work: *The Captive Heart*, a British movie about prisoners of war, had been greeted as a masterpiece by some of the reviewers who, only too literally, couldn't "see" *Monsieur Verdoux*; "So now we know what a masterpiece is: something that isn't either really bad or by any generosity really good . . ." Agee protested that critics were unfair in praising a photographic technique in *The Captive Heart* that they called "archaic, or worse, when Chaplin uses it; and Chaplin uses it all the time, for incomparably richer and subtler purposes."[6]

Since the rejection letter from Chaplin Studios had arrived after both the *Time* review and the column for the *Nation* had gone to press, Agee looked for additional means for contacting Chaplin. Encouraged by his friend Lincoln Kirstein, Agee wrote to Erwin Piscator, the founder of the Dramatic Workshop at the New School for Social Research. Kirstein, who one year later, in 1948, cofounded the New York City Ballet with George Balanchine, had befriended Agee while both were students at Exeter and Harvard. At Harvard, Kirstein launched *The Hound & Horn*, a quarterly literary magazine, and published several of Agee's poems. In a poem entitled "Tudoresque" written while he was stationed in England during World War II, Kirstein recalled their shared schooldays:

My first Shakespeare contacts . . .
Were Jim's reading parts from the Histories aloud, fresh as current
    events . . .
We got drunk on Shakespeare's iambics and Britain's dynastic rain-
    bow.
I most remember him
Flipping the pages of portraits vignetted for the *London News*—
The First War's English dead, . . .
Jim had such charm as Hamlet, I was happy Horatio, his friend . . . [7]

Kirstein was also close friends with Walker Evans, and in 1938 served as curator for Evans's landmark photography exhibit, "American Photographs," at the Museum of Modern Art. To help Agee in his effort to reach Chaplin, Kirstein discussed the predicament with the composer Marc Blitzstein, and the two agreed that Erwin Piscator would provide a likely means of contacting the comedian. Piscator, before emigrating from Berlin, was already a famous and influential avant-garde theater director in Weimar Germany. In the mid-1920s, Piscator developed, in collaboration with Bertolt Brecht, a radical approach to staging, called "epic theater," which merged political subject matter and new theater techniques. Piscator's stage productions were experiments in multimedia. On occasion, Piscator, influenced by the public impact of Chaplin comedies, employed back projection and film in his plays, which typically integrated historical films with disparate everyday elements. Beginning around 1927, many of the artists who later came together in Hollywood had already worked together in experimental theater groups in Germany. In addition to Brecht, Piscator's collaborators had included Hanns Eisler and Berthold Viertel, each of whom later settled in the film colony outposts of Malibu, Pacific Palisades, and Santa Monica. Brecht collaborated with Piscator until Brecht's and Kurt Weill's success with *The Threepenny Opera* took him in another direction. The interrelationships were dizzying; Brecht's partner Weill had provided music for a play by Lion Feuchtwanger, and both Weill and Hanns Eisler had individually provided music for plays by Piscator.

Founded in New York in 1940, after Piscator emigrated to America, the Dramatic Workshop attracted and mentored numerous actors and directors who went on to lead American theater and film, including Marlon Brando, Tennessee Williams, Walter Matthau, Rod

Steiger, Shelley Winters, Harry Belafonte, Elaine Stritch, Ben Gaz-
zara, and Tony Curtis. Both Lee Strasberg and Stella Adler, who
branched off with their own approaches to theater, had been on Piscator's faculty. Another of Piscator's protégés, the actress Judith Malina,
left the workshop to found the experimental Living Theater with Julian Beck; Malina later became one of Agee's several extra-marital
lovers. And Brando later starred in Chaplin's last film, *A Countess from
Hong Kong*.

Agee had hoped to reach Chaplin by exploiting Piscator's friendship with the comedian's close friend Hanns Eisler. The idea to contact Piscator originated with Marc Blitzstein. Ten years before,
Blitzstein's play *The Cradle Will Rock*, which he dedicated to Brecht,
was produced by Orson Welles and John Houseman as part of the
Federal Theater Project backed by the federal Work Projects Administration program. The government, under political pressure, with-
drew its support for the FTP, and blocked the play's premiere
production in New York City on June 16, 1937 at the Maxine Elliott
Theater on 37th Street with padlocked doors and security guards. In
protest, the cast and audience, led by Agee's mentor Archibald
MacLeish, marched across town to the Venice Theater on 58th Street
and Seventh Avenue and performed the play. Blitzstein had first been
exposed to Eisler's music years before in Germany, when he had gone
to study composition with Eisler's mentor, Arnold Schoenberg. Later,
Blitzstein translated Brecht's song *Mäckie Messer Moritat*, from *The
Three Penny Opera*, into *Mack the Knife*, the familiar, modified English-
language version popularized by singer Bobby Darin.

On May 15, Agee sent his request for help to Piscator:

Dear Mr. Piscator
*I must apologize for intruding, and ask you a great favor, and beg your pa-
tience while I explain it. I have an idea, considerably developed for a new
film for Mr. Chaplin's tramp character. I would not think of bothering him
unless I believed strongly that these ideas might be of serious interest and
use to him. I feel it is of the greatest importance to be able to present and
discuss them with him personally. This should not require very much time,
but I realize acutely how beset by requests, etc., he must be, and how naturally he must prefer to avoid them. A friend of mine, Lincoln Kirstein, was
discussing my predicament with Marc Blizstein, who told him that he believed you could arrange an appointment, and would be willing to, if I
identified myself as the person who asked the question in defense of Mr.*

Chaplin, at the press conference he gave, the Monday after his film opened. Needless to say I will be profoundly grateful if you are willing to do this. I realize that Mr. Chaplin has good reason to avoid people who wish to press "story ideas" on him, and I wholly sympathize with him. If you are so kind as to speak to him on my behalf, will you please make my own intentions clear. Money could be useful to me, and further work on my idea could be of interest, but neither is of any concern, beside my desire to put these ideas at Mr. Chaplin's disposal, if they should interest him. If Mr. Chaplin should see fit, he would be more than welcome to these ideas without question of charge or credit or any other kind of commitment, and I would be glad to make this legally binding, if he should so desire. I am sorry to trouble you with this, but I assure you that my motives are in no way opportunistic. I have unlimited regard and admiration for Mr. Chaplin, and am in no way among his enemies or those who would wish to profit off him. I believe I could be useful to him, and that is my desire.[8]

It is not known whether Piscator responded to the entreaty, but in the meantime, Agee's singular action at the press conference had other positive effects. Because the *Monsieur Verdoux* press event had been broadcast live on the radio, Agee's defense of Chaplin quickly became a minor cause célèbre. Friends and admirers reached out to congratulate him for his courageous stance. In a letter dated May 19, 1947, the novelist Henry Miller, no stranger to social censure himself, after reading a report of the press conference in an article in the *New Republic* wrote from Big Sur, California, to applaud Agee's courage in standing up for Chaplin, "My dear Agee: A friend of mine just showed me a clipping from the *New Republic* through which I learned of your wonderful gesture at that meeting of the members of the press which Chaplin convoked recently. It was good to know that someone had the courage to act as you did."[9]

In the *New Republic* column cited by Miller, the critic Shirley O'Hara wrote, "At the press conference itself, however, only James Agee of *Time*, whose admirable control made it possible for him to speak at all, was able civilly to voice the apologies of some of the newspaper and magazine reporters when, in effect, he asked Chaplin what he thought of a country in which a fine artist, whose pity and concern for the downtrodden had made him beloved throughout the world, was given the disgraceful reception just tendered him. Chaplin, still smiling gently, preferred not to discuss that question, and thanked Agee 'very much.'"[10] O'Hara was—along with Max Lerner of *PM*,

Archer Winsten of the *New York Post*, and Bosley Crowther of the *New York Times*—among the very few widely read critics who had expressed any praise for Chaplin's new film.

In 1969 a tape recording of the press conference surfaced and was published in the magazine *Film Comment*. Not surprisingly, the transcription revealed how the event had become romanticized and exaggerated through time and retelling; people's recollections had taken on perhaps more of Agee's heartfelt intention than he was actually able to express at the time. During the press conference, Agee, standing in the balcony, was both nervous and agitated when he spoke—understandably, as he was directly addressing one his life's great heroes for the very first time. He was also angered by the treatment Chaplin was receiving from the largely antagonistic assembly. The tape captured the exchange between Chaplin and Agee.

> Question: [inaudible, voice from the balcony]
> Chaplin: Sorry, I didn't quite get all that you said. That's very nice. Thank you very much. It's needed. I didn't quite hear—I got a little confused. You didn't have the microphone—it is very difficult.
> A microphone is passed up.
> United Artist Spokesman: Would you restate the question, please?
> Agee: [extremely vexed, voice trembling] What are people who care a damn about freedom—who really care for it—think of a country and the people in it, who congratulate themselves upon this country as the finest on earth and as a "free country," when so many of the people of this country pry into what a man's citizenship is, try to tell him his business from hour to hour and from day to day and exert a public moral blackmail against him for not becoming an American citizen—for his political views and for not entertaining troops in the manner—in the way that they think he should. What is to be thought of a general country, where those people are thought well of?
> Chaplin: Thank you very much—but I have nothing to say to that question.[11]

Agee had found himself unable to tackle *Monsieur Verdoux* in his May 10 *Nation* column: Afterward he may have sensed that the best way to build on his new role as Chaplin's defender and advocate was with a bold and unprecedented public act. The question was, how to proceed? Agee found himself in a curious position. He was ambitious to gain Chaplin's support and interest and he was equally anxious to defend a film he honestly considered a work of art, a film that, however flawed, was in Agee's eyes being whipped in the media more for the deflated popularity of its maker than for its own qualities. His options for championing the film at *Time* were limited—for one thing, his *Time* columns were unsigned, and only his prose style and observations could serve to identify his authorship. Agee decided that his column at the *Nation* offered the most promising platform, and he decided to use this bully pulpit to its fullest capacity. Agee took a big leap and devoted his next three consecutive *Nation* columns—on May 31, June 14, and June 21—entirely to an analysis of *Monsieur Verdoux*.

He had twice before written reviews that spanned multiple *Nation* columns. The first was for Laurence Olivier's film version of *Henry V,* published in the July 20 and August 3 issues in 1946. Later that year he devoted the columns in the first two issues of December to an extended review of *The Best Years of Our Lives*. Even so, a three-part review was something striking and unprecedented. Among Agee's surviving papers there is a handwritten manuscript, almost one hundred pages long, comprising the first draft material for his review of *Monsieur Verdoux*. The draft version reveals how hard Agee struggled to find the right tone and approach. The notes make manifest Agee's effort to find a balance that permitted an adulation of Chaplin just short of sycophancy alongside an honest appraisal of the film's weaknesses. To use a Chaplinesque metaphor, Agee's struggle was the critical equivalent of Chaplin's classic high-wire act in *The Circus*, when the Tramp is drafted into performing the act of his AWOL rival, Rex the King of the Air. The Tramp, unknowingly detached from the secret lifeline that has given him the confidence to venture halfway down the tightrope, finds himself under siege from a gang of monkeys who, while scampering over his head, cover his eyes and invade his mouth with groping tails. Agee's monkeys were *Monsieur Verdoux*'s disappointed audience, Agee's fellow critics, and the undeniable weaknesses in the film itself. To pull this effort off would require a bravura performance. In his three-part review of *Monsieur Verdoux*, Agee attempted to work out his highest feelings for Chaplin while fighting to find secure footing from which to celebrate and champion a much-panned film whose subject alone was guaranteed to alienate many in its potential audience.

The film's subject matter, mass murder, was still a bit startling to audiences. There had been dramatic movies about serial killers made previously, including Alfred Hitchcock's Jack the Ripper story, *The Lodger* (1927), and his more recent *Shadow of a Doubt* (1943), with Joseph Cotton playing the lonelyhearts murderer Uncle Charlie. And the German director Fritz Lang had found international success with *M* (1931), the story of a child murderer played memorably by Peter Lorre, a veteran of Brecht's theater. But there were very few precedents for an American comedy about mass murder; the 1944 Cary Grant vehicle *Arsenic and Old Lace* being one of the few. In the years following the release of *Monsieur Verdoux*, England's Ealing Studios released *Kind Hearts and Coronets* (1949), the Alec Guinness tour de force in which he plays all eight members of the D'Ascoyne family, who must be murdered before an ill-treated heir can achieve his due. By the 1960s dark comedies such as *Dr. Strangelove* would wring laughs from total world annihilation. But in 1947, the idea of a charming, remorseless Lady Killer—the working title Orson Welles's had proposed to Chaplin for the story about Henri Landru—was a difficult sell at best, both commercially and critically. The added burden of the low state of Chaplin's American popularity only made Agee's challenge more difficult.

To find the right approach for championing such a film was no easy matter. Agee's draft notes for the reviews are replete with incautious superlatives cut from the final published columns. He wrote, for example, that even with their shortcomings, certain scenes in the movie were "equal with the greatest I have ever seen on film."[12] He declared that Chaplin was "the greatest artist of our time, in any medium, and has come a longer way than any other I can think of." He found that Chaplin's progress from the early Keystone shorts to the more blatant social commentaries, such as *Modern Times, The Great Dictator,* and *Monsieur Verdoux,* reflected the entire arc of historical artistic development: "His evolution it seems to me [encompasses] that of the whole history of art and he has created masterpieces of poetry almost every step of the way. His first work was as pure primitive folk art as I know of."

In these draft notes for his columns in the *Nation,* Agee contemplated the Chaplin films that preceded *Monsieur Verdoux.* He found *City Lights* to be a "thoroughly worthy equivalent"[13] to Shakespeare's *Troilus and Cressida,* and *The Circus* to be Chaplin's "one perfect film, the supreme diamond-like piece of light classicism that I know of in our time." Of *Modern Times*, Agee wrote that though it was "neither politically nor aesthetically the most revolutionary of several great leftist films," it was "nevertheless, the one leftist work of art for which leftists who retain their souls can forever feel immaculate love and pride." Moving from Elizabethan to Biblical comparisons, he noted that *Modern Times* was "practically the Book of Psalms of the angry, hopeful middle thirties." *Monsieur Verdoux*'s unusual mix of black humor, social critique, and slapstick, while challenging for the popular audience, was for Agee simply more evidence of Chaplin's kinship with the great artists of antiquity who had themselves successfully spanned both the tastes of the mob and of the intellectual elite.

In the draft notes, Agee wrote, "Like Shakespeare, Blake and Schubert, [Chaplin] was able to blend the best elements of primitive art with the elements of civilized art." The attempt to work out a sense of Chaplin's significance through comparison with great artists of the past was an ongoing project of Agee's. Years before, after first seeing *Modern Times*, he had written in a spiral notebook, amidst a smattering of unrelated personal observations, similar notes in contemplation of Chaplin: "He shares with Blake and Christ this: that he indicates what is obviously the good way to live: to live that way would mean complete 'withdrawal from the world' for each individual; would mean the destruction of the world as is."[14] Agee had long contemplated the secular saint aspect of Chaplin's Little Tramp; this conception of the Little Tramp—as a Christ or Saint Francis of Assisi-like figure—found it's ultimate expression in *The Tramp's New World*, in which Agee used the character as the model for a new anticapitalist society he imagined forming itself in the wilds of Central Park after the atomic destruction of the city.

Chaplin provided some insight into his own use of Christian principles during the *Monsieur Verdoux* conference. After a reporter asked if he had intended to create sympathy for the film's title character, Chaplin responded, "No. I intended to create a pity for all humanity under certain drastic circumstances . . . certain drastic circumstances . . . in times of stress . . . in catastrophe . . . bring out the worst in humanity . . . and I wanted to show that any time we have a Depression or any time that we have a national catastrophe, that it brings out these cancerous conditions—like the figure of Verdoux."[15] The questioner pushed Chaplin to say whether he thought works of entertainment shouldn't provide the audience with an object of sympathy, to which Chaplin replied, "I intended that the feeling should be that you have a sympathy for the whole human race. I think that's the doctrine of Christianity."[16]

While Agee struggled to write his three-part *Monsieur Verdoux* reviews for the *Nation*—basing all of his analysis and recollections on a single viewing of the film ("So far I have only seen *Monsieur Verdoux* once and thought about it for weeks."[17])—he came to fear that the task he had set for himself was beyond his abilities. The draft notes show him trying out ways to lower the readers' expectations: "After weeks of trying, I am sadly aware that even if granted unlimited leisure and space, I could never write about Chaplin's *Monsieur Verdoux* in a way that was worthy of it."[18] This appeal for a reader to understand the greatness and inherent difficulties of his subject was a familiar element in Agee's writing, and reflected his own personal humility. He had used the same approach in his debut column for the *Nation*, and in the first pages of *Let Us Now Praise Famous Men*: "If I bore you that is that. If I am clumsy, that may indicate partly the difficulty of my subject, and the seriousness with which I am trying to take what hold I can of it; more certainly, it will indicate my youth, my lack of mastery of my so-called art or craft, my lack perhaps of talent."[19] In the hundred pages of draft notes one also finds Agee condemning his fellow critics, who he castigates for being too blind or too lazy to see the virtues of Chaplin's film. For Agee there was an element of Red Scare mob mentality in many of the negative reviews. Agee skewered these critics as "the same great souls who hung Mussolini by his feet,"[20] for what he perceived as their complicity in the rush to lynch the politically radioactive Chaplin.

From these first draft notes, Agee distilled a 4,000-word, three-part review. While the published reviews are in many ways a toned-down version of the themes Agee explored in the draft notes, in their size and scope, and spread over three consecutive issues of the *Nation*, they are equally immoderate. Agee's published defense of *Monsieur Verdoux* is so fervent and adulatory that it remains the subject of controversy and analysis. In these columns, he moved from the conciliatory but positive review written for *Time* to the type of energetic emotional defense one might give a family member insulted by a stranger.

In the first installment of the published review in the *Nation*, Agee began by informing the reader that although his editors had given him dispensation to exceed his column's normal length, it would still be insufficient to cover the ground he wanted to survey: "I can say here only a few of the things that I feel need to be said about Mr. Chaplin's new film. I can only hope that these notes may faintly suggest the frame-by-frame appreciation, the gratitude, and the tribute which we owe this great poet and his great poem."[21]

After beginning with a fairly objective synopsis of the plot, Agee next asked the reader to "disregard virtually everything you may have read about the film," explaining that the mostly negative reaction to the film was mostly of interest as "a definitive measure of the difference between the thing a man of genius puts before the world and the things the world is equipped to see in it." In essence, Agee challenged the reader to be capable of recognizing the truth. He next established the forces aligned against his review with a laundry list of the leading critical cavils about the film, "the film isn't funny; is morally questionable; is in bad taste; that Chaplin should never have stopped playing the tramp; that [Martha] Raye steals her scenes with Chaplin; that Chaplin is no good at casting, writing, directing, producing; that he should have hired people, for all these jobs, who knew the techniques which have been developed since talkies began." Like a boxer in a battle royale, Agee took on each of these complaints one by one.

Responding to the film's supposed lack of humor, Agee placed the blame on critics who lacked the ability to handle a discussion of original subjects being "poetically parodied." He argued that to appreciate the film required a special viewer, one with an "appetite for cold nihilistic irony." Agee took the position that Chaplin must be understood as a brave artist who was willing to risk alienating his audience by subduing his familiar "outrageous fun to the grim central spirit of his work."

On the issue of the film's morality Agee buys time and postpones discussion of the issue for a later column, but adds that any critic who objected to the film on moral grounds was incapable of "recognizing an act of moral and artistic heroism when he saw it." As far as the film being in bad taste, Agee concedes that this must be true if Americans are unable to deal seriously with death (Agee assiduously eschewed the word "murder" for death). He bats away the loud complaints about Chaplin abandoning the much-loved Tramp as simply childish. And as for Martha Raye stealing the show, Agee argues that that is exactly what she's there for, Chaplin being unable by the very nature of the story to have Verdoux, "in his quiet skill and graciousness," get the big laughs. In his response to criticism of the film's casting, Agee simply contradicts the complaint and put his foot down; "Chaplin is the most perceptive, imaginative, exact man alive, at casting."

In discussing Chaplin's script, Agee refuses to give an inch. While he seemed to be willing to concede that the film's writing takes a backseat to it's visuals, Agee spins around and proposes that the Verdoux script is "one of the most talented screenplays ever written." He argues that Chaplin's direction is full of "perfect visual wit and expressiveness and with an all but unblemished grace, force, and economy." The brilliance of the directing, he insisted, was only exceeded by Chaplin's *Modern Times* and by another of his touchstone films, Aleksandr Dovzhenko's *Frontier.*

Although some critics complained that the sets on *Monsieur Verdoux* looked cheap and unconvincing, Agee sees them as a "manifesto against a kind of vulgarity in which Hollywood is drowned—the attempt to disguise emptiness with sumptuousness." He defends the film's production as "handmade, not machine-turned" and "poetic, not naturalistic." Against the charge that Chaplin's movie-lot France was thoroughly unconvincing, Agee responds that the film's scenery was actually a "highly intelligent paraphrase, far more persuasive of its place—half in the real world, half in the mind."

One familiar charge against Chaplin was that his camerawork was static, and had never evolved from the earliest days of filmmaking. Against the argument that *Monsieur Verdoux* lacked modern filmmaking techniques, Agee responds that when handled artistically there is no need to move the camera: "[if] you can invent something worth watching, the camera should hold still and clear, so that you can watch it. That is still, and will always be, one of the best possible ways to use a camera; Chaplin is the one great man who still stands up for it." His defense was that modern viewers have spoiled eyes that keep most in the audience from being "competent to see what [Chaplin] puts before you."

On June 14, 1947, two weeks after the first installment, the second part of Agee's *Monsieur Verdoux* review was published in the *Nation.* If there were any question of his backing off from his solo battle to convert the public, this column's very first sentence put all doubt to rest: "Chaplin's performance as Verdoux is the best piece of playing I have ever seen . . ."[22] Not even a qualified statement would do; for Agee, Chaplin was simply the best.

Sadly, by the time Agee's third and final column about *Monsieur Verdoux* was published one week later in the June 21 issue, Agee was no longer writing to encourage readers to go out and see the much-disparaged film. They couldn't, even if they had wanted to. United Artists had pulled the movie for an undisclosed period to undertake a radical reshaping of its publicity message before re-releasing it for national distribution. Agee's push against the critical tide was now close to futile. He acknowledged the unfortunate turn of events in a brief parenthetical note to his readers which made clear his frustration: "I am grieved to be so late—or early—with this review, but not very; this film has too long a life ahead of it. It is permanent if any work done during the past twenty years is permanent."[23] Agee was now fighting to defend a film for which it appeared even Chaplin's own company had lost faith.

While Agee's reviews of *Monsieur Verdoux* failed to turn the popular tide in the United States in favor of the film, on another level the three consecutive columns were unquestionably successful: The reviews had gotten Chaplin's personal attention. That summer Chaplin wrote what Agee would later call "a deeply kind letter"[24] in appreciation of the reviews. Chaplin, was clearly touched (he is said to have saved Agee's *Monsieur Verdoux* reviews in a drawer in his home).[25] After all of the energy he had expended to reach Chaplin, both before and after the press conference, Agee's effusive *Monsieur Verdoux* reviews had succeeded in motivating Chaplin to seek him out. And now that Chaplin had initiated contact, Agee had his best chance yet to reply and thereby encourage Chaplin's interest for *The Tramp's New World*. But surprisingly, Agee found himself virtually paralyzed by Chaplin's gesture. In this moment of truth he confronted his own moral qualms about exploiting a direct link between his position as critic and his interest in working with Chaplin: It became apparent to Agee that his own ambition had very real self-imposed ethical limits. He did write a letter in response to Chaplin, but he found himself inexplicably unable to send it. Almost a year later, in a rejected section of the draft of a letter that Agee did send to Chaplin, he attempted to explain this personal crisis to Chaplin.

I want to thank you for the deeply kind letter you wrote me, last summer, about my review of Monsieur Verdoux *in the* Nation. *You could only*

begin to imagine the gratitude I felt, and still feel, if you had any full idea
of my opinion of you and your work. I wrote thanking you, immediately—
and didn't send the letter. My failure to send it was not out of ingratitude
or even discourtesy, as it must certainly seem, but for confused would-be
moral and, probably, neurotic reasons which I hope I may explain someday,
but shan't trouble you with now. I have felt miserable shame and regret,
whenever I have thought of it since. I want to apologize and thank you
now."[26]

Although Chaplin appreciated the reviews in the *Nation*, Agee's defense of *Monsieur Verdoux* was neither universally understood nor supported. Henry Luce, the imposing founder of *Fortune* and *Time*, asked Agee to write an explanation of his position on the film. Luce was especially interested in the fact that Agee's reviews in *Time* and the *Nation* differed from each other significantly in tone. Luce may also have noticed that reviews of *Monsieur Verdoux* in magazines and newspapers tended to break along political not artistic lines. As Charles Maland has pointed out "The reviews that gave Chaplin almost unqualified praise came from journals associated with the Left: the *Nation*, *Partisan Review*, *PM* and the Communist magazine *Mainstream*."[27] Agee found it a daunting chore to write a brief to defend Chaplin's film to Luce. He decided instead that his best arguments were contained in the *Nation* reviews. On July 25, 1947, he sent Luce his own personal copies to read along with a note: "I've long intended to write, as promised to, a few extended remarks about *Monsieur Verdoux*. But after trying it, during the past few days, it occurred to me that the piece I wrote for *The Nation* might be clearer than what I can do now. I didn't get down all I wanted to, or say it nearly as sensibly as I wanted to, but a good bit of Parts 2 and 3 is germane, I believe, to the aspects of the movie I had intended to write about to you. I'm sorry to impose on you with so long a piece." After reading Agee's columns, Luce responded with his own note, copied to Agee's editor T. S. Matthews, in which he pointedly commented on the discrepancy in tone between Agee's reviews. In the memo, Luce questions Agee's logic, suggesting not too subtly that Agee had ignored some "grave" issues in Chaplin's film. Specifically, Luce took issue with Chaplin's equation of murder and business, and he challenged Agee to explain the film's position on what constitutes permissible evil.[28] In the remaining days of July, Agee wrote a long response to Luce. He admitted that he was more restrained in his *Time* review but attributed the increased enthusiasm he had expressed in the *Nation* to the fact that the film required time to take full effect on a viewer.

Dear Mr. Luce:

Thank you very much for your comments on the Verdoux *piece. I wish I could at all adequately discuss the important issues you brought up. I do at least want to speak of one or two, briefly.*

Whether Chaplin's paralleling of business with murder is admissible depends, I think, on two things: 1) is ironic hyperbole admissible? And 2) is he *near enough the truth? I don't mean #1 wholly as a rhetorical question, for I fear that irony always distorts the truth, even when it strikes very near some aspect of it, and that the distortion may be more harmful than its revelation. But in a more limited sense #1 depends on #2. I would believe that in business, as in politics and in many branches of science, humane or Christian ethics are gravely enough neglected, or misused, with grave enough consequences, that such an ironic attempt to demonstrate the neglect or misuse is warranted. This use of irony does neglect two exceedingly important facts: 1) that there* are *ethical businessmen and 2) that the ethical practice of business by businessmen in general is certainly and ideally conceivable, and conceivably possible. These two important complications (and perhaps even revolutions) of the general truth, irony is forced by its own peculiar logic to ignore. That seems to me just,—or ethical—according again to the ethics or irony; but that is as far as it can go. Irony is one of the sharpest imaginable instruments, but it is also very limited, very narrow in its usefulness, and its sharpness and its narrowness are one and the same: a deliberate simplification of the truth for the sake of revealing special aspects of the truth. I suspect that a study of irony would show it to be an invariably suspect instrument—fascinated as I am by it.* Verdoux *would be a particularly interesting case to study; its ironies are so crudely simple on the surface, so complex and ambiguous beneath the surface.*

I think I was mistaken in using irony, in paraphrase of Chaplin's own irony, when I wrote that according to the ethics of business realism there is no moral difference between murder and the sale of elastic stockings. I meant it, of course, in paraphrase of the kind of business ethics he was ironically attacking. But it would have been better, I think, to have discussed exactly where the relative complications of the more general truth and the relative limitations of the ironic approach.

But most importantly, Chaplin wasn't making his "metaphor" depend on so cynical a proposition in order to defend the proposition, but in order to attack it as powerfully and bitterly as he knew how—which is why, with various qualifiers and one or two central doubts, I accept his propositions as a whole, with respect and enthusiasm.

I particularly wish I could discuss the distinction between "the attainable good (duty) and the ineffable (love)." I am a hopeless though intensely interested amateur in these matters, but I would suppose roughly as follows. According to unqualified Christianity or Christian idealism, love is regarded as at least somewhere near attainable on earth, and duty (like justice) is neglected in its favor, rather by being swallowed up in it than by transgression. In actual practice all or nearly all people find that they are often, apparently intrinsically, in conflict. But I would suppose that the effort must always be towards love, in the faith that it is in some measure attainable; that when love and duty are sharply segregated and duty is given more priority, as the only kind of attainable good, the moral and other consequences are likely to be grave. (Actually they are likely to be, the other way too, with love given priority over duty; but that is only to say that this is one of the ultimate and tragic problems—unanswerable or unsolvable at least to the degree that many religious men emerge with differing answers.) In the particular aspect of Verdoux that I was writing about, I think it a very powerful parable on a prevalent misuse of duty-for-love's-sake: that is, it seems to demonstrate that when love is deceived and violated, as it were, for its own good, with duty laying down the laws for love and acting in the name of love, love and soul are first corrupted, then destroyed, and duty becomes a sort of mania, self-justifying and self-fueling, and using its own pride of self-sacrifice (even of evil), in its confusion, in place of love.

It seems to me that Chaplin's gravest error is in apparently holding modern society accountable for Verdoux, and—at least on the surface—in holding Verdoux guiltless as an individual. He could reply, "no, the chief meaning of the film is that between his sense of responsibility towards those he loves, and his attempts to fend for them according to ironic extensions of the logic of the world he lives in, Verdoux's conscience is destroyed." This I think would hold water—though in an important sense irony so elaborate holds water just about as well as a knife-blade. But even if he intended this he gave it only subtle, rather than strong surface, dramatization. If he doesn't think personal conscience so much as enters the picture, he is of course as wrong as Verdoux himself (as I tried to point out in the piece). If he does know better he is wrong again, for he failed to make his knowledge unmistakably clear. This again may have been in the interests of irony: but is then a prize example of how a moralist can cut his own throat with irony. On all the evidence I can get my guess is that he knows somewhat though not enough better; was seduced by the peculiar logic of his picture's scheme; and is and has long been in that phase of leftist or even merely progressive sentimentality in which one is so absorbed in all the harm or good that is done to individuals (or for them), that the still more crucial question of the moral responsibility of the individual, is out of focus.

I should have written, in my reviews, a warning about the picture. Most movies are designed to make all their strongest impressions the moment you see them; Verdoux has in common with a great deal of good work, a much slower percolating power. I very much liked and respected it (with reservations) when I saw it; but it was a week or more before I began fully to catch on to it. I mention this as only fair to you, the picture, and my own enthusiasm, when you do see it; also in partial explanation of my Time *review. I did, as you suggested, feel restrained, as I'm bound to whenever I feel my reactions are more strongly subjective than usual; but a good bit of the disparity between the two reviews was not restraint, but simply that when I wrote the* Time *review, I'd only half-digested the show.*

I hope and imagine the picture will interest you. I don't imagine you will care for it, as much as I do, for too much in it, of like or dislike, depends on some basic assumptions—"emotional," rather than philosophical, if emotions can help form assumptions. The chief difference I mean is, that you are relatively hopeful in ways that I am relatively doubtful, so that this kind of tragicomic satire would be likely to please me more—and perhaps unduly more.

I was very grateful for your letter. And I'm very sorry not to have been shorter, and sooner, with this. I've already taken a great deal of your trouble and time.[29]

Agee's self-imposed role as the standard bearer for *Monsieur Verdoux* also met some opposition among his peers. In the spring of 1947, Agee wrote to Dwight MacDonald to ask his opinion of Chaplin's new film and the press's reaction: "Have you seen the Chaplin movie? I'm curious what you think of it, of the reviews of it, and of the general press on Chaplin. There's a lot about the movie that bears argument—or maybe doesn't stand up under it—but in most ways I think it's wonderful."[30] MacDonald later wrote that he considered Agee's defense of the film a critical failing, but one he believed was based on artistic empathy: "I think [Agee's] overestimation of Chaplin's film *Monsieur Verdoux* came because he could see so clearly what Chaplin was trying to do, which was a very admirable thing—make fun of the whole bourgeois system, and so on. But what he had to talk away was the fact that Chaplin in that film fails quite badly in doing it. To Agee, you see, that wouldn't be so visible. But he's still probably our best, certainly one of our best, film critics here."[31]

It wasn't the first time that the two friends had publicly clashed on films. On June 2, 1943, four years before Agee's reviews for *Monsieur Verdoux*, MacDonald had written an angry letter to the editors of the *Nation*, attacking Agee's recent review of *Mission to Moscow*. The film, sponsored by the U.S. government and allegedly instigated by Franklin Roosevelt himself, was developed to build domestic sympathy and support for Russia as it fought against Hitler. The movie, based on a book by Ambassador Joseph E. Davies, depicted his visit to Moscow. Davies was played by John Huston's father, Walter Huston; Jay Leyda, Agee's friend and an expert on Russia, coincidentally worked as a consultant on the film. In MacDonald's opinion, Agee had glossed over the film's handling of Stalin's notorious show trials, and had engaged in critical doubletalk by supporting its political objectives while simultaneously deriding its "moral, aesthetic, and intellectual qualities."[32] For MacDonald, it was a case of Agee ignoring a film's faults while applauding its intentions.

In 1965, *Monsieur Verdoux* was reissued in the United States for the first time since its initial release in 1947. Dwight MacDonald, in his regular film column in *Esquire*, wrote a long consideration of the film and in it an analysis of Agee's reviews in the *Nation*. MacDonald wrote: "it is notable how defensive and often equivocal [Agee] is about it as a movie and how enthusiastic when he analyzes, as he does at length and with subtlety, its social and political meanings or what he says they are; myself I found the glosses much richer than the text."[33] For MacDonald, Agee's greatest flaw was his willingness to see an artist's intention and ignore his failed attempt: "[Agee's] defense of Chaplin's static camera reminds me of the paradoxical reflex by which Miss Susan Sontag defends bad movies . . . precisely on the grounds they are so courageously boring, so defiantly sloppy . . . I suspect that Agee's response is an example of his chief weakness as a critic: his directorial imagination which sometimes remade the movie inside his head as he watched it, so that what came out on his page was often more exciting than what had appeared on the screen."

It was MacDonald's view that Agee's support for *Monsieur Verdoux* was influenced both by its political message and the political climate in which it was released. He argued that Agee was affected by the film "emotionally and personally because of its anti-bourgeois 'black' humor and because of his admiration for Chaplin and his generous indignation at the 1947 campaign of calumny." MacDonald believed that it was difficult for Agee to balance the film's weaknesses against the strong admiration he clearly felt for it: "A great strain must have been put on Agee's fine intelligence by the pressure of his personal feeling for Verdoux, his love and reverence (not critical categories), and the contrary pull of his clear perception of its artistic defects. He was too honest, or better, too serious, to gloss over the conflict by committing either term." MacDonald was troubled by Agee's tendency to review the film that could have been; "that Agee and others whom I respect, take the will for the deed in *Verdoux* is a lapse that is explicable in such intelligent persons—for to call a badly flawed movie great because of its theme and its creator's intentions is like saying an orator is eloquent but inarticulate—only on the hypothesis that they are really interested in something else, something outside my province as a film critic, something that doesn't appear on the screen."

Four

ON THE MOVE: HOLLYWOOD BECKONS

*I*n the middle of May 1947, after six weeks of exhibition, during which ticket sales dropped and the bad reviews mounted, United Artists pulled *Monsieur Verdoux* from its one venue in New York, and went to work retooling the advertising and publicity campaigns. The new ad campaign challenged the ticket-buyer's ability to adapt to the new Chaplin: "Chaplin Changes. Can You?"[1] Hardly bowed by the affair, Chaplin pointedly scheduled the relaunch of the film to take place in Washington, D.C. during the very same week that Hanns Eisler was scheduled to testify under subpoena to the House Un-American Activities Committee. To make his defiant message crystal clear, Chaplin sent a telegram to J. Parnell Thomas, the chairman of HUAC, who had for some time been threatening to subpoena the comedian. Chaplin's biting telegram insisted that if Thomas wanted to know more about his politics he should see *Monsieur Verdoux* for an explicit answer: "You have been quoted as saying you wish to ask me if I am a Communist. You sojourned for ten days in Hollywood not long ago, and could have asked me the question at that time, effecting something of an economy, or you could telephone me now—collect. In order that you may be completely up-to-date on my thinking I suggest you view carefully my latest production, *Monsieur Verdoux*. It is against war and the futile slaughter of our youth."[2]

Chaplin concluded his telegram "While you are preparing your engraved subpoena I will give you a hint on where I stand. I am not a Communist. I am a peacemonger."[3] As a topper, Chaplin later invited all the HUAC members to the film's opening on September 26.

After witnessing the HUAC interrogation of Hanns Eisler, Martha Gellhorn, Ernest Hemingway's third ex-wife, wrote an angry two-page article in the October 6, 1947 issue of the *New Republic*. In the piece entitled "Cry Shame . . . !" Gellhorn referred to the committee members as the "Un-Americans" and took them to task for "three days of sordid, and pointless baying over Eisler."[4] She scoffed that the committee "cannot expect anyone to believe that Eisler, writing background music in Hollywood for a living, is at the head of some furtive movement of music-lovers, vowed to plunge us all into communism."[5] And she concluded that if HUAC were to prevail, "America is going to look very strange to Americans and they will not be at home here, for the air will slowly become unbreathable to all forms of life except sheep."[6]

As the year came to a close, Agee's bold but lonely stance on *Monsieur Verdoux* was partially vindicated when the National Board of Review announced on December 19 that it had chosen Chaplin's film for its highest honor. Lion Feuchtwanger wrote to congratulate Chaplin after hearing the news: "I just happened to read that the National Board of Review of motion pictures picked your *Monsieur Verdoux* as the best picture of the year. Personally I am convinced that *Monsieur Verdoux* is not only the best picture of the year but of the whole decade. But, anyhow, this choice of the National Board of Review is a good sign for the fact that the picture is, gradually, being appreciated on this side of the ocean as it already has been on the other side."[7]

Feuchtwanger and Chaplin had become close friends after the novelist safely emigrated to the United States and settled in California in 1941. Though he is little known today, Feuchtwanger was vaulted to international fame in 1926, following the publication of his historical novel *Jud Süss*. Feuchtwanger's California home, Villa Aurora, is now maintained as a retreat for refugee artists from around the world, funded in part by the German government. As one of the first German writers to recognize and write about the emerging Nazi threat, Feuchtwanger was in the first group of artists to be targeted for retaliation after Hitler came to power. In January 1933, while visiting the United States on a lecture tour, Feuchtwanger was warned by the

German ambassador not to return home. Abandoning his world-class private collection of rare books, Feuchtwanger and his wife Marta relocated to Sanary in the South of France. On August 25, 1933, accused of disloyalty to the German Reich and the German people, Feuchtwanger's citizenship was officially revoked. Safe in France, Feuchtwanger continued to write about the growing Fascist threat. An English film version of *Jud Süss* (released as *Jew Süss* in the U.K. and *Power* in the United States) was produced in 1934, and the British government approached him to write a screenplay of his anti-Hitler novel *The Oppermanns*, but later abandoned the project because it conflicted with the nation's short-lived appeasement strategy.

After France was invaded by the Nazis, Feuchtwanger was thrown into an internment camp in Les Milles and was later moved by Petain's collaborationist Vichy government to Camp St. Nicholas, sixty-five miles west of Marseilles. In a rescue worthy of Hollywood, Hiram Bingham, the local American consulate official, risked his career by snatching Feuchtwanger away from the camp and disguising him in woman's clothing. Bingham told the writer that if they were stopped, he was to assume the role of Bingham's mother-in-law from Waycross, Georgia. After hiding the Feuchtwangers in his own home for weeks, Bingham arranged for the couple to escape to Spain with the help of the American Emergency Rescue Committee. In similar fashion, Bingham helped to save Thomas Mann's brother, Heinrich, and his son Golo as well as the family of the Nobel Prize–winning physicist Otto Meyerhof, the writer Franz Werfel and his wife, Alma, the widow of Gustav Mahler.

Financially, Feuchtwanger was more fortunate than many refugee artists. Though banned in his homeland, his numerous novels remained in print outside of Germany and provided him with a comfortable living. Like many of his friends and colleagues, the writer made his way to Hollywood and settled in Pacific Palisades, where he purchased a showplace villa constructed by the *Los Angeles Times*. Wartime gas rationing made the house's remote location unattractive, and Feuchtwanger was able to purchase it at a bargain price. After getting settled, Feuchtwanger arranged for Bertolt Brecht, who was living in Moscow, to receive the proceeds from sales of his novels in Russia, enabling the playwright to travel to Southern California.

After Feuchtwanger's escape from France, Josef Goebbels, the Nazi minister of information, in an infamous turn of propagandist perversion, had *Jud Süss* translated to the screen in a purposely distorted vehicle of virulent antisemitism. Around the same time, Goebbels assigned Fritz Hippler, the author of the essay "Film as a Weapon," to produce the film *The Eternal Jew*, a notorious antisemitic documentary that included footage of Charles Chaplin and Peter Lorre (the scenes with Lorre were lifted from Fritz Lang's 1931 thriller *M*) as purported examples of how Jews were corrupting world culture. Both films were released in 1940, within months of each other.

Feuchtwanger became a regular guest at Salka Viertel's salon of refugees and émigrés. He also established his own social salon, focused more on literary and classical art than on the film crowd that frequented Salka's. He would frequently read his latest fiction to invited guests, typically arranging one evening for German speakers such as Thomas and Heinrich Mann, Schoenberg, and Eisler, and another evening at which English-speaking friends like Chaplin would be invited. In return, Feuchtwanger was a frequent dinner guest at the Chaplins' home. This close-knit circle of writers, actors, musicians, and filmmakers would soon become very familiar to Agee.

But 1947 ended with Agee still in New York, still writing for both *Time* and the *Nation*. In his last column of the year in the *Nation*, Agee tackled the subject of Congress's hunt for communists in Hollywood. He wrote a heated essay about HUAC's targeting of the film industry and its treatment of the Hollywood Ten writers, directors, and actors. In the same column he also decried what he called "the Catholic Veterans' holy war against Chaplin."[8] He wrote, "I believe that a democracy which cannot contain all its enemies, of whatever kind of virulence, is finished as a democracy. I believe that a vigorous and genuine enough democracy could do so. But I see no reason to believe that this democracy is vigorous or genuine enough by a good deal, or to hope that it can become so; nor am I thoroughly convinced that such a democracy can ever exist except in the most generous and sanguine imaginations."[9]

Whether by happenstance or in an intentional effort to keep up the drumbeat of communication to Chaplin, in the months following the April 1947 press conference, Agee's columns in the *Nation* included a growing number of references to Chaplin. In the movie reviews Agee published from 1942 until the spring of 1947, there had been occasional references to Chaplin. But after April 1947 mentions of Chaplin became frequent, many of them almost arbitrary. There was, it appeared, almost no subject for which Agee couldn't find sufficient reason to drop in a reference to Chaplin. For example, Agee wrote that a scene in *Nightmare Alley* had "some of the hard, gay audacity of *Monsieur Verdoux*,"[10] and a character in Jean Vigo's *Zero de Conduite* was complimented as a "sort of lay Chaplin."[11] Reviewing *Crossfire*, an exploration of antisemitism, Agee praised it as "the best Hollywood movie in a long time"[12] but reduced the praise with the parenthetical explanation that "Chaplin doesn't make Hollywood movies; he makes Chaplin movies."[13] In all, Chaplin is mentioned in eight of the twenty-two remaining columns that Agee wrote for the *Nation* following the *Monsieur Verdoux* reviews.

As Ed Sullivan had hoped, his efforts had helped make Chaplin's film a financial disappointment. While Chaplin and the financially troubled United Artists had hoped *Monsieur Verdoux* would earn $12 million, it ended up grossing only $325,000 in the United States; with overseas revenues it totaled something less than $7 million. In the midst of his business concerns, Chaplin was also occupied with exploring ways to build support for Hanns Eisler. In an effort to take the case to the world stage, Chaplin wrote a telegram to Pablo Picasso asking, "Can you head committee of French artists to protest to American Embassy in Paris against the outrageous deportation proceedings against Hanns Eisler here and simultaneously send me a copy of protest for us here."[14] Picasso and twenty additional artists, including Matisse and Cocteau, complied. Later, along with high-profile artists and intellectuals, including Albert Einstein and Thomas Mann, Chaplin signed a petition that was sent to Attorney General Tom Clark requesting that deportation proceedings against Eisler be abandoned. To help Eisler financially, Chaplin contracted with the composer to create a new soundtrack score for a planned re-release of *The Circus*. Arrangements for payment to Eisler were made through the Chaplin Studios one week before Eisler went to Washington, D.C. to testify.

But Hanns Eisler's battle with the United States government was coming to a close. Providing small consolation, on February 15, 1948, the Motion Picture Academy announced that Chaplin was nominated for best writing for an original screenplay for *Monsieur Verdoux*. On February 28, 1948 a concert of Eisler's music was staged as a joint farewell and protest at Town Hall on 43rd Street in New York City. The event was sponsored by Leonard Bernstein, Aaron Copland, David Diamond, Roy Harris, Walter Piston, Roger Sessions, and Randall Thompson. As part of the performance, a chamber ensemble played Eisler's Suite No. 2 for Septet, which included six excerpts from the score he had written for the reissue of *The Circus*. Chaplin, for whatever reason, ultimately decided not to use Eisler's composition. The Eisler tribute concert in New York was a perfect example of the intersection of Chaplin and Eisler's Hollywood and Agee's New York. Years before, in his volume of poems *Permit Me Voyage*, Agee had included the composer Roy Harris in his list of American artist heroes in the poem "Dedication." David Diamond later put some of Agee's poetry to music, and Copland was inspired by reading *Let us Now Praise Famous Men* to compose his first opera, *This Tender Land*. Leonard Bernstein gave Agee one of his last jobs, hiring him to attempt the libretto for *Candide*.

That March, Hanns and Lou Eisler negotiated a settlement with the Justice Department for what was termed a "technical deportation," which granted the Eislers a voluntary exit visa that allowed them to travel to any country not bordering the United States. On March 26, 1948, the Eislers left New York and flew to Prague. Before their flight from LaGuardia Airport, Hanns Eisler read his farewell statement: "I leave this country not without bitterness and infuriation . . . in 1933 the Hitler bandits put a price on my head and drove me out. They were the evil of the period; I was proud of being driven out. But I feel heartbroken over being driven out of this beautiful country in this ridiculous way."[15] In 1949 Hanns Eisler moved to East Germany where a song he wrote to accompany a poem by Johannes R. Becher was chosen as the national anthem of the German Democratic Republic. Meanwhile, on May 30, 1949, living in Brooklyn, and inspired by Eisler's exile, the folksinger Woody Guthrie was moved to write his own lyrics, for an unscored ballad he called "Eisler on the Go"[16]:

> Eisler on the go
> Eisler on the move
> Brother is on the vinegar truck
> I don't know what I'll do

(Chorus) I don't know what I'll do,
I don't know what I'll do
Eisler's on the come and go
and I don't know what I'll do

Eisler on the farm
Eisler on the town
Sister in the tickly bush
I don't know what I'll do

Eisler on the boat
Eisler on the ship
Daddy on the henhouse roof
I don't know what I'll do

Eisler in the jailoe
Eisler back at home,
Rankin scratch his head and cry
I don't know what I'll do

Eisler him write music
Eisler him teach school,
Truman him don't play so good
I don't know what I'll do"[17]

Years later in a coincidental turn of events, Agee's second wife, Alma Mailman, after their divorce was final, moved to East Germany and befriended the Eisler brothers. In her memoir she wrote: "The Eisler brothers, Gerhart and Hanns, lived nearby, in separate houses, with their wives . . . Hanns and Gerhart played chess together, once a week, tensely, judging by my own memory of one evening playing Ping-Pong with Gerhart in Gross-Glienicke. He played a good game, but I played a better, and after three successive losses he refused to stop, though I had had enough and so had others who had been watching . . . I shall never forget [his] frenzy and his insistence that we continue, until it was past three in the morning and he finally beat me."[18]

Alma and Agee's marriage fell apart in 1941 after he confessed that he was having an affair with Mia Fritsch, a staff researcher at *Fortune*. Alma had herself been in the same position years before, when Agee had fallen in love with her while still married to his first wife Olivia. But Alma had a baby to care for and was unable and unwilling to put up with the emotional stress of an infant and an unreliable husband. With her young son, Joel, in tow, she accompanied Helen Levitt on a photographic excursion to Mexico. The three sailed from New York Harbor while Agee, distraught, watched them from the pier. In Mexico, Alma fell in love with a young German communist writer, Bodo Uhse. After seven years in Mexico, Alma, Bodo, and Joel moved to East Germany. Agee's new love, Mia, an émigré from Vienna, had first settled in Chicago before moving to New York to find a job. She landed her position at *Fortune* as a researcher after a brief stint in an advertising agency.[19] They married in 1945, and had three children—two girls and a boy—over the following ten years. Mia knew and understood Agee's nature fully before they married, and she stayed loyal to him and supported him through all his crises—personal and professional—during the brief ten years that remained to him.

⚮

As Chaplin had steadfastly defended his friend Hanns Eisler under extreme public heat and tangible damage to his own reputation, Agee found himself similarly associated with a highly controversial friend, though one at the opposite end of the political spectrum. As Chaplin had with Eisler, Agee remained loyal to his friend and colleague Whittaker Chambers when Chambers became entangled in the controversial trials of Alger Hiss. Chambers had once been an active member of the Communist Party, but underwent a moving conversion experience that shifted his political views 180 degrees. At *Time* Agee had been partnered with the notoriously anti-communist Chambers, first as cowriters of the Books section and later as a two-man special projects department tasked with devising subjects for cover articles. For a time the two writers even shared an office.

Before joining *Time*, Chambers began his literary career as a translator; in 1928, he was the first to translate Felix Salten's German novel *Bambi* into English. Fluent in German, Chambers also translated novels by Franz Werfel and Heinrich Mann in the years before he joined Time, Inc. Agee's second wife, Alma, recalled how Agee and Chambers first become friends, "No one [at *Time*] seemed to like him, Jim had told me, and Jim, who found something to like in everyone, had befriended him."[20] Both men also shared a preference for late hours. According to their editor T. S. Matthews, "Both [Agee and Chambers] liked to work at night (sometimes all night) when the office was deserted."[21] Agee, haunted lifelong by persistent insomnia, had developed the habit of working through the night when he worked for *Fortune*. At *Time*, the two men kept company in the emptied offices. They were a mixed pair. Matthews noted that the men had very different personalities. Unlike the highly social Agee, who was known for being the last guest to leave a party, Chambers was taciturn: "Physically and temperamentally they could not have been more unlike, and politically they were at right angles, but their preference for working at night led first to a mutually tolerant acquaintance and then to a warm friendship."[22] In 1968 when Mia Agee was interviewed about the bond between Agee and Chambers, she expressed the opinion that Chambers and Agee connected because "they were both essentially poets, their common bond was an interest in writing and in language; and essentially, they were both so American in a romantic, idealistic sense."[23] She also recalled that Chambers, the visionary of the Conservative movement, considered Agee "a child, politically."[24]

Chambers wrote about Agee in his best-selling memoir *Witness* as "probably the most gifted writer who ever worked for *Time*."[25] According to Chambers, "Agee and I soon brought the Books section to the number one spot in the readers' polls."[26] Their success writing book reviews led to the formation of the special projects department, which Chambers explained was created specifically for the two writers: "[Special Projects] was a new department of the magazine whose staff consisted of my friend, James Agee, and me. Its purpose was to provide *Time* chiefly with cover stories which, because of special difficulties of subject matter or writing, other sections of *Time* were thought to be less well equipped to handle."[27]

Chambers was soon to become a lightning-rod figure in American society, viewed either as a hero or a villain. While HUAC investigated communist penetration of the U.S. government, Chambers appeared before the committee and testified that Alger Hiss, a high-ranking official in the State Department, had been an active member of the Communist Party during the days when he himself had been a party member. As the subsequent trials of Alger Hiss split the country, Agee's loyalty to his controversial friend surprised many.

During the height of the Hiss controversy, Chambers considered Agee one of his only friends. In support of Chambers's credibility, Agee wrote a letter to Assistant U.S. Attorney Thomas Murphy, the prosecutor in the Hiss case. Later, Agee was interviewed by the FBI and according to the agents' report told them he had a "high regard" for Chambers and had "absolute faith in him and believed that he was telling a truthful and complete story with regard to Alger Hiss."[28] The extent of their friendship is highlighted by the fact that Chambers added Agee to a list of beneficiaries on his life insurance policy. According to Chamber's biographer Allen Weinstein, Chambers "took out [a group life insurance policy] in December 1945 shortly after returning to *Time* in which, should Esther [his wife] and his two children die before him, three beneficiaries would share his insurance proceeds equally: the Pipe Creek Monthly Meeting of the Society of Friends, his handyman and his close friend at *Time*, James Agee."[29]

It is ironic in retrospect to consider that Agee's friend Chambers helped create the political environment that ultimately resulted in the exile of Chaplin. Chambers had also boosted Richard Nixon's career through the publicity he gained from the famed Pumpkin Papers, the infamous microfilm that Chambers hid in a hollowed pumpkin on his farm. T. S. Matthews, who considered himself a close friend of Chambers, observed that, "Whittaker Chambers certainly didn't invent McCarthyism, though it must be admitted that he helped to loose the McCarthyite madness."[30]

Chambers's landmark memoir, *Witness*, which recounted his voyage into and out of the Communist Party, inspired generations of conservatives, including William F. Buckley and Ronald Reagan. Buckley became Chambers's protégé, hired him to write for his magazine, the *National Review*, and later appointed him to serve on its board. Chambers was in fact actively encouraged to write *Witness* by Agee and David McDowell, a younger St. Andrews schoolmate of Agee's, who in 1950 was working as an editor for Random House.[31] McDowell had to convince his boss, Bennett Cerf, to publish Chambers's book. In 1933 Cerf had been willing to go to Federal Court to break the ban on publishing James Joyce's *Ulysses* in the United States, but he was tentative about publishing Chambers's book. According to Chambers's biographer Sam Tanenhaus, the liberal Cerf saw Chambers as the villain in the Hiss case. McDowell ambushed Cerf by having Chambers show up for a meeting unannounced, effectively shaming Cerf into meeting with him. Cerf took several of Chambers's draft chapters and asked three liberal writer friends for their opinions. The consensus was positive and Cerf decided that the book "was so well written I had to publish it and let the readers judge for themselves."[32] Before the book was published, Chambers published an article, "I was the Witness," in the February 9, 1952 issue of the *Saturday Evening Post*. After reading the article, Agee wrote to Father Flye: "I mainly like Whittaker's opening article. In a sense I even like what I don't particularly like, since it comes out of a degree of faithfulness to one's whole nature, which seems hardly to exist any more."[33]

Surprisingly, Agee's efforts to reach Chaplin seem to have stopped after he received the letter from the comedian thanking him for the *Nation* reviews during the summer of 1947. Within six month though, circumstances would begin to move Agee closer to his dream of leaving journalism for a career as a screen writer. In early 1948, just months before Chambers made his first HUAC appearance, one of Agee's film reviews caught the attention of the director John Huston. Huston had just released *The Treasure of the Sierra Madre*, his first film since returning to civilian life after the war. He had been moved by Agee's enthusiastic comments about this new film and about two of the short documentary films, *Battle of San Pietro* and *Let There Be Light*, which Huston had made for the military while serving in the Signal Corps Photographic Service, where he earned the rank of major. To Agee, Huston was the shining example of successful, intelligent independence working within the confines of the movie studio system. In Huston's eyes, "Agee was a poet, novelist and the best motion-picture critic this country has ever had." In his memoir, *An Open Book*, Huston acknowledged that he was an avid follower of Agee's criticism; "I have read everything of Agee's as it was published."[34] In appreciation of Agee's kind words, Huston wrote to him at the *Time* and *Life* building in Rockefeller Plaza on February 11, 1948.

It was an extraordinary step for Huston to respond directly to a critic: "His piece was so sensitive and perceptive that I sent him a note of appreciation, the one and only time I have ever addressed myself to a critic."[35] Huston's letter reflects the unease he felt at breaking the unofficial barrier between critic and the artist. His prose maneuvered just formally enough to give Agee room to politely refuse his atypical solicitation.

> *Dear Mr. Agee:*
> *I hesitate to put down these lines of appreciation as I'm of the belief that there should be little or no traffic at all between the critic and the criticized. If friendly relations exist between the two, the critic, when the time comes around to criticize, invariably leans over backwards in an effort not to be influenced by his personal feelings, and as a result he is more severe than he would be otherwise. By the same token, if upon making the acquaintance, the criticized appears a thorough going s.b. in the eyes of the critic, he (the critic) in an effort to be fair and unbiased, is generally inclined to give the criticized a break he doesn't deserve. All of which is leading up to this pro-posal—will you have a drink with me next time I am in New York? In the meantime, thank you very much James Agee.*[36]

For Agee, Huston's letter offered a foot in the door to Hollywood: It was an attractive, honest opportunity to forge a friendship with an in-fluential and successful Hollywood filmmaker, and one for whom he had true admiration and high expectations. Even better, Huston was a writer and seemed attracted to bringing serious works of fiction to the screen: His first film, *The Maltese Falcon*, was a fairly faithful transla-tion of Dashiell Hammett's novel. Agee also recognized in Huston a fellow rebellious artist who shared his interest in gritty realism. While Agee had failed to follow up on the opportunity that Chaplin's letter might have offered, Huston's offer of friendship provided Agee a sec-ond front in his effort to pursue a screen writing career.

This time, instead of balking as he had when Chaplin had written to him, Agee wrote back to Huston ten days later and directly ad-dressed the director's concerns about the dangers of mingling the critic and the criticized:

> *Dear Mr. Huston:*
> *That is true about the liabilities involved, if the critic and the criticized know each other. But to quite an extent they are involved, even seeing work of someone you don't know at all; enough so, that any critic is a fool who thinks he can be completely detached and fair—though he is also much worse than a fool if he doesn't try to come as near that as possible. But the only kinds of people I dread meeting or knowing are those who are ex-tremely good in their intentions but show very little ability, and those who*

have real but very small, or uneven, or confused or declining ability. The mixtures of sympathy and distaste in those cases are made much harder to try to handle, if you know the people personally. But I feel no such uneasiness in the thought of meeting people whose ability I consistently and greatly respect, as I do yours. I realize I'm liable through my enthusiasm and satisfaction not to be at the same time as sharp for drawbacks as a good reviewer ought to be; but at least I know I need have no scruples about trying hard to be; also, with any of the work you like best you automatically are applying the hardest standards you know of, according to which it would be impossible as well as unfair to review most things. Yes I would like very much to have a drink. If you'd like to, I hope you'll come down for an evening. My wife also likes your work a great deal, and would I'm sure enjoy meeting you again. (She talked with you once under her office name of Mia Fritsch, working for Fortune, *when you were making* Let There Be Light.*) Thank you very much for your letter.*[37]

As auspicious as Huston's letter promised to be, Agee soon received news as good, or even better. Frank E. Taylor, a close friend from the Greenwich Village literary crowd, had just been wooed from his publishing job at Random House by MGM to try his hand at film production. Taylor had been Arthur Miller's first editor while at Reynal and Hitchcock and published Miller's *Situation Normal* and *Focus*. Miller described him as "a gaunt, sophisticated man of great height . . . an imaginative mixture of aggressive entrepreneur and aficionado of literature."[38] After Random House hired him away from Reynal and Hitchcock, Taylor signed Ralph Ellison to his first book contract. Taylor also launched the American gastronome James Beard when he published the *James Beard Cookbook*, a landmark in the literature of American cuisine. Years later when Arthur Miller was married to Marilyn Monroe, he and John Huston enlisted Taylor to produce Miller's screenplay *The Misfits*, starring Monroe, Clark Gable, and Montgomery Clift.

Taylor's new film job was great news for Agee. The two had an understanding that if it were practical, and depending both on Agee's schedule and Taylor's ability to get approval from the studio, Taylor would invite Agee to work on any film that he was developing. But one other unexpected benefit accrued to Agee from Taylor's move to California. After settling in Los Angeles, Taylor and his wife, Nan, had become good friends of the Chaplins. The two families shared social connections and Nan was heavily involved with a newly founded progressive elementary school to which both families sent their children. Taylor was now in a position to serve as go-between to deliver Agee's screenplay into Chaplin's hands.

And so, in the spring of 1948, through the good graces of Frank Taylor, little more than a year after Agee first began his quest to connect with Chaplin, his goal was realized. Taylor's secretary got word to Agee that Chaplin would be willing to read his film treatment, and Agee excitedly set to work cleaning up and typing his manuscript with the intention to make the best possible impression on Chaplin in hopes of finally interesting him in making *The Tramp's New World*.

Agee already knew from press reports that Chaplin was making headway on preparations for his next film; a discouraging prospect that might spell doom for any chance of getting the comedian to commit to Agee's project any time in the near future. At his current pace, Chaplin was averaging between five and seven years between releases, but Agee counted on Chaplin recognizing both the urgent timeliness of his project's message and the special insight he had into the character of Little Tramp. On May 13, 1948, Agee wrote to Chaplin to thank him for his willingness to read the manuscript:

Dear Mr. Chaplin;
In all courtesy I should write you by hand; but my handwriting is a discourtesy in itself. I'd rather spare your eyes. I am deeply grateful to you for reading what I am sending, and I'm all the more diffident about intruding on you, now that I hear you are already writing a film. I would hold off, feeling that it was hopeless as well as ill-mannered to try to interest you in another project when you are at work. But I feel, and hope and believe that you may feel, that the film I suggest could be of very particular importance and possible usefulness, and that it would have to be made soon if it is to be made at all. Briefly, the idea I am sending could only be carried out by your Tramp character. It could, I believe, summarize and underline all that he has ever been and meant, and could extend his meaning and stature as well, to uncover and to cut very sharply at the roots of a great deal: what is most tragically, preposterously, suicidally wrong with contemporary civilization; how much is conceivably curable and by what means; and what, even if cure seems to be effected, ultimately appears to guarantee the doom of present civilization, and of us all. This would be examined briefly in a prologue on contemporary civilization at its most insane and helpless; then at length and in detail in a story of what happens among the survivors after the "ultimate" Bomb has wiped out virtually every one and every ves-

tige of civilization as it now functions. In the state I'm sending it, I'm sorry to say, this is gotten out by Caesarian in about the fifth month. A fair number of scenes and one or two major sequences are sketched in fair detail; for the rest, I must ask your indulgence and imagination in advance. The general form and the salient ideas are there, but relatively little is worked out specifically or dramatically yet; and a lot of the basic ideas—philosophical or ethical as well as movie—are still not firmly enough defined, or even clearly realized. I wish I could have sent this in a more developed, persuasive and easy-to-read state. But even by continuous typing (in spare time from my job) of this crude, first-draft material, I am late in getting it to Frank Taylor, through whose kindness my opportunity comes of delivering it to you at all. I do hope and believe, however, that there is enough here to make clear to you the movie, emotional and intellectual possibilities of the idea, and to make clear to you whether you are further interested in it. If you are semi-interested but dubious I'll be grateful for the chance to discuss it further. I am grieved to send you anything short of the very best I can do, but there has simply not been time to do better.

I have an immense amount to thank you for, Mr. Chaplin, besides your kindness in reading this: your deeply kind letter to me, last summer, about my review of Monsieur Verdoux *in the* Nation; *and the whole body of your work and all that it has meant to me. If I were not sure that your reading of the manuscript will remain impersonal, entirely unaltered by anything I might say, or do, and that you will trust and understand that my need to say it is disinterested and purely personal, I would not write this. But I will, because it's quite possible I won't have another chance to say it to you. You are the artist in the living world whom I most deeply revere, and one of the few people in the world for whom I feel most fundamental liking, sense of understanding, sympathy, and loyalty.*

You must have suffered as badly from flattery, as from those who are disloyal to you or who so viciously attack you. So please know and believe that I am not trying to flatter you. Within my own abilities, I am an artist, too; and I don't believe that artists flatter; they mean what they say.

My homage, gratitude and affection.
James Agee[39]

Added at the bottom of the last page, Agee wrote, "I've just heard, through Frank's secretary, that you are willing—she said 'eager'—to read the manuscript. I had feared that you might easily prefer not to interrupt your work—so I can only thank you again."[40]

Along with the typed manuscript of the screenplay, Agee included a copy of his satirical short story, "Dedication Day" and wrote on the cover page, "Mr. Chaplin: This is a carbon and may trouble your eyes—don't be concerned to read it—it merely contains some possible material for a different Prologue, and may also convey something of the tone and idea useful for certain parts of the picture."

Fate had now conspired again in Agee's favor. He had made a direct connection to Chaplin through Taylor and there was the very real possibility of studio film work coming from Taylor's new position at MGM. What's more, Agee had commenced a budding relationship with John Huston. Agee saw that he'd need to make some drastic changes in order to take full advantage of these new opportunities. In short order, he devised a new career plan that would provide him both an income and the justification to head out to California. To advance his plan, he compiled a detailed list of freelance story ideas for *Life* magazine. Every one of the freelance story ideas Agee proposed to the editors at *Life* featured a Hollywood angle and an excuse to travel west. Agee's list of story ideas ranged over a wide variety of topics and included proposals for studies of studio heads (Zanuck), silent comedy, maverick directors (Huston), aging child stars (Mickey Rooney), forgotten film artists (Von Stroheim), the red scare's effect on Hollywood, and Hollywood's own image-protecting secret police. In this list of proposed articles are the seeds of what would become Agee's two classic articles for *Life*, the first on the forgotten glories of the silent film comedy era and the other a profile of his new friend, the rebel director John Huston.

Story Suggestions for *Life*[41]

1) LUNCHEON WITH DARRYL ZANUCK
Assigned. Chief problem: can Whitney or Beardwood set up enough lunch dates—under cover of my researching for a conventional close-up—without tipping our hand? I'd guess 3 should be enough, but beyond this, for proper smokescreen, I'd probably need several other interviews.

2) OLD TIME COMICS
Meaning, the silent comics. General substance of piece: 1) medium-length recognition of silent slapstick as about the best stuff ever turned out in movies; brief general story how they were made (about as premeditated as an average drunken charade); brief comparison with good & bad comedy since. 2) What has happened to these comedians since sound killed that kind of comedy? a)—briefly—their

ideas of what their work was, and their reminiscences; b) what has happened to them since and what are they doing now. Probably best done as short sketches of personal interviews, as exact on their personalities as possible. There is good art in contrasting stills from their best shows, with straight clinical shots of them as they are today. Some, of course, have died, but [should] be mentioned in passing & more at length if of special interest. Chief characters: Keaton, Langdon, Lloyd, Charlie Chase, Laurel & Hardy, Lloyd Hamilton, Larry Semon, the old Mack Sennet Company (James Finlayson, etc.), the old Chaplin stock-company (Mack Swain, Kalla Pasha et al), and some typical one of the Sennett bathing girls who, unlike Swanson & Haver, never went on to be stars. Chaplin I think should be mentioned only in passing: [he] always was & remains too much a case by himself. No peg: nostalgia & personality story.

3) JOHN HUSTON

Possibly the ablest living director: certainly as good as any in sight; and still relatively young (early 40's) More or less a straight close-up (he is an extremely colorful guy) but it would also be well worth doing, to go into considerable detail about his directing methods, and what gives his pictures their particular quality & individuality. (Of course he is also a first rate screen writer, and combines these skills; we should recognize this, & get into it some.) He was planning to work, this Fall, on an episode about an attempt on the life of Cuba's Machado. Hope I could watch him at work and base how-he-does-it copy on this; story could peg on picture's release. Of additional interest: he is probably the happiest contemporary example of the guy who has *always* worked in Hollywood, & has successfully used & bucked it.

Huston could be the director story we discussed. But I suggest that he's worth a story to himself and that that director should be a medium-talented reliable journeyman, not so far above the average as Huston, Ford, Wyler & such. Say, a good director like Victor Fleming.

4) MICKEY ROONEY

Most housebroken hides crawl when the mere name is mentioned— and there are good reasons. Nevertheless Rooney is one of the finest actors in pictures, here or abroad; and I think that copy which would interest and surprise habitual Rooney-haters (and admirers), could be made out of examining that point in some detail. Much of it is, his incredible skill at mugging and at handling subtle gradations between mugging and straight good acting; some of it, the pure & inspired—and hundred percent resourceful—pieces of first-rate acting he has done. The rest of the story is bio perse, with special interest in trying to understand for what reasons, both "Hollywood" and deep in his own personality, his abilities have come to so little. My impression is that he has become a tough Metro problem—several years too superannuated to play brats any more; what do we do with him now? Maybe he is even on skids. But both need careful checking and even if so, it doesn't impair story as I see it, for the story is: You can be something close to a great artist without having an ounce of "artist" or highbrow in you (he is the essence of pure commercial, deep-vaudeville skill and experience), and can be almost the perfect embodiment of the "popular artist" (his great popularity after all, has always been chiefly among pale-oliths)—i.e., you can be the ideal kind of movie actor—and still crack up, or use only a fraction of your potential talent. How & Why?

If peg is needed, this could run with release of his next picture, whatever it is.

Art: Clip-shots (far preferable to stills) from his finest moments and from his most extreme mugging; candid work on Rooney en pantoufles, or cups, or whatever.

Unless a miracle happens and they cast him for something he could really show his stuff in, this story should be done, if at all, before very long—if my guess is right that he is slowly coming apart like an elderly child-prodigy.

Another possible angle of bio-perse: Rooney, from adolescence on, as a Metro problem child (i.e., in his private life. Best done from angle of worried people who are paid to "protect" him, but such information [would] have to be gathered indirectly and, I assume, used with such discretion it might nullify its interest).

5) HOW A PICTURE GETS MADE
Take one through from start to finish, in every kind at detail & interlocking of detail which could possibly interest or enlighten the reader; candid illustrations, plus one or two picture-series say, building a scene (or a single shot) from the bones on out to the ultimate soft polish seen on screen. Ideally, should be a near-average show, but a little above average if we want to tackle some of the most interesting & typical stuff: i.e., what happens when something a little out of line, and better than average, is tried? If the show was perfectly accommodating to us we would be able to point out in it one or two gratifying victories, one or two lousy defeats, a great deal of intricate

compromise of the kind that is scarcely to be suspected by those who see it on the screen. This would be a long job to research & write and I hope if you're interested in it, that I can do it in the future rather than now.

A FEW OTHER IDEAS, MORE BRIEFLY

1) If we can find a good-average, or a top-grade *IDEA MAN*, there might be quite an amusing story in how he got where he is and how he keeps earning his keep.

2) GUARDIANS. Undoubtedly libel dangers if we got far enough into this to have any fun; yet a possible and fascinating, thin-ice story. I have no clear idea yet of its extent, but am sure it goes far beyond just the press-relations people—for habitual drunks, creepers, perverts & swinehounds, assume there are people on 24-hour duty, trying to protect them from the Beast in them—or rather, from the Beast in the public. Best-known sample: The Protectors of the Keenan Wynn—Van Johnson—Mrs. Wynn-Johnson Private Lives menage. Metro seems to have all this most highly developed. See above; & Rooney; and the successful protection of Walter Pidgeon when he was caught among Charlies in a Brooklyn male cat-house. Art: Perhaps mere facial studies of the Guardian Angels, and of their little charges a) at their worst, b) in their dream version, as the public sees them.

3) POST-WAR Directors (and, secondarily, actors & writers). A whole bunch of the best people in Hollywood went to war, grew up considerably while away, came back to work with the evident determination not to fritter around anymore—to make first-rate pictures no matter what; to lick every obstacle to that. How successful [was] this resolve in performance, and how long has it lasted? Consider a few of the people—Wyler, Huston, Ford, Capra, Montgomery, Litvak, Stevens . . . They have done some pretty fine work since their return. It may be too early to be sure whether, or to what extent, they'll get beaten or get discouraged; yet it seems a good stage of things for a sort of assessment. The more so, because there is virtually no "new blood" in American movies. These guys, thanks to their war experience, *are* the "new blood," such as it is, and [on] the whole it has been good—about a hundred times better, for instance, than Hollywood's record during the war years.

4) EFFECTS OF THE PROBE, and of the general swing to the Right.

We [would] not try in this to go into the merits or demerits either of the Congressional Probers or of the ten Hollywood men cited for contempt; merely to examine, in specific detail, the effects: chiefly a job of learning from one writer or director after another, what had to be modified or killed in work they were doing or planning. Even in the little I have learned about this, it extends very far beyond any sort of movie stuff which could be regarded as politically suspect—extends, even, beyond "social-minded" movies. This might be an interesting kind of shocker, on censorship from an angle seldom considered by itself.

5) WHAT I WOULD MOST LIKE TO DO. The general assumption is, that all real talent is frustrated in Hollywood. True of some kinds of talent, a damn silly lie about others. But here, we would run through say 15 or 20 of the best writers, directors & players out there asking them what, under ideal circumstances they would like most to do (i.e., to make, as a movie); what prevents them; what movie or mere passage in their achieved work they feel best about; ditto on what (for reasons of personal failure or defeat from work) they feel worst about—and how come they did these bests and worsts. May sound too technical but could I suspect be of more personal interest, through the various personalities talking, than seems clear on the surface.

6) ERICH VON STROHEIM. When the great Griffith died recently, he hadn't made a picture in 15 years, nearly. Once he was dead, everybody recognized him as a great man; but still also recognized him as a great has-been. [Von] Stroheim is another "unemployable" of close to the same stature. It would be interesting to get at him while he is still alive and through him, and through every other source possible, try to understand why he hasn't been entrusted with a picture since about 1926. There are various good reasons of course: he is as arrogant as the whole crowd of Junkers distilled into one; he has fantastic ideas of the kind of sexual & other material which ought to be in movies if only all these swine weren't out to play safe for the dough; he is insanely extravagant. But his pictures also show that he is a man of terrific force and talent. We should get into some detail about the best things in his best pictures (and the craziest); some fair samples of his extravagance & intransigence; for the rest, a highly personal story.[42]

The editors at *Life* approved two of Agee's ideas, the proposed Huston and Silent Comedy articles, and Agee made arrangements to travel to California. In August, he resigned his positions at *Time* and the *Nation;* his last column for the *Nation*, a reconsideration of D. W. Griffith, was published on September 4, 1948. Meanwhile, at MGM, Frank Taylor was struggling to get one of his own dream projects off the ground. Taylor had first hoped to produce a film version of F. Scott Fitzgerald's *Tender is the Night* or Malcolm Lowry's *Under the Volcano* with a script by Graham Greene. Instead, he found himself assigned to helm a *noir* thriller, a staple of MGM at the time, set in Boston and called alternately *Murder at Harvard* and *Mystery Street*. Taylor found working in the studio system frustrating. It was difficult for a fledgling producer to enlist leading actors and competent directors. The film's protagonist was a young detective derisively nicknamed "Portuguese Pete," who had to overcome ethnic prejudice while investigating a murder. For the role the studio considered John Hodiak and Van Heflin. Taylor played with the idea of getting James Whitmore and ended up giving the job to a young Ricardo Montalban. He tried to get Joseph Losey to direct (Agee wrote to suggest Nicholas Ray, a boyhood friend of Manny Farber) but the job ended up going to John Sturges.

For help with the screenplay, Taylor enlisted Ben Maddow, a veteran of the New York progressive documentary movement. As a member of the communist-affiliated Workers Film and Photo League, Maddow had worked on socially progressive films with Sidney Meyers and Jay Leyda. In the 1930s Maddow wrote numerous documentaries, including *Heart of Spain*, *Native Land*, and *Valley Town*, and worked with Meyers on films such as *People of the Cumberland* and *China Strikes Back*, a 1937 movie featuring footage of Communist forces in the Shensi region. *People of the Cumberland*, codirected by Leyda and Meyers, was a combination of documentary footage and dramatic reenactments that told the story of a progressive school, the Highlander Folk School, and the struggle of local workers to organize unions for coal miners and mill workers. Ten years later, Meyers, with Helen Levitt and Janice Loeb, used similar documentary techniques to depict another progressive school, The Wiltwyck School for Boys, in *The Quiet One*. Agee, who knew Helen Levitt and Sidney Meyers's former collaborator Jay Leyda through their mutual friendship with Walker Evans, was hired to write voiceover commentary for *The Quiet One*.

Frank Taylor desperately wanted Agee to help edit the *Mystery Street* screenplay, but Agee was falling behind on his *Life* pieces. On January 3, 1949, Taylor wrote to Agee to ease his anxiety about the possibility of losing out on the opportunity to work on Taylor's first film. "So far as you go, Jim, please do not fret. As you can see, my plans are just as hypothetical as your own and subject to all kinds of change. I have still not spoken to Dore [Schary] about your possible role and will not until my final sessions with him in ten days or so. I think the only safe thing for each of us to do is to proceed independently of each other, and then if and when we can work out an arrangement, it will be a happy surprise. I am so grateful to you for all of your suggestions, each one of which I am going to do my damnest [sic] to use."[43]

Since Agee was unable to make a full-time commitment to the film, Taylor mailed the *Mystery Street* screenplay to him and encouraged his input. The two maintained a constant correspondence in which Agee wrote detailed suggestions in his notoriously difficult-to-decipher handwriting. He sent Taylor multi-page letters with dialogue, casting, and scene construction suggestions, all of which Taylor found indispensable; "I can't possibly tell you how touched and grateful I am for your most excellent, constructive notes." But Taylor was less than thrilled with the task of reading Agee's notorious scrawl. At one point, Taylor wrote to Agee:

> *I was very grateful to you for your rapid reply, however I would have been more grateful had it been (even!) more easily decipherable. I am sure you will not be offended if I admit quite openly that for two-and-a-half days I had three people at work trying to make out your script. If I did not value your opinion so highly I assure you that I would now not stoop to an admission of our inadequacies at reading your writing, but since I do not wish to miss a word of it, and because I think you might be amused at the extremely garbled translation, I include them herewith hoping that someone closer to you than I will come to the rescue. Please then dispatch same at your earliest possible.*

⧼⧽

While Frank Taylor learned the ropes at MGM, his wife, Nan, became increasingly involved in the founding and organization of the Westland School, a progressive elementary school founded on the precepts of John Dewey. As the red scare heated up, the school provided a refuge of sorts for children of blacklisted filmmakers. There the children were free from the redbaiting taunts they might face at other schools. Still in operation today, the school describes its founders as "a group of parents and teachers for whom living one's political and social beliefs was a way of life. . . . They were risk-takers, passionate in their hopes for a better world, and certain that that world could begin by educating their children in a humanistic, democratic way."[44] Oona Chaplin became a supporter of the school, and the Chaplins enrolled their oldest daughter Geraldine. Nan Taylor, serving as the school's chairman of the board of directors, enlisted Chaplin's help to create a fund-raising benefit. The comedian allowed the school to hold a rare screening of *City Lights*, which had been out of distribution for years. Nan Taylor oversaw the benefit, which was held in December 1949 at the Gordon Theater in Los Angeles and raised $2,000 for the school. An account of the benefit in the *Daily People's World*, a communist-oriented newspaper, was added to Chaplin's voluminous FBI file and later played a role in his exile; the article was referred to by the attorney general after journalists pressed the Justice Department for evidence proving Chaplin's alleged un-American activities.

Chaplin's FBI file also contains a document that includes the elementary school in a list of organizations it identifies as dangerous to the welfare of the United States. The document, under the heading "Affiliation of Charles Chaplin with Groups Declared to be Communist Subversive Groups or Reputedly Controlled or Influenced by Communist Party,"[45] lists a total of fifteen organizations, including the Westland School, and ranges from the National Association of Mexican-Americans and the National Council of American Soviet Friendship to the Hollywood Ten. The document also quotes an "informant (blacked out) of known reliability . . . [who] learned that Charles Chaplin and his wife were interested in the Westland School and that all Progressive children are sent there if their people can afford it."[46] The report also describes the article from the *Daily People's World*: "In the previous week Chaplin's movie, *City Lights*, had been shown for the benefit of the Westland School, and [the article] states that after the showing, at which Chaplin was present, Chaplin received a tremendous ovation. The article continued by stating, 'It was more than an ovation of one of America's greatest motion pictures, it was more than a salute to the only genius of the English language cinema, to a timeless pantomimist who will be remembered for his artistry as long as man has memory. It was a political demonstration, too, of a solidarity with a man whose every screen appearance has

Nan and Frank E. Taylor were close friends of Agee's in New York City. After Frank Taylor came to Hollywood as a film producer for MGM, Nan Taylor became involved in the management of a new progressive elementary school, the Westland School, supported by the Chaplins, whose oldest daughter Geraldine was a student there. (Photo courtesy of Curtice Taylor)

been a brilliant attack on a dying society. This was an audience that understood his barbed darts at pompous politicians, at wealthy maniacs, alternating maudlin and ruthless at the stupidity of the police, at the heartlessness of a society that has no place for the little man, except in the hearts of his fellows.'"[47]

Coincidentally, progressive education was on Agee's mind around this time, too, because of his work on the groundbreaking documentary film *The Quiet One*. This film was made to raise awareness and support for the work done by the Wiltwyck School, a pioneering school founded by the Episcopalian Mission Society in 1936 as a refuge for troubled black Protestant boys. In 1942, after the Mission Society decided to close the school, Justine Wise Polier, with the help of Eleanor Roosevelt, arranged to have it moved to Esopus, New York, where it reopened without its previous religious and racial exclusions. The school's progressive approach toward childhood development was guided by the renowned child psychologist and social activist Dr. Viola Bernard, who served as its psychiatric consultant. Eleanor Roosevelt was an active supporter of the school and held an annual picnic for its students at her estate on the Hudson.

Agee became involved with *The Quiet One* through his friendship with the photographer Helen Levitt. Levitt had first met Agee at Walker Evans's studio. Around 1946 Levitt, together with her brother Bill and her best friend Janice Loeb (later Bill's wife) formed a documentary film company, Film Documents, to make socially progressive films. Loeb decided to produce a film to raise money and support for the Wiltwyck School. Levitt and Loeb brought Sidney Meyers on board to direct the film, which dramatized the efforts of a counselor at the school, played by Clarence Cooper, to break through to a withdrawn lonely boy from a troubled home. Donald was played by a ten-year-old amateur actor Donald Thompson. The film's musical score was supplied by the African American composer Ulysses Kay, the nephew of the legendary jazz musician Joseph "King" Oliver, and a recipient of the Prix de Rome and a Fulbright award. Originally made in 16mm *The Quiet One* cost $28,000 to produce. Bill Levitt had the film blown up to 35mm and it was first screened to wide acclaim in late 1948 at the Little Carnegie theater in New York City. Soon after it opened, the *New York Times* reported that the film "has reached a degree of enthusiasm which defies ready comparison even by those who have long observed the Broadway movie scene."[48]

What made the film notable, according to Bill Levitt, was its move away from the traditional documentary nuts-and-bolts presentation of facts: *The Quiet One* ushered in a new era of artistic storytelling in documentary film. On December 18, 1949, the National Board of Review included it in its list of the top ten pictures of the year. The following February, Helen Levitt, Janice Loeb, and Sidney Meyers were nominated for an Academy Award for Best Writing, Story, and Screenplay. The film was also nominated for another Academy Award the following year, for Best Documentary.

Although the film's voiceover commentary, written by Agee after *The Quiet One* was shot and edited, wasn't recognized in the Academy Award nomination, it helped raise the film to a higher artistic level. In the *New York Times*, Bosley Crowther, who called the film a "genuine masterpiece,"[49] lauded Agee's contribution to the film as a "truly poetic commentary."[50] Film Documents had actually considered having Agee record the narration, but his reading had come across as too mannered: "He read like a poet,"[51] recalled Bill Levitt. In the film, Agee's prose is read by the actor Gary Merrill, who soon afterward married the actress Bette Davis.

The commentary for *The Quiet One* was in fact Agee's first contribution to a completed and released film, and provided a perfect vehicle for him to combine his interest in realism with lyrical prose:

> That's the most we can hope to do, here at Wiltwyck, for any of the boys who lie sleeping here: to clear away some of the great harm they suffered in the difficult world they came from; to make them a little better able to take care of themselves in the difficult world they must return to: A little better able to live usefully and generously, in that world; a little better able to care for the children they will have, than their parents were to care for them: Lest the generations of those maimed in childhood, each making the next in its own image, create upon the darkness, like mirrors locked face to face, an infinite corridor of despair; To keep open a place of healing, courage, and hope, for as many as we can afford to care for, among the thousands of those children who lie sleeping, tonight, in impoverished little rooms, and in poor fugitive, derelict holes, in the rotten depths of the city: Whom poverty, bewilderment, hunger, pride, fear, lovelessness, may drive into sickness, into crime: And who, in a world which disfigures them cannot be cared for, and are not wanted.[52]

The 1948 Academy Awards were held on March 24, 1949, at the AMPAS Theatre in Los Angeles. When Bill Levitt and Janice Loeb came out to Hollywood to attend the ceremony, they were fêted as the "hot new kids"[53] and Frank Taylor arranged for them to meet Buster Keaton and Charles Chaplin. Coincidentally, Taylor first met Bill Levitt when Levitt held the post of educational director for the United Automobile Workers of America in Detroit during the war; Taylor had been brought in to help organize book clubs for the workers. After seeing *The Quiet One*, Taylor offered to help promote the film and arranged for the Film Documents crew to visit Chaplin at his Summit Drive estate. They brought with them a print of a short art film, *In the Street*, shot on the streets of Spanish Harlem by Helen Levitt and part-time cameraman James Agee. Chaplin was so taken by the short film that when it ended he did a spontaneous pantomime of one of the film's memorable children, a dancing gypsy boy. Chaplin also provided a promotional quote for the filmmakers: "Splendid. . . . Has qualities of poetic and dramatic impact rarely achieved in films."[54]

Helen Levitt later recalled how the short film *In the Street* had been created: "I had been taking pictures (in Spanish Harlem) and I was also interested in movies at that time. I got to wondering if a film could be made there. I spoke to Jim Agee about it, and I asked Jim if he thought by just shooting wild, shooting the sort of thing I had been taking with the still—camera—whether one could possibly cut that together and make a film. He said he thought so, absolutely. So I borrowed a 16-millimeter camera from a friend, and Jim and I went up to Spanish Harlem. I gave him the camera, and I had my still camera. He shot a lot in the street . . ."[55] Levitt and Agee adopted a hidden camera approach similar to one that Levitt had helped devise in 1938, when she had assisted Walker Evans in taking a series of portraits of unwitting New York City subway riders. Evans's biographer Belinda Rathbone credits Agee with having encouraged Evans to undertake the subway project. Using a 35mm Contax camera painted black to hide any metallic reflections, Evans hid the camera in his jacket, its shutter controlled via a cable fed through his sleeve to a palmed trigger.

In the Street begins with an uncredited preface, likely written by Agee: "The streets of the poor quarters of the great cities are above all a theater, and a battleground. There unaware and unnoticed, every

human being is a poet, a masker, a warrior, a dancer; and in his innocent artistry he projects against the turmoil of the street, an image of
human existence. The attempt in this short film is to capture this
image."[56] When the film was finally released in 1952, Agee's friend
Manny Farber, who had inherited the film critic post at the *Nation*
("He made sure I got the job, and I made sure I lost it,"[57] Farber
would later say), wrote that *In the Street* "has been beautifully edited
(by Miss Levitt) into a somber study of the American figure, from
childhood to old age, growing stiffer, uglier, and lonelier with the passage of years. Let me say that changing one's identity and acting like a
spy or a private eye are more a part of the American make-up than I'd
ever imagined before seeing this picture. This not only holds for
Levitt, Inc., who had to disguise their role of filmmakers to get the
naked truth, but also goes for the slum people who are being photographed."[58] Farber described Levitt's surreptitious gear: "The Film
Documents group used an old model Cine-Kodak, which records the
action at a right angle to the operator who gazes into his scenefinder
much as was done with the old-fashioned 'Brownie.' The people who
wound up in this movie probably thought the camera-wielder was a
stray citizen having trouble with the lock of a small black case that
could contain anything from a piccolo to a tiny machine gun."[59] After
Agee had to drop out of the project because of conflicting commitments, Levitt recruited her close friend Janice Loeb to help out: "I got
my friend Janice Loeb to help, and we went on and made the film. A
lot of what Jim shot that first day is in the film. He was an all around
genius—he was able to shoot marvelous stuff, even though he'd never
shot anything in his life."[60]

In the years following the release of *In the Street*, Film Documents
made several more documentaries, including one to educate people
about rheumatic fever, directed by Bill Levitt. The company considered branching out into feature films and explored producing a film
version of the Carson McCullers novel *The Heart is a Lonely Hunter*. In
the spring of 1953, the company contracted Agee to develop a screenplay, a thinly veiled depiction of the breakup of his first and second
marriages, called *A Love Story: Bigger than Both of Us*. Agee described
the subject of the unproduced story as "three essentially kind and well
meaning people, trying as a general rule to do their best under the increasing stresses of love and longing and jealousy."[61]

$\mathscr{I}$CARUS $\mathscr{F}$ALLS

$\mathscr{I}$n late 1948 after quitting his movie reviewing jobs at *Time* and the *Nation*, but still living in New York City, Agee began to research material for his *Life* magazine articles. He explored the Museum of Modern Art's outstanding collection of silent comedies and contacted John Huston to make arrangements to visit Hollywood and interview him. Shortly after Agee arrived in California, Huston and his wife, Evelyn Keyes, planned an adventurous hunting trip to Idaho and invited him to join them on the wilderness excursion, along with Huston's friend, actor Gilbert Roland. The four drove from California to a hunting lodge in Idaho's Salmon River mountains. There they hired a professional guide who led them through the snowy terrain on horseback. Huston wrote of the trip:

> We chose a place in the Bitterroot Mountains run by a bush pilot named Ben Bennett. It was so remote and so hard to get to that, so far as I know, no other plane ever ventured in there. Agee had never been in the Western wilderness before. He loved it. He didn't want to shoot a gun, to kill anything but on the other hand he didn't want to miss anything either. He went on every outing. Evenings, we would sit around and play poker or listen to Ben's stories about his days as an Alaskan bush pilot. Agee liked to listen, and I doubt he ever forgot anything.[1]

Not long after the trip, Keyes ended her marriage to Huston: "John later said that that hunting trip was the best part of our life together. Go figure that."[2] For a short while after, Keyes dated Sydney Chaplin, Charles's son.

The month after he returned home Agee was making headway on the Huston profile and wrote to the director from New York on February 18 with encouraging news from his editors. "My bosses at *Life*, I am happy to say, would like as much as possible on how you work."[3] Agee sent Huston a long and detailed questionnaire on his approach to film directing. Huston had in the meantime fallen in love with Ricki Soma, a beautiful eighteen-year-old ballerina. Agee, himself a veteran of two failed marriages, wrote on May 25 to commiserate with Huston on the breakup: "I'm sorry about you and Evelyn. By my own past performance I know how asinine it is to be merely sorry. It's so often incomparably better than to try to insist that things are as they damned well aren't. Being so aware of this I hesitate to speak of it at all. But regardless of that I damned well am sorry, because I like you both so much."[4]

Huston, attentive to Agee's expressed interest in screen writing, arranged a job for him writing the script for an adaptation of Stephen Crane's *The Blue Hotel*. The job came through Huntington Hartford, who wanted Huston to direct the film. While Hartford ultimately left Agee's script unmade, Crane's writing became a familiar subject for both Agee and Huston; Huston, after completing his next project, the film-*noir* classic *The Asphalt Jungle*, written with Ben Maddow, was hired to direct Crane's *The Red Badge of Courage*. And a couple of years later, Agee was again hired by Huntington Hartford to write a screenplay based on a Crane short story, this time for an adaptation of *The Bride Comes to Yellow Sky*.

While Agee was wrestling with his profile of Huston for *Life*, Frank Taylor continued to struggle to get his first film *Mystery Street* in front of the cameras. On April 26, 1949 Taylor wrote to Agee from the MGM studio in Culver City, to deliver a progress report on the obstacles he was facing:

> *I can't possibly tell you how touched and grateful I am for your most excellent, constructive notes. They came at a time when we had been forced by one circumstance or another to so contort our material that we felt all we had left was a pile of garbage. When I see you I will tell you the whole saga.*

For the moment things are at a standstill while we get a director and lay plans for a location trip. There are still many complaints which I do not share being leveled at the script. The whole project is becoming an unfortunate lesson in how to make turkeys. I am still hoping to salvage something. It has been suggested that still a third writer come on and taking the best out of both previous scripts add his own fine touches. This would unquestionably make a potpourri so odiferous that you might catch whiffs on Bleecker Street. In other words, things here at Metro are not so different . . . I do not know whom I will get as director, but what I want now more than anything else is enthusiasm and imagination. To hell with a long line of mediocre credits. Metro is in the process of grinding out so many of this genre that it is difficult to get a contract director to take one of them on. This is fine with me. Having been turned down yesterday myself by Roy Rowland, I just came out and asked for Joe Losey who very much needs a job and whom I think I could work with. Cast-wise, we are also up in the air. Van Heflin whom "they" wanted for a Portuguese Pete turned it down. This means I will either have John Hodiak or perhaps have the opportunity to introduce James Whitmore who did such a splendid job in Command Decision *on the stage. I wanted Ann Southern for Grace since she was on the lot, but it's not big enough for her. If enough of the local folk turn it down it may just be that I will have a chance to use unknowns, but of course if I get the wrong kind of director this could be more of a liability than an asset. Ben was very grateful for your criticism and there are very few points where we disagree. I think Pete is something of a failure as a character and we intend to add a dimension. How I wish we might have several hours to discuss this with you. I intend to go to Boston by way of New York, and must see you. As soon as my plans are definite I will let you know. Again many, many thanks to you.*[5]

Taylor's letter ended with a note encouraging Agee to start thinking about likely subjects for a follow-up project they could collaborate on: "Meanwhile I am reading and reading hoping to locate a second project. If you have any hot flashes, particularly one which you might wish to work on yourself, do drop me a line."[6] Filming for *Mystery Street* was completed on December 9, 1949, and the movie was released the following September. Its screenplay was credited to Sydney Boehm and Richard Brooks, its story to Leonard Spigelgass; Maddow's and Agee's contributions went unacknowledged. When the Academy Award nominations were announced, *Mystery Street* earned Spigelgass a nod for Best Story, but he lost to the writer of *Panic in the Streets*.

Agee had missed out on the opportunity to work full time on Taylor's film because of his inability to complete the first of his two freelance articles for *Life* as quickly as he'd hoped. Agee's celebration of silent film comedy was finally published as "Comedy's Greatest Era" in the September 3, 1949, issue. He had hoped to finish the article in a few months, but it took almost a year to complete. The finished article, though, was a great success; it was widely credited with reviving general interest in silent film comedy and also helped to renew appreciation of Buster Keaton. In a doff of his squat porkpie hat, Keaton later showed his own appreciation for Agee in the very first paragraph of his autobiography, *My Wonderful World of Slapstick*, by quoting the *Life* article's discussion of his famous impassive visage, his Great Stone Face: "That kindly critic, the late James Agee, described my face as ranking 'almost with Lincoln's as an early American archetype, it was haunting, handsome, and almost beautiful' . . . I sure was pleased."[7]

Agee was devoted to silent films from an early age, and when talking films first appeared he disliked them immensely. During April 1929, while a student at Harvard he had written to Dwight MacDonald to describe his reaction to the advent of sound in film. He imagined the new technology's best potential usage, but felt guilty for even entertaining the thought of betraying his beloved silent movies: "I'm trying to write a paper on the possibilities of the talkies—which I despise. Nevertheless, great things . . . could be done with them. . . . One is that they could be a fulfillment of all that Blake wanted to do—great pictures, poetry, color and music—the other is the chance they offer Joyce and his followers. I should think they'd go wild over the possibilities of it."[8] He imagined making a "test case" film based on a story he had written, but feared that he would "somehow feel a traitor to the movies as they should be, even to think of such things."[9]

The *Life* article was Agee's one-man campaign to remind the public of the power of those now distant, receding images. In the original story proposal Agee wrote that he intended to discuss Chaplin only in a cursory fashion, and planned to devote the weight of the story toward comedians who had passed from public prominence and visibility: "Chaplin I think [should] be mentioned only in passing."[10] But the published article instead paid as much attention to Chaplin as to Keaton, Harold Lloyd, and Harry Langdon. In fact, in the article Agee used Chaplin as the measure by which to evaluate the other actors. He quoted the director Mack Sennett to establish Chaplin's preeminence: "Of Chaplin he says simply, 'Oh well, he's just the greatest artist that ever lived'"[11] For Agee there was no doubt of Chaplin's superior rank. He asserted in the *Life* article that "Chaplin's former rivals . . . speak of him no more jealously than they might of God. We will try here to only suggest the essence of his supremacy."[12] To convey the depth of Chaplin's accomplishment, Agee was compelled to compare the comedian's work with poetry: "The finest pantomime, the deepest emotion, the richest and most poignant poetry were in Chaplin's work."[13] The *Life* article contains Agee's now classic, frequently quoted description of the final moment of Chaplin's *City Lights*, when the once-blind flower girl suddenly recognizes that the benefactor to whom she owes her sight is not a millionaire but actually just the Little Tramp. Here Agee's praise reached its apex: "It is enough to shrivel the heart to see, and it is the greatest piece of acting and the highest moment in films."[14] Agee also took the opportunity in the *Life* article to take one more stab at defending *Monsieur Verdoux*'s virtue. He remained steadfast in his estimation of the film: "Verdoux is the greatest of talking comedies . . ." But in a clever turn he pointed out that Americans were unlikely, thanks to their fortunate history, to ever appreciate a film "so cold and savage that it had to find its public in grimly experienced Europe."[15]

After the silent comedy article was published, Huston wrote to congratulate Agee and to ask about what progress the writer had made on his novel. Agee's first novel, *The Morning Watch*, is a coming-of-age story set on Maundy Thursday, the day before Good Friday. Huston wrote: "I intended to write you about the old-time movie article in *Life*, which was superb from every standpoint. How is the book coming? Are you nearly finished? If you want to give me something let it be your promise to send me one of the first copies off the press."[16] On September 14 Agee sent Huston a three-page synopsis of the novel, and described the story as "a long, very slow, winding, deeply introvert [*sic*] story . . . developing in its last pages into a short piece of violent action with heavy symbolic and ambiguous charges."[17] He wrote to Huston that the story's protagonist was a "12-year-old boy (roughly myself) at edge of puberty, peak of certain kinds of hypersensitive introversion, isolation, and a certain priggishness." Revealing the sway that Joyce had over his literary life, Agee shared some insight into the nature of his young subject: "The 'hero,' though authentic and I think in some ways interesting, meaningful, and even sympathetic, is in so many respects a complete little shit. By his most favorable comparison he is a kind of backward, scrub-team version of Stephen Dedalus at the same age, but Stephen, from the age of two on, had tremendous charm and glamour—and I both love Joyce for that and hold it against him; This little shit has none."[18] While Agee feared that the subject and style of the novel would hold no interest for Huston, he was proud of his book—"I really feel good about the story, which is enough of a novelty to me that it's a pleasure to say so."[19]

Meanwhile, Agee's postatomic Tramp idea had gotten no further than Chaplin's willingness to read it. Mia Agee remembered the screenplay:

> [Agee] had an idea which I think would have been a very good film; a film that Chaplin should make with a return of The Tramp as one of the few, if not the only, survivor in a post-atomic world. And Chaplin liked the idea very much. If that's the last person in the world, then it's also, in a way, the first person, so then the circle closes and there are lots of possibilities. It might have been complicated for him because of the sound when, after all, the films with The Tramp were all silent. But then, you see, you could conceivably, at least in large parts, have justified a silent film, which is what Jim was after anyway. In the post-atomic explosion world, this would probably go quite well, since of course there wasn't anybody for him to talk with. There were no sounds. What would there be? So it would have had to go into pantomime. He was so involved in the visual scenes of what the world would be like. Just think what you'd do with a place like New York City without a soul in it. The images are so fantastic that he never got as far a worrying about the plot. He started writing an outline, not a real script. All I remember is the shadows that had been burned into rock by some atomic explosion. I don't think he worked out more than a third of the film, if that much. He was very interested in it for a while, but he never did it, due to a combination of things. Chaplin was working on *Limelight*. They had started talking about it before, but he had already done most of the work for *Limelight* so he obviously had to follow through and finish it.[20]

Although Chaplin had kindly encouraged Agee to send him the script to read, he apparently never developed sufficient interest in the idea to consider turning it into a film. He did find the manuscript interesting enough to lend to friends, including Norman Lloyd, to read. Lloyd also recalled playing tennis with Chaplin one day at the Summit

Drive estate when the butler appeared to say that Mr. Agee was on the phone. Lloyd remembered that Chaplin, afraid to hurt Agee's feelings by so quickly rejecting the offered project, requested that Agee be informed that he was not available. This was apparently a common maneuver for Chaplin, whose close friends would sometimes resort to writing letters when they found it too difficult to reach him on the phone. Lloyd's recollection of why Chaplin didn't pursue Agee's project was that Chaplin was convinced that he was too old to play the Tramp again, that his body had changed too much, and that his age wouldn't permit a proper performance.[21]

While Agee's dream of having Chaplin make his film went unfulfilled, he was well on the way to realizing a different fantasy: He and Chaplin had again made social contact and would soon become close friends. Agee wrote to Frank Taylor at the end on January 30, 1950: "I'm so sorry to have had to ask you, twice in a row, to bother to find addresses for me, and I'm very grateful. Particularly that you thought also to tell me where Chaplin is staying; for I'd decided I shouldn't try to enquire through United Artists but, emboldened by your wire, called him up this morning. He was nice as hell ('cordial' being too chilly a word), including all he said of you, and I'll be seeing him Thursday."[22]

In an interview with the documentary filmmaker Ross Spears, Mia Agee described the growing affection between Agee and Chaplin:

> When Jim went out to Hollywood, they were good friends. He absolutely adored Chaplin . . . we spent quite a lot of time with [Chaplin]. He was an enormously stimulating person. I mean he was interested in so many different things—very articulate and very warm. Once he trusted you, or once he accepted you, he was very open, very free, and very, very nice to be around. He and Jim set each other off in terms of the kinds of things they talked about since they were largely interested in very similar things, you know, that sort of pleasure when somebody else's mind clicks with yours, and you can really have a kind of exchange and bounce the ball around. You can't do that with most people; it is a great pleasure, you know, if you happen to hit it. [23]

Agee's friendship with Huston was also growing stronger. Though his profile of the director was months away from being published in *Life*, the two maintained their communication and correspondence.

On May 23 Huston's newest film, *Asphalt Jungle*, was released. Agee wrote a month later to tell Huston, "I saw *Asphalt Jungle* a second time last night. I liked it the first time. I was nuts about it the second."[24] Agee pointed out that a few scenes in the film disappointed him and struck him as "soft" or "art" ("I'm afraid I tend to blame Ben, but you too, as the boss in the team?"[25]), but he also admitted being driven to "uncontrollable" tears by the ending. At the time, Huston was already deep at work preparing to film *The Red Badge of Courage*. Agee cheered him on: "I think this new one will be your best yet, and as good as anyone ever made."[26] Agee concluded the letter with an assessment of Huston's work, ranking him almost as highly as he did Chaplin, "I bar Chaplin, in the special world he moves in. Outside of him, I think you're the best there is."[27]

Like Agee, Huston had also been deeply affected by Chaplin at a young age. In a strange and memorable encounter, Huston was given a private audience with the comedian when he was a little boy. At the age of ten or eleven years old Huston had been diagnosed with chronic nephritis. The potentially fatal condition enlarged his heart. In desperation, his mother took him to see a series of heart specialists across the country. The two traveled from the Mayo Clinic in St. Paul, Minnesota, to New Orleans, and to Phoenix. Eventually, the boy and his mother moved to California in hope that the warm weather would help. One day, while staying at the Alexandria Hotel in Los Angeles, the phone rang, after which Huston's mother informed the incredulous child, "That was Charlie Chaplin! He heard there was a sick boy in the hotel, and he's coming to see you!"[28] Chaplin came up to visit and encouraged Huston's mother to let him entertain the boy while she took some time to herself. Huston later wrote, "No one today holds a position in a child's world even remotely comparable to the one Charlie Chaplin held then. He was more than a picture star; he was myth incarnate; nobody thought of him as a real being."[29] Chaplin kept Huston spellbound for over an hour with a pantomimed flea circus and a puppet show made out of handkerchief. As an adult, Huston came to know Chaplin socially and they frequently played tennis together, but Huston hesitated to ask the comedian about the childhood visit. Years later, they found themselves at the same party. His inhibition weakened by champagne, Huston asked, "Charlie, do you recall, some twenty years ago, coming to see a little sick boy in the Alexandria Hotel?"[30] According to Huston, Chaplin's reaction was odd; "He stiffened, gave me a strange look, then abruptly turned and hailed someone across the room. It was a mystifying reaction. It was as though he was ashamed of my mentioning a good deed."[31] Many years later, when filming *The Bible*, Huston tried to recruit Chaplin to play Noah. "He was tempted and toyed with the idea for some weeks . . . but finally said no; he couldn't conceive of being in someone else's picture."[32] Huston ended up playing the role himself.

Huston's life was filled with strange adventures like his encounter with Chaplin, and Agee put many of these stories to use in the profile he wrote for *Life*. The article, "Undirectable Director," was finally published on September 18, 1950, almost a year after the silent comedy article. Much of the new article covered Huston's colorful upbringing and unbridled manner. In an effort to characterize Huston's politics, Agee argued that although Huston was seen by many as a "fellow traveler"—especially after his involvement in a group of Hollywood celebrities that had traveled to Washington in support of the Hollywood Ten and his subsequent support for Henry Wallace's run for president—Huston was "a political man chiefly in an emotional sense,"[33] and "rather less of a Communist than the most ultramontane Republican, for like perhaps five out of seven good artists who ever lived he is—to lapse into technical jargon—a natural-born antiauthoritarian individualistic libertarian anarchist, without portfolio."[34] Agee would probably not have objected to having had himself described in the same fashion.

In the *Life* article, after a discussion of Huston's filmmaking technique, Agee assessed Huston's place in the ranking of his film heroes and declared Huston the "most inventive director of his generation." Agee singled Huston out as the one director who "has done more to extend, invigorate and purify the essential idiom of American movies . . . than anyone since the prime of D.W. Griffith."[35] But, perhaps sensing that Huston would not have respected a profile that did little more than sing his praises, Agee tempered his adulation and wrote that when compared to his own frequently cited pantheon of silent film greats and artistic European filmmakers, Huston fell far short: "[Huston's] work as a whole is not on the level with the finest and most deeply imaginative work that has been done in movies—the work of Chaplin, Dovzhenko, Eisenstein, Griffith, the late Jean Vigo."[36] The Huston profile closed with a list of the reasons why the director had not yet achieved greatness, and what it would take for him to achieve it.

After reading the article, Huston wrote on September 14 to Agee to let him know that the profile's honesty, while cutting close to the bone, was respected and appreciated: "I think that writing about a good friend must be just about as tough a thing to do as there is for a writer. Several times, reading your piece over, I thought—Jim must have sweated blood here Maybe friends shouldn't write about each other until they're dead—both of them."[37] Huston continued, "Objectively speaking, I think your article is excellent, in fact one of the best things of its kind I've ever read—often penetratingly humorous. . . . But let me get around to the real point of this note which is that I felt every line, including the lines you believe to be most critical, was written with affection and for this, most of all, I'm grateful."[38]

It was part of Agee's nature to fear his own artistic inadequacy: He was, in this regard, almost compulsively self-effacing. On September 13, the day before Huston wrote his letter, Agee had already written to Huston, perhaps preemptively, to express his own reservations about the *Life* article:

> *I just want you to know that I don't feel good about the* Life *piece either. I may not know much but I think I understand both your work and you, better anyhow than there's any evidence of in the piece as it appears. But somehow I made a good deal of a mess of it, all the way down the line. The long piece I turned in was better than what is run, more coherent, making more points, and I think more perceptive—yet somehow I never got hold of it right; I always felt I knew better than I knew how to get onto paper. When I finally turned it in I couldn't feel it was really good but only that it was the best—for some undefeatable and for that matter undiscoverable reason—that I could do. They cut a little more than sixty percent out. Not their fault by my funeral. They had to cut for space and cut, I think, about as well as could be; but I feel even unhappier about the result than about what I turned in. Quite aside from all that, I have a feeling of breach-of-something, not so much of confidence as of friendship, on some points in it; the waterfall story, which seemed important to me; Blanke's opinion of the importance of the second marriage; some of the adverse comment and conjecture at the end. Of the latter in particular I feel: if you feel misgiving or qualifiers, either say them in private to your friend's face, or not at all— above all, not in public print. Against this, of course, there was and is the fact that if as a critic you are trying to evaluate, you omit nothing; and that*

friendship should have no more influence on that, than enmity. All true enough, but I guess I don't really like criticism, including my own. Almost worse; at least if you are going to say something, say it accurately and unmistakably. I think I failed to do this close to half the time, both in praise and dispraise. In the main way, when you feel you have botched something, yet know that at least you have done your best, you should keep your mouth shut, or open it only to take your medicine. That's probably what I really ought to do. But both on the work itself and in affection, I would hate for you to be able to imagine that I feel satisfied. I'm satisfied that there is some good in the piece, and that it may be of some indirect use to you, and that it may clarify some things for some parts of an audience and may help bring better recognition from people who see and write better than I do. So far as that goes I feel better than not, that it's in print, even as it stands. Beyond that I feel lousy. I only hope you'll feel frank with your own reactions. For whatever good regrets and apologies are, and it's a damn thin good, you certainly have them . . ."[39]

The next day, before either man could have received the other's letter, the two spoke on the phone and made plans to have Agee travel to California to watch the filming of *The Red Badge of Courage*. It is likely that on this call Huston also suggested that Agee work with him on the screenplay for his next film, *The African Queen*. Huston remembered: "When it was time to start on *The African Queen*, I phoned [Agee] in New York and said, 'How about it?'"[40] That same day, September 14, after the phone call, Agee wrote again to Huston, to vent more of his concerns about the *Life* profile and to express his hope that the writer Lillian Ross would be able write the profile of Huston that he had intended: "to come out in 3 or 4 weeks as you suggest would work fine on my end; I may even come out before that though I doubt it. . . . What irks and sickens me about my *Life* piece, beyond the things I mentioned already, is that up to then I'd never had nearly enough room to write about your work as I've wanted to . . . and to a great extent I flubbed the chance to get down a lot . . . someone ought to get down." Agee put his faith in Ross's ability to succeed where he thought he'd failed: "Of one thing I'm damn glad and that is that Lillian is on hand during the shooting of this . . . I count on her."[41] Ross was closely following Huston's filming of the Crane story and later turned the experience into a classic work of nonfiction reportage, *Picture*, first serialized in the *New Yorker*, then published as a book in 1952.

Huston's understanding reaction to the *Life* article must have come as a major relief for Agee—he was still working on *The Blue Hotel* screenplay, a job that Huston had arranged for him; a rift at that point would have been a major setback. On September 19, 1950, he thanked Huston again and reported on his progress on *The Blue Hotel* script:

> *That was kind and thoughtful as hell of you to take the time out, as busy as you must be now, to send me a wire and a letter. I'm more deeply grateful than I can say. I'm exceedingly glad you like the piece on the whole. Reading it over when I got the magazine, I felt less badly about it than in the getting-it-to-press stage. I don't feel good about it but such as it is, as far as it gets, it's better than I had thought. You're right that only the dead should bury or unbury the dead. If I ever have to do such jobs again, and doubtless I shall, I hope I have the sense to work on things I feel moderately interested in, where little if any affection—or disaffection—is involved. I'm above all glad it was clear to you reading, that whatever was done was done in affection; it sure as hell was . . . I'm sending out the first draft today . . . a kind of combination treatment and shooting-script; a form which was perhaps ill-advised; I only hope not: anyhow it seemed the best way to try it at the time. There are things in it, I now realize, which need shaving and tightening; and possibly (though I don't feel so) there should be more of my own invention in ration to Crane's story; but at this stage I'm spending no more time on it—I type too slow for all that retyping and it's time it was sent along. On the whole I feel good about it and about some things in it I feel very good. I only hope that you will and that they will.*[42]

After Agee arrived in Hollywood to work on *The African Queen* script with Huston, he found himself quickly embraced by the overlapping social circles that Frank Taylor, Huston, and Chaplin traveled in. Chaplin recalled hosting Agee at his home, "We had open house on Sunday and saw many of our friends, among them Jim Agee, who had come to Hollywood to write a script for John Huston."[43] In early December 1950, Agee wrote to Father Flye to share his impressions of Hollywood and report on his growing friendship with Chaplin:

> *I have particularly been seeing a great deal of Chaplin and his wife. Very interesting, (to put it mildly) to see what a man of real genius—which I am convinced he has—is really like. Few if any mysteries or surprises about that. A very active, self-taught, interesting, likeable man: a blend of conflict in him of sensitiveness and tenderness with icy coldness, which some-*

times disturbs me and would I think put you off. Perfectly unpretentious.
The "genius" is a mixture of these things with tremendous self-discipline
and technical mastery and hard work, with incandescent feeling and intu-
itiveness when he is working. The roots are emotion and intuitiveness; the
chief necessity is discipline. Well, I'm not getting a bit [of discipline].[44]

Lillian Ross remembered first meeting Agee a couple of years earlier, in 1948, at a party at the Chaplins' home with other guests including the director Jean Renoir and Oona Chaplin's close friend
Carol Marcus, then married to William Saroyan. To Ross, the Chaplins' home "always served as a refuge from the Hollywood frenzy . . .
which they shared graciously with other refugees of all kinds, both
foreign and domestic."[45] In Hollywood, Agee, a refugee of the domestic sort, found himself in the middle of a vibrant intellectual social
scene, a heady mix of progressive and leftist artists, writers, composers, and film people from California, New York, and Europe. The
European crowd in Hollywood included both recent political refugees
and their predecessors, the first wave of emigrants who had come to
Hollywood before the rise of fascism. At the center of this circle was
Salka Viertel, a native of Polish Galicia, who held a revered position,
according to John Huston, as the scene's "universal mother."[46] Salka's
home, a near legendary cottage at 167 Mabery Road in Santa Monica
Canyon, was close to the ocean, and at the time, before the advent of
freeways, situated in a fairly remote location. Salka's salon provided
one of the few cultural islands in the near semi-arid cultural desert of
the Los Angeles film colony. At Salka's, sophisticated conversation,
controversial politics and European manners thrived.

In the early 1950s Hollywood began to attract a new generation
of New York actors and writers, many of whom had studied or
worked with Erwin Piscator at the New School. It was inevitable
that Salka's home would provide the up-rooted New Yorkers an attractive political and cultural oasis. Salka wrote in her memoir, *The*
Kindness of Strangers, about the New York crowd that found its way
to her cottage:

One of them was Norman Mailer, who seemed a mixture of ancient
wisdom and astonishing naiveté, somehow thrown out of balance by
his world fame; and much too young and complicated to be married.
We were very fond of him. Then there was James Agee, critic and
essayist, passionately addicted to films but essentially a poet. After a

long day's work with John Huston, for whom he was writing a screenplay, he would come to Mabery Road and, if no other guests were present and no discussions and arguments going on, we would sit and listen to music . . . sometimes he, Agee, would sit down at the piano and play his favorite Schubert sonata, not ostentatiously and not very well.[47]

Chaplin, too, was a frequent guest at Salka Viertel's. Chaplin first met Salka at a dinner party in the 1930s and soon after, began making regular appearances at her evening gatherings. In his memoir he fondly recalled her friendship and support during the dark days of the Joan Barry paternity trials. Chaplin described Salka's home as a *"une maison Coppet,"*[48] comparing her to the celebrated Madame de Stael who fled from Paris after the French Revolution and established a salon of exiles at her father's property in Switzerland: "Salka Viertel, the Polish actress, gave interesting supper parties at her house in Santa Monica. Salka attracted those of the arts and letters: Thomas Mann, Bertolt Brecht, Shoenberg, Hanns Eisler, Lion Feuchtwanger, Stephen Spender, Cyril Connolly and a host of others."[49]

Gene Kelly was one of the young actors that found their way to Salka's. Kelly recalled, "there was sort of a New York group that usually met at my house—everybody that came from the New York theater, the New York artistic establishment. (John) Garfield was around, and we also saw a lot of Monty Clift. Salka Viertel and her son, Peter, a novelist and screenwriter, had a famous salon of expatriates. Bertolt Brecht, Thomas Mann, the Feuchtwangers all gathered at Salka's house, and Charlie Chaplin was there two or three nights a week. Salka wrote screenplays for people like Greta Garbo."[50] In Kelly's analysis, Salka and Peter "had the intellectual European salon, while we had the fun salon for New Yorkers at our house."[51] Kelly noted that the two social groups, while different in mood, shared similar political views: "Our group was predominantly liberal and left-wing, so there was naturally a lot of political discussion. The same was true of Salka's. The town was very divided at that time. Unlike New York, where you could sit in Ralph's on Forty-fifth Street and discuss something, Hollywood had hard lines drawn up."[52]

The Viertels were among the earliest European artists to emigrate to Hollywood. They first arrived in Southern California in the late 1920s after Salka's husband Berthold, a successful writer and director for stage and screen, was hired to write the script for *The Four Devils*, the second American film made by F. W. Murnau (the German director of *Nosferatu*). This job led to a contract offer from the Fox Studio. Salka's position in Hollywood was enhanced by the close relationship she developed with the enigmatic Greta Garbo, then the most popular female screen star. Salka acted in several films, including Garbo's *Anna Christie*, and at the star's urging wrote the screenplay for Garbo's *Queen Christina*.[53] She became known as the gatekeeper and advisor through whom the studios could communicate and negotiate with the reclusive Swede. The Viertel's marriage ended amicably in 1934 after Berthold found film work in England.

Raising her three sons alone, Salka found herself assuming a new role as the maternal host of the growing European émigré crowd. Over the years a seemingly endless stream of leftist intellectuals, artists, and celebrities made their way to Salka's salon, including Albert Einstein, W. H. Auden, Aldous Huxley, and Sergei Eisenstein. After the Second World War began, the writer Christopher Isherwood traveled to Pacific Palisades and moved into a small room in the back of Salka's home. Isherwood, whose collection of Berlin-based short stories, published as *The Last of Mr. Norris* and *Goodbye Berlin*, were later turned into the musical *Cabaret*, had worked with Berthold Viertel in England. Isherwood's experience working on Viertel's *The Little Friend* in 1934, inspired his acclaimed 1945 novel *Prater Violet*.

Agee was instantly at home in this mix of East Coast artists and refugees from European fascism. There was a natural rapport between the two social crowds, and in one notable instance, the actor Oskar Homolka, who in 1949 was nominated for an Academy Award for his performance in *I Remember Mama*, brought the two circles together through marriage. Homolka, before emigrating to the United States from Germany to escape Hitler, had a promising career in theater and film. His relationship with the Viertels began in 1923, when, at the suggestion of Brecht and Lion and Marta Feuchtwanger, he was given the lead role in Berthold Viertel's Berlin production of Eugene O'Neil's *Emperor Jones*.[54] Three years later he starred in a film directed by Berthold Viertel in Germany, *Die Abenteuer eines Zehnmarkscheines (The Adventures of a Five Mark Note)*. Around this time he also befriended Brecht and starred in *Baal*, the writer's first play to be produced in Berlin. Homolka had also worked for a while in England, where he gained fame as the saboteur Verloc in Alfred Hitchcock's

1936 film *Sabotage*, and the same year he starred with John Huston's father, Walter, in Berthold Viertel's English film production *Rhodes of Africa*.

After joining his émigré colleagues in Hollywood, Homolka fell in love with Florence Meyer, an artistically inclined New Yorker who'd found her way to Pacific Palisades in 1943. Florence was the daughter of Eugene Meyer, the owner since 1933 of the *Washington Post* newspaper, which he bought after serving in government office under Herbert Hoover. Among other prominent positions, Meyer had served as a governor of the Federal Reserve Board and was a founder of the World Bank. Florence Meyer's connection with the Pacific Palisades crowd came though her mother, who was a close friend of Thomas Mann. The Meyers's older daughter, Katherine, after marrying Phil Graham, took over the reins as publisher of the *Washington Post* and was pivotal in revealing Richard Nixon's role in the Watergate scandal.

Florence and Oskar's marriage failed after a couple of years. In the summer of 1947 while she was getting divorced, Florence developed an interest in photography. At the suggestion of John Becker, a New York gallery owner who had hosted the first gallery exhibition of Walker Evans's photos, Florence hired Evans to come out from New York to teach her the art of photography. With her budding interest in portrait photography and her countless friendships among the leading artists of both the "New Weimar" émigré crowd and their New York associates, Florence soon became the unofficial court photographer to the progressive artist colony. Over the years she captured numerous candid and formal portraits of her friends including Schoenberg, Chaplin, Huston, Feuchtwanger, and many other directors, composers, painters and actors. Bertolt Brecht was approached for a profile by *Vogue* magazine, but declined the offer after his insistence that Florence provide the photography was ignored. While Agee was in Hollywood working with Huston on *The African Queen* script, Florence arranged a portrait shoot of the writer that resulted in some of the most famous photographs of Agee. In 1951 while filming *Limelight*, Chaplin invited only Florence and the renowned photographer W. Eugene Smith to photograph the daily production. In 1962, shortly after Florence died, a book of her photography was published—its introduction contributed by Aldous Huxley. Included in the book were some notes she had written on Agee: "Jim had a deep

James Agee, photographed by Florence Homolka (Collection of the author)

sympathy for the poor of this world—for those who were materially poor in terms of this world's goods, certainly, but most especially for those who were at a loss in life, whose minds were inadequate, whose feelings were of little account to anyone."[55]

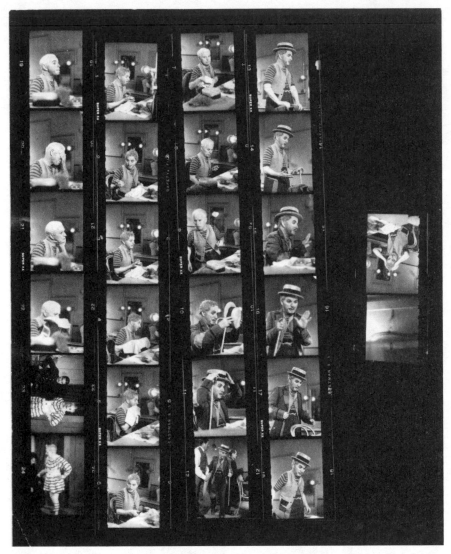

Proofsheet of images taken of Charles Chaplin by Florence Homolka during the production of *Limelight*. (Photos by Florence Homolka; collection of the author)

Salka Viertel's efforts weren't confined to screen writing and entertaining. Her influence among the European's in the film colony played a key role in helping a new wave of emigrants escape from their uncertain fate after Hitler came to power. Along with the talent agent

Paul Kohner, himself an immigrant born in Teplitz in Bohemia, Salka was one of the founders of the European Film Fund. The European Film Fund was organized in late 1939 after requests for aid from European artists became increasingly numerous and urgent. In order to find ways to help as many potential refugees as possible, a meeting was held at the home of the director Ernst Lubitsch, and was attended by many of the leading and most successful European filmmakers in Hollywood. In addition to Salka and Kohner, the group's founders included several influential European émigrés such as William Dieterle, Bruno Frank, Gottfried Reinhardt, Billy Wilder, and William Wyler. Their task was to create a process whereby the artists and intellectuals could be saved through the simple means of an affidavit for a work contract. Armed with proof of a film studio job the trapped artists would be allowed to emigrate to safety. Already, through other means, numerous Europeans had escaped Hitler to find refuge in Hollywood, including the brothers Thomas and Heinrich Mann, Franz Werfel, Erich Maria Remarque, and Alfred Neuman. Kohner took on the lead of the Film Fund and approached the most powerful studio heads for help, and succeeded by appealing to their need to outdo each other. Jack Warner agreed to provide four jobs. At MGM Kohner played to Louis B. Mayer's competitiveness and convinced him to outdo Warner, which he did by committing to six positions. Harry Cohn, at Columbia, not be outdone, agreed to provide ten jobs.

Kohner, before forming his own talent agency, had worked for years at Universal as the protégé to its founder Carl Laemmle. At Universal Kohner developed a special niche, creating parallel foreign language versions of American market films for distribution to foreign countries. Kohner's innovation was to use the same sets as the English-language films but with actors who spoke the appropriate foreign languages. His Spanish-language version of Todd Browning's *Dracula* featured a young Mexican starlet named Lupita Tovar, whom he later married. After Universal was sold, Kohner found himself unemployed and decided to start what would become one of Hollywood's most influential talent agencies. His first marquee client was John Huston. On Huston's word Walter Huston signed on for Kohner representation. Later, due in part to fan letters his actress wife, Tovar, was receiving from the enigmatic novelist B. Traven, Kohner was able to develop a deal for John Huston to film an adaptation of Traven's *The Treasure of the Sierra Madre*.

At Huston's instigation Agee signed on with Paul Kohner's agency for representation in film work. Kohner also represented Salka Viertel. As McCarthyism spread through Hollywood, Kohner apparently shifted representation of his more controversial screenwriting clients to the care of Ilse Lahn, the head of his literary department. The screen writer Michael Wilson, who later wrote the blockbuster *The Bridge on the River Kwai*, recalled the political pressure Kohner was under late in 1951: "Shortly after my appearance before HUAC, Kohner was at a bullfight in Tijuana, where he saw John Wayne. Kohner walked up to him and said, 'Hello, how are you?' Wayne stared at him and said, 'I don't shake hands with people who represent Commies.' This did it for Kohner. He knew from that time forward he was not going to represent me. He would let his assistant Ilse Lahn do it, but not he himself. He never took a militantly hostile position toward any of the blacklisted people, but he didn't go out of his way to get them work with the independents—and he did have such contacts."[56] As she had for Wilson, Lahn also took over the day-to-day representation of both Agee and Salka Viertel.

Agee, now under Huston's wing, was poised to make his mark in Hollywood, and the two began working on the screenplay for *The African Queen*. Lillian Ross witnessed the early days of their collaboration:

> One day in the middle of December, Huston and James Agee, the novelist and former *Time* writer, who had been hired to collaborate with Huston on the script for *The African Queen* were working in the Horizon cottage, trying to finish the script in time for Huston's and Spiegel's departure for Africa, where the picture was to be filmed . . . Agee was saying, as Huston paced in small circles, that the trip the river captain, Humphrey Bogart, and the missionary's sister, Katherine Hepburn, would make together down the river on the captain's boat in *The African Queen* could symbolize the act of love. "Oh, Christ, Jim," Huston said. "Tell me something I can understand. This isn't like a novel. This is a screenplay. . . . People on the screen are gods and goddesses. We know all about them. Their habits. Their caprices. But we can't touch them. They're not real. They stand for something, rather than being something. They're symbols. You can't have symbolism within symbolism, Jim.[57]

Huston soon found that the undivided attention he and Agee would require to translate C. S. Forester's novel into a workable script was difficult to find in Hollywood. He decided that if he and Agee were to be productive, they would need to escape from all social and business distractions. So, the two headed north to a remote exclusive resort ranch called San Ysidro, a 500-acre estate in Montecito, near Santa Barbara, with calming views of the ocean to the west and the mountains to the east.

Although Huston claimed to be incognito, shortly after they were settled at the resort, he sat with Agee and Ricki Soma, now his fourth wife, for an interview with the local newspaper, the *Santa Barbara News-Press*. The resulting article ran on the front page of the newspaper on January 9, 1951. Headlined "Director John Huston Visits City Before Trek to Africa," the article featured a large photograph of Agee and the Hustons poring over the draft screenplay; the photo caption read "John Huston . . . Academy Award-winning movie director, Mrs. Huston and James Agee, writer check over a film script Agee is adapting from S. C. [*sic*] Forester's novel, *The African Queen*. The trio is spending several weeks here preparatory to going on location in Central Africa."

The article provides a fascinating snapshot of the earliest stage of the film project:

A tall, friendly man welcomed us into his cottage at the San Ysidro Ranch yesterday. The talk that followed ranged from new developments in ballet to his experiences in the Aleutians. John Huston, one of Hollywood's best directors and son of the late actor Walter Huston, his charming wife, the former ballet dancer, Ricky [*sic*] Soma, and James Agee, movie and magazine writer, were in on the discussion. "Agee's doing the work of preparing C. S. Forester's novel *The African Queen*, in movie script form," Huston said. "We came up to Santa Barbara with him for a few weeks to help him whip the story into shape. In about a month I will leave for Kenya Colony in Central Africa to pick out locations for the movie." This picture will star Humphrey Bogart and Katherine Hepburn and a third actor who dies early in the story, Huston said. So only a small company of actors will be needed, with the African natives only as background— much different than the current *King Solomon's Mines*, which uses so many Africans in mass scenes and as actors. It will be produced by the Far Horizon Co. [*sic*], a firm owned by Huston and Sam Spiegel.

In early January, 1951, Agee and John Huston retired to a resort in Santa Barbara to work on the script for *The African Queen* ("John Huston . . . Academy Award-winning movie director, Mrs. Huston and James Agee, writer check over a film script Agee is adapting from S. C. [*sic*] Forester's novel, 'The African Queen.' The trio is spending several weeks here preparatory to going on location in Central Africa."). Agee, attempting to mix tennis, drinking, and writing, suffered a nearly fatal heart attack. (*Santa Barbara News-Press*)

"I'm looking forward to directing Miss Hepburn," Huston said, "since I never have, and I consider her one our finest actresses. Bogart was in the first movie I ever directed in 1941, *The Maltese Falcon*.

Winning the Academy Award for directing *The Treasure of the Sierra Madre* in 1948 established Huston as a top director, quite independent of his father's fame as an actor. But he went through the rough-and-tumble of Hollywood to get there.

Huston described for us the sweating and actual melancholy which he goes through on each picture. After months of work, when he sees a new movie in its rough cut state "It makes me sad and only a year or two later can I get up enough courage to see it in its finished form."

Such keen feeling for drama and story seems to drive him to great lengths to turn out a picture. And he works hard, he plays vigorously too, owning several horses and racing two of them currently at Santa Anita.

He is under contract to Metro-Goldwyn-Mayer, but his contract specifies that he can make other pictures too, hence his own company. He makes a movie for MGM, one for himself, another for MGM, etc.

"Will *The African Queen* be a good movie? I don't know. I never know how a film will be until the public sees it," Huston smiled. "Another one, *The Red Badge of Courage*, still unreleased, may or not be a good one."

This is the first time that Agee and Huston have worked together, but they seem to be getting along fine.

"We love to come to Santa Barbara for a visit," the director said, "since it so quiet and conducive to work. Miss Nan Huston lives here too, the last of my four aunts and uncles."

"Yes, it's wonderful here," Mrs. Huston agreed. "It's great to get away from the city. Even though we live at Malibu, we call it the city."

Agee shrugged. "I'm the guy that's doing the work here right now," he smiled, "and in less than a month I'll be on my way back to New York. Lucky me, eh?"[58]

While at San Ysidro, Huston planned to take full advantage of the resort's solitude to make headway on the script while using its recreational amenities to get in shape physically. Huston wrote, "I thought this an opportunity to live the good life and get into shape, so I proposed to Jim that we follow a stiff regimen of work and exercise. We decided to play one or two sets of tennis each morning before breakfast, and at least two sets each afternoon after work. We swam a couple times a day, avoided nighttime activities and cocktail parties, and so far as I know, Jim, like me, hit the sack before ten P.M."[59] Many years later, Peter Viertel reported in *Dangerous Friends* a memoir about his relationships with Huston and Ernest Hemingway, that Huston and Agee had also "indulged in some fairly heavy drinking"[60] while at the resort. In their comfortable seclusion, Agee and Huston quickly found that they were making good progress and working well together. Huston remembered, "I would write a section and give it to Jim. Jim would write and give it to me. Most of what Jim wrote stayed as Jim had written it, and most of what I wrote, Jim rewrote. So the collaboration was a one-sided one, and much to my benefit." Huston was surprised by the quantity of Agee's output, "Jim was forever bringing more pages. He was doing an enormous amount of work, and I didn't see how he managed to turn so much work out . . ."[61]

Agee, a lifelong insomniac, was in fact working through the night, writing as much as he could on little or no sleep. Huston confronted him about pushing himself too hard, but Agee, who must have sensed that this project could be his big break, refused to slacken his pace, and assured Huston "there was no problem—his normal work hours were at night."[62] It wasn't long before the unfamiliar athletic exertion and numerous sleepless nights took a tragic toll.

One day, while Huston took a break to appraise a sale of pre-Colombian ceramics in San Francisco, Agee suffered a near-fatal heart attack. The doctors, summoned to the resort, found Agee's condition to be touch-and-go and were afraid to move him from his room to the hospital. After he'd improved enough to be moved to a hospital, Agee wrote to Walker Evans from his bed at the Cottage Hospital in Santa Barbara on January 22, 1951:

> As you've doubtless heard, I am in a hospital with the effects of a heart attack . . . I got off light. Four weeks in hospital and strictly in bed, then a few more weeks' slow convalescence & I'll presumably be all right . . . if I'm careful. And yesterday Ricki [Huston] brought up a long-player and every l-p record she had—So I've had about 35 hours music since. And a great deal of fun with John—gags, general discussions, etc., because of course, there was for a couple of days uncertainty whether I'd live, or whether I'd come through other than bedridden or semi-invalid—so, there was lot to go through, mostly in silence but some in talk . . . not that I felt very ill—just that, short of 2–3's testing and graphing, there apparently isn't much telling how grave the clotting may be or may be becoming. We arrived, more or less independently, at a same ringing affirmation of the minimal, inalienable rights of a man: That he has the right, even the obligation, to write (or other vocational work) and to fuck as much as he can and in the ways he prefers to, even if doing so shortens his life or kills him on the spot. And that he hasn't got one other fucking right in the world that can't be taken away or proved invalid in two seconds.[63]

While Agee convalesced, Huston left for Africa with the unfinished screenplay, which glaringly lacked a satisfactory ending. Huston quickly hired Peter Viertel to work with him to complete the script. Peter had begun his film-writing career rewriting the screenplay for Alfred Hitchcock's first American thriller, *Saboteur*, which starred Chaplin's friend Norman Lloyd. During World War II, Peter volunteered for the Marines and his fluency in German led him to a post in the OSS, the predecessor of the CIA; Viertel trained foreign agents for undercover assignments in Nazi territory. After the war, he and Huston together wrote the script for *We Were Strangers*. Viertel recalled first meeting Huston at his mother's home when he was fifteen years old. A bon vivant and a natural athlete—he is credited with introducing the surfboard to Europe after stashing one aboard a plane shipment of film production equipment and hauling it to the beach at Biarritz—Viertel was a popular companion for both Hemingway and Huston. He later married the actress Deborah Kerr.

For Huston, Peter Viertel was a natural choice to replace the ailing Agee and accompany him to Africa, where making the film would occasionally be secondary to Huston's goal of shooting a wild elephant. After returning from Africa, Viertel wrote a sometimes stinging *roman* à *clef* about his experiences witnessing Huston at work. The book *White Hunter, Black Heart* unflinchingly portrayed Huston's self-absorbed personality, perhaps giving Huston another reason to contemplate his earlier suggestion to Agee that a friend not write about a friend until both are dead.

In Viertel's novel, his alter ego, Peter Verril, "one of the best skiers in the Screen Writers Guild,"[64] receives a phone call in Switzerland from John Wilson, a talented but notorious filmmaker with a "screw-you-all personality" inviting him on a trip to the "very darkest bloody corner of Africa we can find." "Who's going to pay," asks Verril. "Not us kid. You know that. What a damn fool thing to ask. I'm going to make a movie down there." "And what am I supposed to do?" "Help me. Keep me company. There's a little work to be done on the script. And then you can stay on and we'll hunt." "Hunt what?" "Everything. Haven't you always wanted to shoot an elephant?"[65]

In *Dangerous Friends*, Viertel's nonfiction account of his friendship with Huston and Ernest Hemingway, he recollected that, "[Agee's] incomplete effort was heavily laden with brilliant descriptions, but there were practically no dialogue scenes, which Huston explained was the reason I had been hired. . . . My contribution had mainly been sitting for hours with John while we laboriously invented the sparse lines of dialogue he required."[66] The screenplay's lack of a coherent ending haunted the early stages of production. The ending for *The African Queen* that Viertel and Huston finally settled on mixed a makeshift wedding and the miraculous intervention of a torpedo, but was an ill fit for many critics. Huston defended the jarring resolution on the basis that Forester himself had changed his book's ending for its American edition. Many viewers shared Bosley Crowther's reaction in the *New York Times:* "The fantastic climax that is abruptly and sentimentally contrived appears the most fulsome melodrama, unworthy of Mr. Huston and this film."[67]

Writing to a friend in 1953, Agee described his contribution to 160-page first draft of the screenplay for *The African Queen:* "The first hundred [pages] were mine and brought it through almost exactly half the story. The last 60, except a few scenes and interpolations, were Huston's."[68] Agee was given screenplay credit, shared with Huston, and their work was nominated for an Academy Award. Peter Viertel recalled that Huston's partner Sam Spiegel raised the issue of the screen credit with him just before he was to leave Africa: "Shrewder than I was, which wasn't difficult at that point, [Spiegel] asked me about the ultimate screen credit on our script, and I told him that I didn't give a damn whether my name was included or not."[69] Viertel, judging by what he had witnessed in Africa, had little faith that Huston would deliver a memorable film; he agreed to settle for Academy Credit which would ensure that his name would appear in the Academy of Motion Pictures's film yearbook, a costly decision he came to regret. Viertel remembered that Spiegel used Agee's health to help convince him not to fight for more credit: "Sam also said that he thought it would be nice to award credit to James Agee, who had not yet recovered his health after the heart attack Spiegel said his collaboration with John [Huston] had caused. Magnanimously, halfway out the door, I agreed with Spiegel and fled."[70]

When the Academy Award nominations were announced on February 11, 1952, *The African Queen* was recognized as one of the best films of 1951. The year before, Huston, who won Best Director in 1948 for *The Treasure of the Sierra Madre,* had been nominated in the same category for 1950's *The Asphalt Jungle.* Now he was again nominated for Best Director for *The African Queen,* the second year in a three-year streak of nominations—he was nominated the following year for *Moulin Rouge.* Humphrey Bogart, playing Charlie Allnut, another of Agee's friendly drunks, in *The African Queen*, won his only Oscar for Best Actor. Katherine Hepburn's performance in the film was nominated in the Best Actress category but she lost out to Vivien Leigh's performance as Blanche DuBois in *A Streetcar Named Desire*. Agee shared a nomination with Huston for Best Screenplay. Agee, like Huston, was on a sort of streak himself: This made the fourth year running that a film in which Agee was involved had been nominated for an Academy Award, counting the two consecutive years that *The Quiet One* was nominated, and *Mystery Street*'s 1950 nomination for Best Story. Even so, Agee at forty, his health ruined, now faced the possibility that his career momentum was stalled and his prospects questionable. He knew that his drinking, if he kept it up, would kill him, but he also knew himself and his own nature all too well. He wrote to a relative on April 6, 1951, "I am certainly a naturally hard drinker. After one drink it's very hard not to take another, and after three it is even harder not to take three more, and after that I'm apt to lose count and stop caring how much I drink."[71]

Six

*L*OSING *C*HAPLIN

*W*hile still in the hospital Agee's worst fears about his prospects for work were dispelled when he received an unexpected call from Robert Saudek, his former roommate at Harvard. Saudek called to offer Agee a new project, not for the big screen, but for television. With funding from the Ford Foundation, Saudek had recently developed and launched a groundbreaking new television magazine program called *Omnibus*, hosted by the English journalist Alistair Cooke. The innovative program had no formal boundaries save a mission to deliver a mix of quality entertainment and documentary programming. Its ambitious charter was to improve the quality and cultural level of television fare. Saudek tapped Agee to write an extended piece, *Mr. Lincoln*, about the youthful development of Abraham Lincoln. The result was a landmark five-part series, much of it filmed on location in the places of Lincoln's youth—Kentucky, Indiana, and Illinois. To direct the series Agee suggested and got Norman Lloyd, whom he knew socially through his friendship with Chaplin. Lloyd, a veteran of Orson Welles's Mercury Theater, was best known as the villain of Hitchcock's 1942 film *Saboteur*, who famously falls from the top of the Statue of Liberty's torch at the film's climax. For some of the series's location filming in Hodgkinsville, Kentucky, Lloyd hired a novice cameraman named Stanley Kubrick to serve as second unit cinematographer.

Agee handpicked for the part of Lincoln Royal Dano, the gaunt actor who had played the Tattered Soldier in John Huston's film version of *The Red Badge of Courage*. So effective was Dano in the role of Lincoln that the Disney Studios later chose him to provide the voice for the animatronic Lincoln in Disneyland's Hall of Presidents. Ann Rutledge, Lincoln's love interest in the series, was played by Joanne Woodward. Agee also wrote himself a role, Jack Kelso, "a slender, shabby, charming man of forty; clearly a souse in a sober moment."[1] Agee used the unrepentant, hard-drinking Kelso to express Lincoln's tolerance and empathy for the common man. Underlining his ability, like Chaplin's, to find the poetry within the downtrodden, Agee wrote a scene for the series's fourth episode in which Kelso, while fishing on a river, recites poetry to the young Lincoln. According to Lloyd, Agee embraced—accidentally or not—a true method acting approach and showed up for the scene with a massive hangover. As Kelso, Agee recites "quietly and quite beautifully; Abe listens, spellbound." Agee had Kelso speak the identical scene from *King Lear* that he had chosen years earlier for the preface to *Let Us Now Praise Famous Men;* a plea for God and man to shelter and care for the impoverished and homeless:

> *Kelso:*
> Poor naked wretches, where so e'er you are,
> Who bide the pelting of this pitiless storm,
> How shall your houseless heads, and unfed sides, Your loop'd and
>   window'd raggedness, defend you,
> From seasons such as these?
> Oh! I have ta'en
> Too little care of this. Take physick, pomp,
> That thou mayst shake the superflux to them,
> And show the heavens more just.

Clearly, this cry for empathy and compassion for the world's "houseless heads, and unfed sides" had great significance for Agee, with its demand for disparity in wealth to be replaced with social justice. After Kelso's surprising Shakespeare recital, Agee develops the scene to expand on Lincoln's tolerance and broad-mindedness toward the poor man's drinking: "He is silent; so is Abe. After a long pause, Abe solemnly shakes his head, and clucks his tongue, Jack, after a moment, un-stoppers his jug,

Kelso: Come on, Abe. I hate to drink in front of a man who isn't drinking.

Abe, smiling, shakes his head. Jack, reluctant, balances the jug on his shoulder and drinks deep,

Kelso: I can't make you out. You're the only temperance man I can stand the sight of.

Abe: I'm not a temperance man; I just don't drink.

Kelso: You go to temperance meetings,

Abe: I like people that take a thing so much to heart.

Kelso: A lot of busybodies.

Abe: Yes; that I *don't* like.

A pause.

Kelso: Well: if I've got to drink fer two . . .

He takes another swig.

A pause.

Abe: Tell me some more poetry, Jack.

Kelso (nods): This is Shakespeare, too. "When in the chronicles of wasted time, I read descriptions of the fairest wights; Of beauty, making beautiful old rhyme . . ."

In this scene, Agee's quotation from Shakespeare's "Sonnet 106" comments simultaneously on both his and Lincoln's fears of their own inadequacy: The poem's subject is the poet's fear that he lacks the talent to successfully express himself, a familiar theme of Agee's. In a later scene, Agee had Lincoln deliver an impassioned defense of drinking men to the crowd at a temperance meeting:

> I have not spoken here before, and I'm not sure I ought to now; but I earnestly feel that some members of this society go to extremes, I agree that the use of liquor beclouds some men, and brings misery and waste and ruin to others; but I cannot stand by and hear it said of all drinking men that they are evil men in league with the devil. Now I don't want to offend any good and earnest person but I must say this: I have known as many drinking men as teetotalers, and it is my experience that for good company, and for tolerance, and for kindness and forgiveness towards those I trouble and disgrace, the drinking man, as a general rule, compares favorably with the teetotaler.

It struck Lloyd that Agee used Lincoln's life story as a vehicle to examine his own life: "He was using historical events and the facts of Lincoln's childhood, youth and young manhood . . . he was really writing about himself. He used Lincoln to say a lot of the things he wanted to say."[2] Coincidentally, when Agee's screenplay for *The Bride Comes to Yellow Sky* was filmed, Agee was given the small but memorable role of the town drunk who locks himself into the jail cell while the sheriff is out of town.

The first episode of the *Mr. Lincoln* series was broadcast on CBS on November 16, 1952. The series received accolades, especially for its moving depiction of the funeral train bearing the assassinated president's coffin through the heartland, passing groups of citizens holding vigil by the railroad tracks. The scene was played without accompanying music. Instead, Lloyd read Walt Whitman's poem "When Lilacs Last in the Door Yard Bloomed." A little less than eleven years later, this somber and affecting scene was shown repeatedly on television in the days after John F. Kennedy's assassination.

Agee's artistic handling of Lincoln's love life did bring some quibbling from academic circles. Protests about the historical accuracy of his version of events led to a pseudo-debate on a follow-up episode of *Omnibus*, in which Alan Nevins, then professor of history at Columbia University, joined by an uncomfortable, shy-voiced Agee were induced to confront each other in a mock trial with scenes from the series introduced as evidence. The historian argued for the facts as known while Agee defended artistic interpretation in which facts were ambiguous. The strange debate ended with the professor unambiguously acknowledging that Agee's effort was clearly a success as an artistic interpretation, and Agee accepting the graceful gesture as a sufficient ground for agreement.

While Agee was working on the Lincoln scripts, Frank Taylor, still trying to make his mark as a producer in Hollywood, had moved from MGM to Twentieth Century-Fox. On June 1, 1951, Agee wrote to Ilse Lahn that he was reading A. B. Guthrie's *The Way West*, "which Frank Taylor may do at Fox."[3] Although that particular project didn't materialize, Taylor did get involved with two other westerns, *Bloodline* and *The Gun and the Cross*. Taylor, loyal to Agee, brought his friend to Twentieth Century-Fox to help him work on the projects. Agee, the true bohemian, found it difficult to fit into the fashion-conscious studio culture. At the time, while still recovering from his first heart attack, Agee, his wife Mia still on the East Coast with their children, became involved in an affair with Taylor's sister-in-law, Pat Scallon. The two shacked up and kept company with the hard-drinking writer

Dorothy Parker in her nearly empty home.[4] In his unpublished memoir,[5] Taylor recalled how Agee's disheveled appearance upset the studio management:

> The meeting took place in Zanuck's office which was even larger than [Louis B.] Mayer's and [Dore] Schary's. Despite an attention span of seconds and disconcerting attention to a polo mallet, Zanuck seemed to connect with me. My literary background interested him as it had Dore and I soon joined 20th as a producer. My first act there was to convince the studio to hire James Agee who had left Time-Life and come to Hollywood to write. We had an idea for a fancy western to be called *The Gun and the Cross*. Jim was as bohemian in appearance and dress as he was gifted. We were both excited about the opportunity of his writing an original screenplay and my producing it. At the studios it was the custom then for screen writers to informally lunch together in an alcove room adjacent to the main commissary. The writers' status in those days was, with few exceptions, definitely below the salt. They were treated like carpenters, not creative artists. This did create a special camaraderie among them. They also showed and expressed more peer respect than was Hollywood custom among professional competitors. When Hollywood's *Variety* announced that James Agee was coming to Twentieth Century-Fox, interest in him among the resident screenwriters was high. Most, if not all, were aware of his distinguished career as movie critic. A number of them had been praised or panned by him in *Time*, *Life* or the *Nation*. It is customary on the first day of a writing assignment for the producer to take the screen writer to lunch in the studio commissary to celebrate the working beginning of the filmmaking process.
>
> On Jim's and my first day I had made a reservations for two. However when we entered the main glitzy dining room, I noticed there were vacancies at the writers' table. This prompted me to change my plan and I guided Jim toward two empty places. The men and women put down their forks, stood up politely and in a few cases deferentially asked to be introduced. In his customary shyness and head-bobbing modesty, Jim shook all the way around. Like all movie-making people, the writers were elegantly dressed—superbly tailored slacks, tasseled loafers, and open-necked, brightly colored silk or fine cotton sport shirts, plus always, an expensive gold wristwatch and a ring or two. The first-day excitement had quite blinded me to Jim's dress. There was no way to ignore the contrast between him and them. He was wearing a black workman shirt, black trousers

and black laced high work shoes. The fact that Jim perspired more than most—probably due to hangovers—resulted in heavy sweat stains on his shirt. His hair was usually in need of a haircut, just as his body was in need of a bath. This typical condition was familiar to his legion of friends who so admired him that they paid no attention. The lunch got off to a nervous beginning, but so brilliant and enthralling was Jim that I was confident he had completely won over his sleek peers. After lunch Jim went to his writer's bungalow across the Twentieth Century lot and I back to my quarters. Within 15 minutes my phone rang. It was the corporate head of the office which contracted, processed, and supervised all matters dealing with writers.

"Frank, I am sorry about this, but dressed as he is, Mr. Agee will not be allowed to eat in the commissary."

"I can't tell a grown man what to wear. What possible difference does it make? If his fellow writers object, Jim and I will in the future simply lunch alone together."

"It wasn't just the writers who were offended. Everyone, including the waitresses, was horrified by his appearance."

"If I mention this flap to Jim, he would quit on the spot."

"In that case, you and he had better have your lunch delivered to your offices."

This is what happened. I never mentioned the fuss and if he knew, he didn't mention it to me. Our friendship survived and we worked hard and well together. Three months later, Zanuck rejected our synopsis. Jim's short-term contract with 20th was over and he left."[6]

This awkward episode wasn't the first time that Agee's bohemian attitude toward clothing had gotten him in trouble. While at *Time*, Agee's appearance had garnered a strong complaint from the magazine's advertising salesmen. Winthrop Sargeant, *Time*'s music critic, recalled that on one occasion "*Time* advertising execs were so embarrassed that they asked management to have him fired because it was embarrassing to them to have their customers and clients come into the office and see Agee riding the elevator."[7] Sargeant interpreted Agee's behavior in psychological terms: "Agee had had trouble with his mother too, and his reaction to it had been more overt than mine. He had been brought up by his mother to bathe regularly and to brush his teeth, so, as an adult, he seldom bathed or brushed his teeth. He refused to dress like the Ivy League boys, though he was, in fact, a Harvard man. He wore tennis shoes and often had holes in his pants."[8]

While Agee's work on Taylor's project *The Gun and the Cross* is lost, the treatment for *Bloodline* survives. The film scenario, dated September 21, 1951, is set in "Middle Tennessee" in the aftermath of the Civil War. The story tells how Captain John Ransome, after returning to his ruined plantation, is reunited with Isaiah, one of his family's former slaves, now freed. Ransome tells Isaiah, "You're a free man, now, but all the same you stayed." "Free?" says Isaiah. "That I am. But you know how a snake feels, right after he casts his skin? Just wants to lay still a while? Take the sun? See where he's goin' next? Besides—you think I'd leave all this for you to find? All by yourself?" In Ransome's absence, Isaiah has been taking care of Shiloh "a magnificent three-year-old stallion . . . the one thing he managed to save from the holocaust—awaiting Ransome's return." The two set out on the road in an effort to recover the rights to Ransome's treasure and property, unscrupulously acquired by Fenton Mabry "a tired, silky patrician."[9] Together they confront white and black racism and come to terms with Yankees, while Ransome falls in love with a lady doctor and Shiloh gets involved in a race for honor with a Comanche Indian tribe and its noble chief Stone Hawk.

After Twentieth Century-Fox passed on the film, Agee found himself in financial straits. Four weeks after the project fell apart, on October 24, 1951, Agee wrote to his agent, Paul Kohner, "I am now in such a bad way financially that my need for work is immediate and desperate. What has made it so particularly urgent, of course, was the falling through of the *Bloodline* job."[10] While Kohner and Ilse Lahn, the head of his literary department, looked for jobs for Agee, an unusual project emerged, the first of what would be several foreign-film translation jobs he'd undertake.

Earlier that year, after winning a popularity contest run by the *Philippine Herald*, Manuel Conde, a young actor and filmmaker, headed to Hollywood with a print of his newly completed film, an ambitious all-Filipino epic biography of Genghis Khan. Conde's experience promoting his film *Gengis Khan* in the United States was later researched by Agustin V. Sotto, a Filipino film historian and archivist.[11] According to Sotto, Conde made the rounds in Hollywood, trying to interest anyone who could help him gain a distribution deal. He arranged to screen his film at the Warner Brothers studios and succeeded in attracting the attention of Carl Foreman, the writer of *High Noon*. Foreman, who was subpoenaed by HUAC in September 1951, had been subsequently blacklisted by the film industry. Foreman liked the film, but suggested that Conde ask Agee for help. Conde contacted Agee and arranged to screen his film for Agee at Consolidated Lab. Conde recalled that after viewing the film Agee said, "O.K. son, I'll work on it." Agee thought the film should be submitted to the Venice Film Festival, but Conde was nearly broke. Agee responded to Conde's predicament by saying "I don't want to lose my professional standing. I will charge you one dollar."[12]

Conde recalled that he would occasionally host Agee and his wife, Mia, in his apartment, where they would dine on the Filipino national dish, chicken adobo. Conde said of Agee that you could "cut his sincerity with a knife."[13] Later, when he learned more about Agee's reputation, Conde reflected, "If I had known who he was, I would not have fed him leftovers."[14] Agee spent a month working on *Gengis Khan*, writing English narration and overseeing the editing of the film to shorten and tighten up the story. He wrote to Father Flye on November 23, to say "The main thing to cheer me up has been getting a short quick job which I expect to finish in another few days: writing 'narration', and paraphrasing dialogue for a quite likeable movie, made in the Philippines, about the youth of Genghiz [*sic*] Khan."[15]

Agee was wrong about how much time it would take to finish writing and editing the film. Conde recalled that he and Agee worked on the movie from 9 P.M. on Christmas Eve until 7 A.M. Christmas Day, and noted that Agee worked without complaint.[16] The film was successfully shown at the Venice Film Festival, and its international acceptance established a milestone in the history of Philippine cinema. United Artists arranged for distribution of the film in the United States and Europe. Two years later Agee, Conde, and the cinematographer James Wong Howe explored the possibility of developing film projects together. It was Agee's commitment to a film project with Conde that resulted in his passing up John Huston's offer to write the screenplay for his screen version of *Moby-Dick*, a decision Agee would live to regret.

In the last months of 1951, Agee found his relationship with Chaplin growing stronger. He wrote to Father Flye on November 7, to describe their deepening friendship: "I've spent probably 30 or 50 evenings talking alone most of the night with Chaplin, and he has talked very openly and intimately. The last thing I could ever do is make an article of this; the only way it could ever belong on paper, if at all, is in a journal or in letters, the kind of thing which is never public until long after both people are dead. Both because he is the man he is and I so much respect him, and because he's also an intrinsically interesting man, I wish I had kept a record of this. But all I've done of it is in a couple or three letters to Mia, and a good deal of it, though all of it interested me so much, I'm bound to have forgotten . . ." Chaplin was then in the process of filming *Limelight*, his first film since *Monsieur Verdoux*. Originally called *Footlights*, Chaplin's semiautobiographical story set in London was an examination of his roots, both theatrical and personal. It was the story of Calvero, a once-popular comedian, now aged and at the end of his career; the comedian falls in love with a beautiful, young, suicidal ballerina and through her finds the will to perform again. For this film, Chaplin had taken the unusual step of first working out his ideas by writing a novel, not for publication, but as a deeper way into his material. He worked on the novel and the subsequent screenplay for three years. The writer Joyce Milton claims that Agee was instrumental in helping Chaplin translate the hundreds of pages of prose into a workable screenplay.

The end of 1951 also found Agee continuing to struggle with his potentially lethal habits. Contemplating the state of his health and his odds for survival, Agee wrote to Father Flye on November 23, 1951, "I am on a non-fat, non-cholesterol diet. . . . The prospects on smoking and drinking are harder. I keep the smoking down quite well. The drinking is much harder. . . . Unless I can keep within a few quite strict rules, I am virtually promised very serious trouble within a year or two. If I hold them, I am virtually promised 10, 15, 20 or more years before any serious return of this trouble."

While working on the screenplay for *Limelight*, Chaplin spent spare hours at the Circle, a theater founded by his son Sydney, William Schallert, the son of *Los Angeles Times* film critic Edwin Schallert, and their friend Jerome Epstein. The Circle was an immediate success in a town starved for serious theater, and the group quickly made their mark with their first production, Elmer Rice's *The Adding Machine*. They later landed the premiere production of a new play by William

Saroyan, the husband of Oona Chaplin's friend Carol. Chaplin supported the theater by providing the young actors use of his studio's sets and costumes and directed one of the their productions, a version of Somerset Maugham's *Rain*.

William Schallert was studying music with Arnold Schoenberg at the University of California, Los Angeles when he was recruited into the theater. The instantly recognizable character actor, known by many as the father on "The Patty Duke Show," later replaced Ronald Reagan as the president of the Screen Actors' Guild. He recalled meeting Agee during the Circle Theater days. He remembered Agee being around on occasion and hearing Agee play some blues piano. To Schallert, Agee came across as a man looking to make a success.

Sydney Chaplin remembered that around this time Agee was a frequent guest at dinner parties at his father's estate. Sydney, who could be counted on to escort beautiful young starlets to these dinners, recalled how his father would, in Agee's absence, render a spot-on pantomime of Agee's idiosyncratic hand gestures. According to Sydney, his father would hilariously, but in good nature, play off the way Agee's conversation would often be diametrically opposed to the tortured motion of his hands. Chaplin's mimicry at parties is the stuff of legend. Countless stories survive of the comedian's spontaneous entertainments at private parties.

One notable victim of Chaplin's mimicry was philosopher Theodor Adorno. Adorno and Hanns Eisler had collaborated on a book about film soundtrack composition, *On Composing for the Films*, which was published in Germany in 1944. The book was the result of work done for the Film Music Project financed by the Rockefeller Foundation with a grant of $20,000 funneled through the New School for Social Research. Eisler was the project's director. In the preface of their book, Eisler thanked his friend Chaplin: "The art of Charles Chaplin proved to be a continuous inspiration." When the English-language version of the book was finally published in July 1947, it bore only Eisler's name: Adorno had insisted that his name be removed. In a 1969 reprint of the book, Adorno explained the conditions that had led him to request the removal of his name: "[Eisler's] brother Gerhard was under severe attack in the United States because of his political activity. . . . In view of the scandal I withdrew my name from the book."[17]

In early 1947 Adorno was on the West Coast and at a party in Malibu experienced firsthand the mixed charm of ending up one of Chaplin's pantomime subjects:

> He once imitated me, and surely I am one of the few intellectuals to whom this happened and to be able to account for it when it happened. Together with many others we were invited to a villa in Malibu, on the coast outside of Los Angeles. While Chaplin stood next to me, one of the guests was taking his leave early. Unlike Chaplin, I extended my hand to him a bit absent-mindedly, and, almost instantly, started violently back. The man was one of the lead actors from *The Best Years of Our Lives,* a film famous shortly after the war; he lost a hand during the war, and in its place bore practicable claws made of iron. When I shook his right hand and felt it return the pressure, I was extremely startled, but sensed immediately that I could not reveal my shock to the injured man at any price. In a split second I transformed my frightened expression into an obliging grimace that must have been far ghastlier. The actor had hardly moved away when Chaplin was already playing the scene back. All the laughter he brings about is so near to cruelty; solely in such proximity to cruelty does it find its legitimation and its element of the salvational.[18]

When *Limelight* went into production, Chaplin invited Agee into the process, both as an interested viewer and as an informed consultant. On December 13, 1951, while in the middle of helping Manuel Conde, Agee wrote again to Father Flye to report: "During whatever time I can take from the job [*Gengis Khan*], I have great interest and pleasure in watching Chaplin make his new movie." His wife Mia recalled that Agee had never given up on the hope of collaborating with Chaplin; "He had all sorts of ideas of films that he wanted Chaplin to make." The *Limelight* shoot provided Agee with his first real opportunity to watch Chaplin at work. According to Mia, Chaplin actively sought Agee's reactions and critical reception as the film unfolded; "Chaplin used him as a critic, though he never paid any attention to any criticism. But he was always very interested and he made Jim write out what he thought. He was then shooting *Limelight*, and Jim was at all the shootings. So he'd have Jim tell him what he thought about various scenes. And Jim would, of course, tell him very honestly. Of course, Chaplin never paid attention to what he said. But it didn't

Charles Chaplin, in costume during the production of *Limelight*, reviews dailies of his own performance. (Photo by Florence Homolka; collection of the author)

matter. As far as their relationship was concerned, this was perfectly all right. This was a sort of dance that you went through."[19]

It is widely believed that it was encouragement from Agee that led Chaplin to offer Buster Keaton a role in *Limelight*; it was the first and only time that the two great silent comedians would appear on screen together. Agee brought Mia to witness the filming of the historic pairing of Chaplin and Keaton. The photographer W. Eugene Smith, hired by *Life* to shoot a feature on the making of the film, captured images of Agee and Chaplin together on the set, deep in conversation, the comedian still in costume, Agee's hands in constant motion. As Chaplin assembled the finished film, he repeatedly used Agee as a sounding board, inviting him to view rough-cuts and advance screenings. According to one Chaplin biographer, David Robinson, "On 15 May [1952] Chaplin showed a rough-cut to James Agee and Sidney Bernstein and was gratified by their reactions. . . . By 2 August the final prints were ready for a preview at the Paramount Studios Theater, which held two hundred people and on this occasion was packed."[20] Agee clearly relished the opportunity to give advice to Chaplin. He provided the comedian with detailed notes on scene se-

Agee was often on the set while Chaplin filmed *Limelight*. While photographing a profile of Chaplin at work for *Life*, W. Eugene Smith captured the two artists in conversation. (© The Heirs of W. Eugene Smith; courtesy Kevin Smith)

lection and other aspects of editing. Two pages of Agee's handwritten suggestions to Chaplin survive:

> Trim as short as possible: orange business on stairs; 2nd staircase; dialogue with Mrs Alsop—to retain 2 points: we'll pretend we're married; she is sick . . . Trim to minimum C's first fight-talk, *re* suicide, intercutting CB—repeat shots if need be & with C's lines over . . . *Restore* his falling into basin, & all kidding *re* disease . . . Trim or cut if possible, the maid & Claire & C's entrance; repetitive in exposition . . . On flea number hold o.s. laughter longer, over pan over empty theater at end maybe going into echo filter soon after this shot starts; and cut sharp to silence over C's watering face—or fade over this face. As is, the live audience laughter lasts so long as to kill the point. If still possible, in scene with Claudius, use the *cold* take of C., and cut to the cocked head of Claudius. It gives warmth & life to Claudius, and adds immensely to one's realization that C is a highly complex and impressive character. It deepens our interest and sympathy in him and is, I believe—and I'm not alone—one of the greatest pieces of acting in the picture. I feel this the more because, by neutral lighting, and many lines to say without much detailing of the

man facially, or in business, he is slow to enter in any way deeply to involve us in him . . . Scene with Pharmacist, at door, can be drastically cut, through intercutting C and Dryden. Latter hints the same point 4 times, which contemporary audience is more quick than that to accept and sufficiently understand . . . too questionable whether C & Dr. [would] have known of Freud. But cut to minimal exposition—a *single* rather than quadruple statement—and keep mention of Freud, regardless of possible anachronisms—and C's remark that he'll have to see what *he* can do . . . Clare's bursting into tears isn't, actually, reduced from August showing. Her crying tends to be monotonous . . .

Business: It is charming but too extraneous to the main meaning. Once too often, you eat, or hold up food. Trim the herrings, or, in this long dialogue, if possible, cut to Claire, still thinking of her breakfast.

Claire: She isn't up to varying sufficiently, various emotional scenes. Always the same too-loud sucking of breath. Trim them, except in her "I'm walking" climax. And maybe there too . . . After the opening, with C in the bar with the gaffers you had a much more endearing take of C, quite soused, ad libbing, pointing to barmaid's bosom and saying, approximately, "there's a pleasant place." Much funnier and warmer than the take which is used. I would use it, instead of the take now used. It engenders great liking for Calvero; it is funny as hell and in terms of "the new Chaplin"; and only adds piquancy to his character—not inconsistency—that we next see him behind door, overhearing CB's love scene with Sydney . . .[21]

Agee's friendship with Chaplin coincided with a narrowing of the comedian's social circle. The swing to the right in American politics had taken a distinct toll on Chaplin's popularity both at the box office and in Hollywood society. In the years following the release of *Monsieur Verdoux*, McCarthyism had taken root and Chaplin's star lost much of its luster in the United States. His oldest son, Charles Jr., wrote, "When I came back from the East to play my part in *Limelight*, I was saddened to see the effect his [political] stand had had on his own life. It was no longer considered a privilege to be a guest at the home of Charlie Chaplin. Many people were actually afraid to be seen there lest they, too, should become suspect." Norman Lloyd recalled New Years Eve in 1950 when, entering a party with his wife and the Chaplins, a guest spit in Chaplin's face.[22]

During this period, Agee frequently shuttled back and forth between New York and Hollywood. On several occasions, the Chaplins also made visits to New York City. Jane Sargeant, married to Walker Evans before she left him for music critic Winthrop Sargeant, described to Evans's biographer, Belinda Rathbone, one uncomfortable night at the Agees' when she and Walker were invited for dinner to meet the Chaplins. According to Rathbone:

> One evening Jim and Mia Agee invited the Evanses to their apartment for dinner to meet their new friends, Charlie and Oona Chaplin. . . . To both Agee and Evans, Chaplin was the god of movies; there was no greater honor than his presence among them. But as far as Jane was concerned, the evening was a trial. Mia, who had just had a baby, and Oona, who was expecting one, talked about nothing but children, while Jim and Walker sharpened their wits for the sake of their honored guest, who did not seem to be feeling at his most garrulous or amusing. At her usual bedtime, Jane announced that she was going home. Though he said nothing at the time, "Walker was so furious he wouldn't speak to me for a week." . . . "Nobody leaves before Chaplin!"[23]

After *Limelight* was completed, Chaplin decided to premiere the film in Europe. His thought was to combine the launching of the film with a family vacation that would provide his wife and their young children their first look at the England of his youth. The Chaplins made plans to sail from New York on the ocean liner the *Queen Elizabeth* and left California with a print of the film, which they screened for small audiences of friends before departing. During their last week in New York, the Chaplins socialized and reconnected with old friends. Lillian Ross, who had profiled Chaplin for the *New Yorker*, spent a memorable day accompanying the comedian throughout Manhattan walking with him for hours all over the city as he explored his old haunts.

Their long walk through New York was reminiscent of earlier walking tours, taken in disguise, that Chaplin would make into poor and working-class neighborhoods in Los Angeles. In his memoir, *My Father*, Charles Jr. recalled that his father "liked occasionally to pay a visit to Skid Row in Los Angeles, and he would start his preparations several days in advance by allowing his beard to grow. In shabby clothes, to complete his disguise, he remained, so far as I know, unrecognized during these visits." Chaplin would sometimes bring his son on these excursions. The chauffeur dropped them off downtown: "From there we were on our own. Dad would saunter around the grimy streets that perhaps reminded him of the London slums, and go into bars and sip a drink while he watched the people around him and listened avidly to their conversations."[24]

On his last full day in the United States, Chaplin visited photographer Richard Avedon's studio to have his portrait taken. Chaplin gave the photographer a classic parting shot: Posing with index fingers shooting hornlike from his white hair and a leering smile, Chaplin played the Nijinsky-like satyr of American opinion, the lusty devil of popular imagination. That night Charlie and Oona dined with Lillian Ross and the Agees at the Stork Club. Frank Taylor, writing to Oona years later, on the eve of Chaplin's death, also recalled meeting the Chaplins and Agees at the famed nightclub "21" that same evening.

On September 16, 1952, the night before sailing into unwitting exile, barred from re-entering the U.S. by the State Department, Oona and Charles Chaplin dined with Mia and James Agee and the writer Lillian Ross at the Stork Club. (Courtesy Mia Agee)

The next day, Agee went to the dock to say his farewell to the Chaplins. On his lawyer's advice, Chaplin was below decks avoiding an expected subpoena from a business-related civil suit. The poignant scene of Agee desperately searching for one last view of Chaplin made a lasting impression on Chaplin, who described it in his memoir:

I boarded the *Queen Elizabeth* at five in the morning, a romantic hour but for the sordid reason of having to avoid a process server. My lawyer's instructions were to steal aboard, lock myself in my suite and not to appear on deck until the pilot disembarked. Being groomed for the last ten years to expect the worst, I obeyed.

I had been looking forward to standing on the top deck with my family, enjoying the stirring moment of a ship's severance as it glides off and away into another life. Instead I was ignominiously locked in my cabin, peering through the porthole.

"It's me," said Oona, rapping on the door.

I opened it.

"Jim Agee has just arrived to see us off. He is standing on the dock. I shouted that you were hiding from process-servers and that you'd wave to him from the porthole. There he is now at the end of the pier," she said.

I saw Jim a little apart from a group of people, standing in fierce sunlight scanning the boat. Quickly I took my fedora hat and put my arm through the porthole and waved, while Oona looked out of the second porthole. "No, he hasn't seen you yet," she said.

And Jim never did see me; and that was the last I ever saw of Jim, standing alone as though apart from the world, peering and searching. Two years later he died of a heart attack.[25]

Just as years earlier, Agee had watched his second wife, Alma, and their son, Joel, sail away and out of his life, now he watched his life's greatest hero, a man whom he had almost miraculously befriended, sail away from America, never again to return during the little more than two years left to Agee. Mia Agee recalled that Agee and Chaplin "were still talking about possibly doing a film together. Then [Chaplin] went to Europe, and of course he didn't know he wasn't going to come back until the last minute. In fact, he didn't know that until after he had left on the boat. He had only left with the idea of a vacation and showing his children Europe. And, of course, he never came back.

He wasn't a citizen and the government wouldn't give him a reentry permit."[26]

Accompanying the Chaplins on the trip to Europe was Harry Crocker, the publicity man for *Limelight*. The scion of a prominent San Francisco banking family, Crocker had earlier helped Chaplin manage his money and had even acted as Rex, King of the Air in Chaplin's feature film *The Circus*. It was Crocker who first learned that the State Department had taken steps to prevent Chaplin's return to the United States.

In his unpublished memoir, Crocker described the scene, "On Friday, the Nineteenth, just two days after we left New York, Oona, Charlie and I were dining with Nela and Arthur Rubenstein, and Adolph Green. I was midway through a delicious slice of larded beef when a white-coated steward informed me that there were four radio-telephone calls for me."[27] The messages were from reporters seeking Chaplin's reaction to the news that Attorney General of the United States James P. McGranery had rescinded Chaplin's reentry permit. Chaplin drafted a straightforward response, "Through the proper procedure I applied for a re-entry permit which I was given in good faith and which I accepted in good faith; therefore I assume that the United States government will recognize its validity."[28]

McGranery had likely hoped for a publicity coup resulting from his move on Chaplin, but if he wished for headlines, he was disappointed—the Chaplin story was driven below the fold by the breaking scandal involving Richard Nixon, Dwight Eisenhower's running mate in the upcoming presidential election, and accusations of a mysterious slush fund. The scandal dominated the news for days until Nixon went on television to deliver his infamous "Checkers speech," during which he defended his wife's Republican cloth coat and swore to keep the little dog named Checkers that he admitted accepting as a gift for his daughters. Nixon's television appearance successfully swayed public opinion in his favor and Eisenhower was induced to keep Nixon on the ticket.

On September 22, 1952, three days after Chaplin received word that he was no longer welcome in the United States, the *Queen Elizabeth* reached port at Cherbourg, France. Chaplin was greeted by a friendly throng of hundreds of fans and reporters. He took the opportunity to publicly state, "I am not political. I have never been political. I don't want to create any revolutions. I just want to create a few more films . . . I have never been a super-patriot. I think super-patriotism leads to Hitlerism and we have had our lesson from that. I assume that in a democracy one has a right to a private opinion."[29] Soon after, on October 2, McGranery held a press conference during which reporters pressed him for details on the evidence he had for barring Chaplin's return. The attorney general disappointed the journalists with his scanty reply: He declared that Chaplin was reported to have made "sneering references in response to attending a show for a children's benefit on the West Coast,"[30] a reference to the FBI's report on the Westland School benefit showing of *City Lights*. The *New York Times* reported on McGranery's press conference the next day; "One instance [McGranery] cited concerned an invitation for a children's affair on the west coast." Chaplin, the attorney general announced, was also said to have spoken with "contemptible regard for the high estate of womanhood" and "if what has been said is true, he is an unsavory character."[31] These claims established the sum total of the government's publicly stated case against Chaplin. Afterward, the government made an effort to shore up its position. Harry Crocker recorded the following from an Ed Sullivan column, "Immigration Department Investigators are calling on Broadwayites and interviewing performers who knew Charlie in the good old days. They are trying to put together a portrait that will aid Attorney General McGranery when Chaplin is examined at Ellis Island."[32]

In the November election, Harry Truman was beaten by Dwight Eisenhower, and Herbert Brownell was picked as McGranery's successor. Henry Luce ran an editorial entitled "Heretics or Conspirators,"[33] in the December 22 issue of *Life*, calling on Eisenhower and Brownell to go easy on Chaplin and to recognize the difference between a communist who actively conspires to overthrow the government and a heretic: "heresy is no crime in this country; it is every citizen's guaranteed right." The editorial offered the Truman administration's treatment of Chaplin as an example of the failure to discern between the two. Questioning the government's threat to prevent Chaplin from returning to the United States, the editorial cast doubt on the attorney general's case: "Attorney General McGranery seems to suspect [Chaplin] of being 'unsavory.' If he means morally unsavory, many an alien denizen of Hollywood will not dare to go abroad again. If he means politically unsavory, then the conspiracy-heresy test becomes applicable. The law is pretty clear against conspirators. Unless Chaplin can be proved to be one, then the Europeans who are howling at our cultural barbarity on his account are right."

The editorial concluded that Chaplin was most likely guilty only of political naiveté and that the new attorney general, Brownell, should dismiss the case with an off-hand joke. Encouraged by the *Life* editorial, Agee wrote to Chaplin on December 21, offering any help he could provide to create public support for Chaplin's return:

> *Dear Charlie and Oona—this is mainly just to wish you and the children a very happy Christmas and New Year. Beyond that, to gabble a little. All the McGranery filth is sickening and infuriating beyond any words, even unprintable, that I can think of. I gather (confidentially, through Norman Lloyd from Jerry [Epstein]—and will keep it confidential), that you have no intention of coming back if you are required to be subjected to that kind of Ellis Island grilling. And though I suspect it is a fight you would win, I certainly don't blame you. In relation to that, I'm much interested what use, if any, may come of the editorial in* Life, *of this week—which I assume United Artists has sent you. I have an idea it may turn out to be some real use. The thought of you being in any way beholden to that eminent libertarian Henry R. Luce is a little preposterous; but if the whole mess could be cleared up in any way, to make it easy for you to go and come when and where you please, I frankly can't much care how it's cleared up. Certainly the people who instigated and wrote it are for you, much more strongly than they thought politic to say; The interesting thing is, that the top brass approved it.*
>
> *I've been wondering, of course, from the start, whether there is any useful thing I could do, and if so, what. The best idea I can get is the drafting of a statement, or petition, probably more useful to send to Brownell than to McGranery, urging that you be permitted to return without any detainment whatever, and stating several of the main reasons why: some of these in relation to you, and to you as an artist; others, in relation to the world at large. My idea is that such a statement should be so drafted that people of many or all political colorations—any sensible and civilized people at all—would sign it; so that it isn't dismissible as a liberal-to-leftist pressure job. Beyond that I have two ideas: to circulate for mass-signing; or to go, on the whole, after eminent names, in whatever profession, etc. I think on the whole, the latter might work better for two reasons: because the variety of political character would stand out more unmistakably, and impressively; and because it could be done more quickly.*

This is a hell of a funny Christmas note, but the whole thing has been on my mind, and once I got started, I went on. I hope it's legible enough not to be a torment to read.

Anyhow, if you think there's any point in the idea, please let me know, and I'll do anything I know how, and get the best help I know how.

For the rest, we have been only delighted in all we have seen and heard of the really royal progress of the The Chaplins, and Limelight, *through all those backwaters of civilization like England and France and by the time you get this, Italy. Another great pleasure was Oona's lightning trip.*

We are always so late that it has become practically tradition, not to say mania. This probably won't reach you til mid-January. So, in order to get word to you by Christmas, we'll send a cable.

Our love to you and warm regards to Harry—
Jim and Mia

Friends in California also wrote to Chaplin in Switzerland to keep the comedian up to date. After seeing *Limelight*, Lion Feuchtwanger wrote to say how much the film "stirred and pleased me . . . it accomplishes the mission which Molière requires of a real work of art: it satisfies the professor as well as the cook."[34] He wrote again in June to report that the government was keeping the pressure up. United States government immigration investigators were interviewing "everybody including my friends' housekeepers [regarding] what they think about me politically and morally."[35]

Seven

THE WALKING WOUNDED

Back in New York, Agee lived in the heart of the West Village. He was plagued with insomnia and frequently spent nights in local taverns until the last call. At the San Remo bar, Agee met the actress Judith Malina, a protégé of Erwin Piscator, and the founder with Julian Beck, of the experimental theater group The Living Theater. In her published diaries, Malina recounts details of her love affair with Agee. The two often spent nights in a small second apartment on Cornelia Street that Agee kept for writing and used for extramarital liaisons. Through May, June, and July of 1953, Malina observed Agee working with a young director, David Bradley, on plans to film *Noa-Noa*, Agee's screenplay about the life of painter Paul Gaugin. In a diary entry for May 19, she describes Agee at work in the apartment at 17 King Street where he lived with his wife and three young children:

> King Street is one of those dark, quaint vestiges of old New York and the route to it from the café is dank with garbage pails and 'the yellow smoke that curls.' The room on the first floor floods the street white. It is fearsomely bright. Inside, Agee sits at his typewriter acting out each sentence before he writes it. His face moving to the rhythm. I watch for a long time before he sees me though the window and lets me in. Jim reads me long portions of his scenario for a film on Gaugin. His simplicity seems incompatible with life in this world. I think it is. He reads each line between

Gaugin and Van Gogh with an exaggerated weight as though each one were an epigram.[1]

Free from the earlier restraint he had been under as a film critic for the mass audience that Luce's magazines served, Agee returned to a consideration of the link between murder and business in the *Noa-Noa* screenplay. Agee has Gaugin respond to Vincent Van Gogh's statement that Gaugin was "a successful businessman" before devoting himself to painting:

> *Gaugin:* O yes—a young man of shining promise. When people couldn't meet payments on mortgages, it was my business to slit their throats and to catch every drop of the blood.
> *Vincent:* Tsk-tsk . . . but—after all, you had a wife and children to support, Paul. People have to do all kinds of sad, difficult things, for the sake of that, don't they.
> *Gaugin:* (with a bitter smile): O yes indeed.
> *Vincent:* But you really were very *good* at business, weren't you?
> *Gaugin:* "Good?" It's just a machine for making money. If you're a part of the machine you make some of it; that's all; and if you get caught between the rollers, you get the life crushed out of you.[2]

Agee has Vincent accuse Gaugin of being a socialist, to which he responds, "Perpetuate all this filth? . . . No thanks. Civilization nauseates me. To make it a little better is only to make a little worse. All I want is to be free of it."[3]

Agee found in Gaugin a kindred spirit: Gaugin wrestled terribly with the choices an artist confronts between obligations to family, the demands of making a living, and the siren call of creativity. Like his portrait of Lincoln for *Omnibus*, Agee's script *Noa-Noa*, the Tahitian word for fragrance, provided a vehicle to express his own personal struggles and demons. It also recapitulated "anticlerical" themes in his Chaplin script as well as its concern with the corruption of civilization and the loss of human innocence. In Agee's screenplay, Gaugin, confronting a bishop in the Marquesa Islands, vows to "do my best to 'corrupt' the natives back into their innocence." Agee saw himself, like Gaugin, as a "nonreligious" religious man. This was the same secular religiosity that Agee recognized in Chaplin. Whittaker Chambers, after Agee's death, wrote that Agee "was not a religious man . . . but he was, among all men I have known . . . the one who was most about religion."[4] Agee's Gaugin, dying from a weak heart, discusses his burial plans, "God knows I'm no Christian . . . much as I regret it, I'm a civilized man . . . ," to which a friend replies, "Gaugin: in some ways you're a religious man, in caring at all."

Gaugin's final speech in *Noa-Noa* is a life summation from a sick and dying artist, who, having neglected his family and devoted his life to art, takes stock of the choices he has made in life: "You see, essentially I'm a very limited and stupid man. When I left my family I was sure *that* was temporary. And so it has gone: straight through . . . I was foolish enough to think that I might have fame during my lifetime; and foolish enough to care."[5]

On May 23, Malina wrote, "Agee's room. He says to me, 'I am a drunk.' We talk about sleeplessness. He says, 'Alcohol is my substitute for both sleeping and fucking.'"[6] By August, Agee is talking about traveling and holding out hope for the film he'd planned to make with Manual Conde. He tells Malina on August 6 that he plans to go "In the autumn, perhaps, to the Philippines to make a big film, for half a year, and/or to Tokyo."[7]

The next month, in September 1953, Agee heard from Ilse Lahn that Salka Viertel was on her way to New York and would contact him when she arrived. As McCarthyism strengthened and the political climate worsened for left-leaning artists in Hollywood, Salka decided to leave the United States. She sold her house to the actor and director John Houseman, a close friend and collaborator of Norman Lloyd, and drove from California to New York with Jay Leyda as her passenger. Her plan was to move in with her son Peter at his home in Closters, Switzerland. Meanwhile, Lahn's boss, Paul Kohner, was in Europe trying to make a deal for *Noa-Noa*. To help sell the project Kohner had Agee's screenplay translated into German.

That same September, Chaplin wrote from Vevey in response to a letter from Lion Feuchtwanger to describe how he and his family had settled comfortably into their new existence in Switzerland: "glad to hear from you in that distant, remote country of California. It is so wonderful to be away from that creepy cancer of hate where one speaks in whispers, and to abide in a political temperature where everything is normal contrasted to that torrid, dried-up prune-souled desert of a country you live in. Even at its best, with its vast arid stretches, its bleached sun-kissed hills, its bleak sun-lit Pacific Ocean, its bleak acres of oil derricks and its bleak thriving prosperity, it makes me shudder to think that I spent 40 years of my life in it."[8] In October, Feuchtwanger wrote again to the comedian to relate how he had himself luckily missed being vilified by the American press for being honored with the East German government's National Prize for Literature: He was "saved" through the fortunate timing of having also been similarly honored by the West German University of Munich. He added, "I read an excellent short story, 'A Mother's Tale,' by James Agee whom I met at your house. Do you know the story? If not, I shall send it to you."[9] Agee's story, published in *Harper's Bazaar*, was a parable against conformity set among a herd of cattle destined for the slaughterhouse.

In early November, Agee was rocked by the sudden death of the poet Dylan Thomas. Thomas, following a legendary series of whiskey shots at the nearby White Horse Tavern, was hospitalized, fell into a coma, and died four days later on November 9. Just before Thanksgiving, Malina wrote in her diary that Agee, shocked by the poet's death, had decided to make a serious attempt to cut back on his own booze intake; "Jim is much troubled by Dylan's death. He makes efforts to cut down on his drinking, boasts about it less, attends a meeting of Alcoholics Anonymous, rations himself to five drinks a day."[10]

Soon after, Agee returned to California for film work and began an affair with Oona Chaplin's friend Carol, who had ended her second marriage to William Saroyan the year before. In her memoir Carol (later married to the actor Walter Matthau) recalled first meeting Agee in 1951 at a party the Chaplins threw to celebrate her second ill-fated marriage to Saroyan. She came to know Agee socially and recalled seeing him "quite a few times at the Chaplins." In California, around Thanksgiving time in 1953, Agee was alone, his family on the East Coast. One evening he dropped by to visit Carol, who lived only blocks away from the little cottage Salka Viertel had just vacated: "We talked a lot about the people we knew and, of course about Oona and Charlie. Jim told me he kept in close contact with Charlie, writing to him often." During this time Agee was working on the *A Love Story* script for Film Documents. Carol remembered that Agee, "always brought a manuscript with him in the evenings. It was a story he was working on. It had to do with his first marriage and falling in love with

Mia. He would read it to me . . . and he always wanted to know if he was correct about how women felt in this or that situation . . ."[11]

Agee returned to New York and wrote to Chaplin to say that Salka was staying in his home. From New York, Salka flew to Shannon, Ireland, where her son Peter was working with Huston on a screenplay based on Rudyard Kipling's *The Man Who Would Be King*.

A single letter that Chaplin wrote to Agee during this period survives. That Chaplin actually wrote to Agee, and likewise to Feuchtwanger, is a sign of the high regard he held for both men. To receive a letter from Chaplin was truly a rare occurrence. One longtime associate of Chaplin, Carlyle T. Robinson, estimated "in his whole life Chaplin had written no more than a dozen [letters]."[12] He was notorious for never writing even to his two oldest sons, Charles Jr. and Sydney, while they were serving in the United States Army in Europe during World War II. Charles Jr., for example, was amazed when one day, on the German front, he was delivered a letter from his father—"One day the unbelievable happened. I received a long personal letter directly from my father." Typically he would only hear from his father through Oona.[13] The week before Christmas in 1953, Chaplin wrote to Agee from Switzerland:

Dear Jim,

Received your bountiful letter; you certainly went from soup to nuts and I must say it was heartening to hear from you.

As for your qualms, wondering whether I was offended in some way, I believe it was just a ruse of yours to make me answer to your letter quickly. How could I possibly be annoyed, or offended, or anything of that nature? However, you have succeeded in getting me to reply at once.

Now for the news and bulletins as they come to me.

Firstly, I am so glad to be out of that stink-pot country of yours. I should have done it in 1930 when I was over here the last time. I never really wanted to come back then, but the fates knew best because I would never have met Oona and our five children! To be over here, away from that torrid atmosphere, is like stepping out of the death house into the free sunlight. Occasionally, someone sends us a New York Tribune—*its dark news makes me shudder. It's nothing else but Dulles' vomit all over the front page. And the belly-aching about the charity they are giving to the world. Oh, what a stink-pot country! As the negroe [sic] says about living in Paris: "Colored folks is quality here," so I say about Europe: "Charlie's the tops."*

But seriously, we are very comfortable and happy living in Switzerland. We have 37 acres and we grow the best corn-on-the-cob I have ever eaten. We also have cherries, strawberries, asparagus, apples, pears, plums, greengages. Apart from the orchard, we have beautiful, magnificent trees which have been artistically spaced over the 4-acre lawn, framing a 14th century church that appears below the slope of the lawn with the lake and the mountains in the distance. You really must come over, you and Mia. Vevey is where Rousseau lived and wrote for a while and, of course, Corbet, the painter, lived just below us.

We are a couple of hours from everywhere; Oona and I go back and forth to London, to Rome and Paris. It's like taking a trip to Santa Barbara.

The Swiss government are splendid people, stolid and reliable and have been most hospitable to me. As for our neighbours, there are plenty of interesting people around, painters, writers and socialites and quite a few Americans who live here part time, so we can have any kind of life we want. Fortunate for me, Oona is not social minded and, as you know, she is somewhat of a recluse, almost like her father, so everything works out very well. She is extremely happy here and the children are beginning to speak French and are making friends. They go to the local village school which is excellent for they are very disciplined and they have plenty of work and study to do by comparison with other schools. In all, everything is working out wonderfully; I have sold all my properties in the States and have the money all here so there is no way in which they can heap on their revenge in future.

Strangely enough, I am not the least bit bitter, neither is Oona and she is most sincere in her liking for Switzerland.

As for my work, naturally I have had many distractions. It took me about a year to rearrange my life and we are just about getting it into shape. Nevertheless, I have written about 80 pages of the new script and made lots of notes. It is a story about an exiled King and will give me an opportunity to comment on current events. I have a few comedy sequences which are very funny, but the characters are a little dim at the moment. However, I am certain they will take shape but it means digging my chin in my chest for a week or so.

As for Limelight *it has been a tremendous success over here and has grossed more than any other picture bar* Gone With The Wind *so they tell me.*

I am glad to hear that you have had a nice year—you deserve it. As for your new script being almost poetry I don't think you could write anything without it having that flavour. So let us have more of it. It will be wonderful if you can come over next year, I will be able to show you around a bit.

As for other items, I am glad to hear that Salka is living with you; I was getting a little worried about it, especially if it is true that they wouldn't

let her out of the country. What bastards they are! Seems all the decent peo-
ple are getting it in the neck. Tell her I have seen Peter several times and
that I saw Hans in London for a moment and that they seem well and
happy. However, give her my love. I believe Oona is writing to her.

I think this will be enough for one session—I have run out of thinking!
So Oona and I send Mia and yourself all our love and best wishes for the
Xmas holidays and the coming year.[14]

As 1954 began, Agee had no shortage of potential projects. Although word came from Ilse Lahn in February that the producer
Alexander Korda, who had earlier shown interest in the *Noa-Noa*
script, had decided to pass on the project, Lahn reported that Kohner
was going to offer the project to the producer Walter Mirisch. In
March negotiations were underway for Agee to write a screenplay
from an original story for Mirisch about Lincoln's assassin, John
Wilkes Booth. But news of Agee's next big job came on March 15;
Kohner wrote to tell Agee that the producer Paul Gregory, a business
partner of Charles Laughton, was interested in having Agee write the
screenplay for *The Night of the Hunter*, based on Davis Grubbs' novel.
The film would be Charles Laughton's directorial debut. Laughton,
too, was a habitué of the Viertel social circle. He had collaborated
with both Brecht and Eisler on a production of Brecht's play *Galileo*,
which had been directed by Norman Lloyd. Laughton's wife Elsa
Lancaster, best known for her title role in *The Bride of Frankenstein*,
had coincidentally played a significant supporting role in *Mystery
Street*.

Grubb's novel was ideal fodder for Agee. The frightening story
depicted a psychotic murderous preacher hunting two young children for the loot their father hid before his arrest. Played by Robert
Mitchum, the evil Rev. Harry Powell, with the words *LOVE* and
HATE tattooed on the knuckles of his hands, became a film villain for
the ages. For years, Agee's involvement in the writing of the *The
Night of the Hunter* screenplay has been controversial. The film, now
considered a landmark of the film noir genre, was released after Agee
died, and many believed that the screenplay credit given to Agee was
more a gift than actually deserved. Posthumous reports over the
years from witnesses to the production, including Laughton, Lancaster, Laughton's partner Paul Gregory, and the film's star, Robert
Mitchum, painted a picture of Agee being too debilitated by alcohol

to write a useful screenplay. Recently, Agee's long sought-after first draft has emerged from where it was stored for over fifty years. The manuscript is over three-hundred pages and contrary to the legend, Agee's first draft is clearly the direct source for the final film.

Recently discovered business correspondence provides additional ammunition against the negative legend of Agee's tenure on the film. Lahn wrote to Agee on August 23, 1954 to inform him that there were rumors of discord on the set of *The Night of the Hunter*. Specifically, she told Agee, Mitchum had his doubts about Laughton's suitability for the material and she had heard that the star wished to arrange a deal to allow Agee to return to set to provide support.

Furthermore, there is no indication in the numerous pieces of correspondence of any dissatisfaction with Agee's services. A contract had been arranged to pay Agee $1,000 a week for ten consecutive weeks for writing the first draft. If the first draft was deemed satisfactory, a final payment of $2,500 would be made. If the script needed more work, Agee would receive an additional $5,000 for five more weeks of work. Any additional work beyond that would be paid at a rate of $1,000 a week until the script was completed. On July 3, the Gregory Associates acted on their option to extend Agee's contract for an additional five weeks beyond the original five. There is no mention of any dissatisfaction with Agee's performance in any of the correspondence.[15]

More projects were lining up. In late August, while Agee was at work on *The Night of the Hunter*, Kohner wrote to say how disappointed the Columbia film studio was that Agee couldn't take on a project writing a screenplay called *Joseph and His Brethren*. In the same letter, Lahn asks Agee if he'd ask Montgomery Clift, whom he likely knew through Salka Viertel, whether had any interest in a screenplay based on the novel *The Man Who Killed the Deer*. On October 4, Lahn wrote that Jerry Wald, who was still waiting for Agee to accept the *Joseph and His Brethren* project, now wanted him to first write a script about Franz Liszt. By October 20, both jobs had disappeared, and were given instead to a writer named Noel Langley. But Lahn had some good news, too: The Rockefeller Foundation wanted to fund the writing of a half-hour show for the Williamsburg Reconstruction Project and the job was Agee's if he wanted it.

Before tackling the script for Laughton, Agee had made significant progress on a screenplay written jointly with Howard Taubman, the music critic for the *New York Times*. The script, *A Tanglewood Story*, was a love story about ambitious musicians set at the famed Tanglewood Music Festival. Agee and Taubman had succeeded in interesting the director Fred Zinnemann in the project, and Ilse wrote to ask if Agee wanted Paul Kohner's help in representing him in the project. Zinnemann's most recent film, *From Here to Eternity*, had won eight Oscars just seven months earlier, including best director and best picture. Lahn reminded Agee that Zinnemann's involvement promised a big payday for the writer. At the same time, Agee was being approached by the famed cinematographer James Wong Howe, who was also interested in developing a project with him. As Agee began his work on *The Night of the Hunter* script in April, Lahn wrote to say that Howe wanted Agee to write the script for a story about a young Chinese boy in San Francisco's Chinatown. Howe wanted to feature the tension between traditional values and modern technology through the eyes of the child. Agee asked Lahn to "Show Jimmy Howe *The Blue Hotel* script—revised version if you have copy. He was interested when I saw him last."[16] Lahn wrote back to say that Huntington Hartford had promised to get her a copy of the script to show to Howe, but that she doubted that Hartford would ever part with the rights. On November 22, 1954, Ilse wrote to Paul Kohner about an offer for Agee to write a television pilot based on a radio program called *Doorway to Life*. According to Lahn, Agee turned down the contract because the project was too similar to his unfinished novel *A Death in the Family*, which he told Lahn was about three-fourths complete.

That Christmas, Agee wrote a long letter[17] to John Huston. He confessed that he had attempted to write four times previously, but, as he had with the letter to Chaplin before, he found himself unable to mail anything:

> *This won't reach you by Christmas or perhaps even by New Year, but it does seem to me about time I not only wrote but mailed some kind of word to you. So to begin with: Merry Ex-Christmas and a happy Ex-New Year.*
>
> *I know (or believe) I both hurt and displeased you in never writing in all that time—particularly in never writing you all, or anything, I thought of* The African Queen. *And I'm afraid the hurt and displeasure could be permanent;—not, I hope and suppose, to the degree of destroying a friendship, but quite possibly to the degree of discoloring or slightly queering it. I feel tempted to try to describe the kind of depression and virtual paralysis*

which caused my failure to write, but the simple fact is that nothing short of Dicease (Passing Away, I mean) could make my failure excusable, either personally or professionally. So can only say how much I regret it, and hope the failure, and the effects of it, will drift and thin out in the course of time.

Since I saw you, incidentally, I've three times gotten a long way into long letters, and have finished still another and never mailed any of them.

Quite the neurotic, huh?

I want to tell you something which I think will amuse you, as much as it gripes and amuses me, about my connection (or non-connection) with Moby Dick. *When the chance came, to work on it, I knew it was the job of a lifetime—or one of the very few jobs of a lifetime anyhow. And so I came gradually to realize that that is the one thing which not only excuses but requires, getting out of any conflicting commitments one possibly can. (My commitment was purely verbal to a nice rather crazy guy named Manual Conde, involving also Jimmy Howe.) Well, I sweated around trying to be "honorable" just too damned long; and within literally hours after I made myself sufficiently "dishonorable" I learned the* Moby Dick *job was lost. Now the place you're to laugh is here: within three weeks after that, the project to which I was committed [disappeared]; with nary a word from Conde. So much for that kind of honor; we have seen the enemy, and you can have them.*

I very much enjoyed Beat the Devil, *John. And how wrong I was about it! To me it had the gayety and pleasure of a 'vacation' picture, a thing done purely for fun; only through talking with Ricki—with whom I had a wonderful time did I realize anything of the difficulties it was made under.*

I learned about the showing of some of Moby Dick *on the* Ed Sullivan Show. *Just 3 days too late. Natch. (Around the house they call me Old Unfaithful.) By everything I hear of it, it's going to be the best of yours and quite possibly the best of any—if there were such a thing in art, which thank God there isn't. God! How I'd give my ass and every other ass available to have worked on it!*

Currently I'm having a lot of fun writing lyrics for Lillian Hellman's adaptation of Candide; *and fun and misery starting script on a toilsome original about musicians, which, now that I'm into full detail, begins to show signs of getting off the ground.*

I can't imagine you having time to write before Moby Dick *is entirely put to bed, so don't add that flea to the tons you must have on your mind.*

Since Agee had balked at the opportunity, Huston gave the job of writing *Moby Dick* to the novelist Ray Bradbury. After accepting the job from Huston, Bradbury read in *Variety* that it had earlier been offered to Sherwood Anderson. Later, Bradbury discovered that Huston had also offered it to Agee. Bradbury tried to reach out to Agee: He recalled, "I wrote to Agee to apologize for Huston going behind his back."[18] Bradbury traveled to Ireland to work with Huston on the script; Peter Viertel was there also, simultaneously working with Huston on the script for *The Man Who Would Be King*. Bradbury's experience in Ireland was a mixed affair; Huston and Viertel continually taunted the writer, famed for stories about rocket ships to Mars, for his fear of flying. Bradbury later wrote a fictional account of his experiences with Huston and Viertel in *Green Shadows, White Whale*; the title of his *roman à clef* a sly nod to Viertel's own novel about working with Huston.

Agee had passed up the chance to write *Moby Dick* for a project he had developed with Conde and Howe. Their proposed film, *Twilight of the Pagans*, was a paradise-lost tale set in Polynesia, in which a European and Asian castaway depict "the legends and rituals of the place of innocence before the coming of the Westerner."[19] Their Eden comes to an end when "three symbols of Western civilization are seen setting foot on the island—a syphilitic sea captain, a Chinese businessman and a missionary."[20] In the forward to a twelve-page treatment for the proposed film, Agee wrote, "Our purpose is to show one kind of human and natural perfection—the version of the ancient dream of an earthly paradise during the last days before its invasion and destruction. . . . It must have the accuracy of a good documentary film and properly handled will greatly transcend that—will stand as a good passage of heroic poetry."[21] The outline further stated: "There is a great deal of this kind of wild, naive, legendary material to draw on. What we propose to assemble is a set of adventures through which every major aspect of courage, skill, wisdom and honorableness of a whole man may be displayed and developed in visually exciting or pleasing terms and—through which any 'incomplete' man is bound to come to grief. Some of these obstacles are to be human, others non-human, some will be tinged with the supernatural."[22]

Agee had explored similar themes in his *Noa-Noa* script: He had Gaugin encourage Tioka, the old Marquesan sorcerer, to recall the pre-Christian days before the priests, military, and merchants had ruined the culture: "Gaugin: Where are your gods? Their images? Tioka: They have all gone. The French took them away, to the Paris exhibitions. Gaugin: Tell me about the old days, Tioka."[23] Earlier, Gaugin discusses the destruction of Paradise with his friend Vernier: "Vernier: But civilization brought deadlier things than bullets. . . . A Peruvian ship brought smallpox; the Chinese brought leprosy . . . the whole civilized world brought venereal disease. Gaugin: And France brought Law and Order and Taxes and Moneygrubbing and Servility and Hard Work: and you and the good Fathers brought Christianity. And that was the deathblow. You Missionaries killed all joy and courage in the soul itself."[24]

In early 1955, Agee took on another small foreign-film narration project. This time the film was an Italian travelogue-documentary set in Peru, a predecessor to the series of *Mondo Cane*–inspired exotic travelogue films. *Magia Verde* (Green Magic) was the account of a crew of adventurers traveling from east to west across South America from the Atlantic ocean, through the Amazon, and over the Andes, all by jeep. Released in the spring of 1955, Bosley Crowther called the film "a beautiful, thrilling and sometimes gruesome travel experience." The film's gore was provided by the fate of an unlucky heifer sent across a river to distract a school of efficient piranha. Crowther faulted Agee's translation of the documentary's commentary as "sometimes gaudy."[25]

Agee also became involved with the creation of an English-language narration for a short film about a young boy and a wild stallion in the coastal Camargue region of France, directed by Albert Lamorisse, who would later gain fame for his classic film *The Red Balloon*. Though Agee is not credited on the surviving film version, sound recordings of him reciting the narration survive, and after his death, the *Omnibus* television program broadcast the short film with Agee's version of the commentary.

During Agee's last months, Norman Lloyd and Royal Dano, the actor who had portrayed Lincoln in the *Omnibus* series, dropped in to visit him at his Greenwich Village apartment at 17 King Street. They brought Agee some ice cream, which unbeknownst to them was on his list of forbidden foods. Agee ate some anyway, and soon after had a bout of angina, which he quelled with a nitroglycerin pill. Lloyd recalled that Agee claimed that writing his autobiographical novel "was killing him."[26] Late in January of 1955, he had written to Father Flye that for almost a month he had become "vulnerable to frequent heart attacks. At best I skip a day or two. At worst they are very painful, and

I have as many as 8 a day."[27] On March 17, two months before he died, Agee was still hoping to travel and apparently had patched up his relationship with Huston. He wrote to Father Flye that he might travel to Ireland to work with John Huston on *The Man Who Would Be King;* he also added that he was now averaging twelve to seventeen attacks a day.

Another witness to Agee's last days was the photographer Robert Frank, who, through his friendship with Walker Evans, had become friends with the ailing writer. Frank is now famous for his collection of photographs *The Americans,* published in 1955, his Jack Kerouac film *Pull My Daisy,* and his association with the Rolling Stones (he designed the artwork for their album *Exile on Main Street* and directed the legendary "banned" documentary *Cocksucker Blues).* His friend Helen Gee, in her memoir of Limelight, the photography gallery she founded and named after the Chaplin film, recounted Franks's brief but moving relationship with the weakening Agee. According to Gee, Frank and Agee found common ground in their artistic and political viewpoints. The photographer was moved by Agee's conversation: "[Frank] spent several long evenings in Agee's King Street apartment, listening to him hold forth. Agee talked about everything—books, movies, photography, life." As Frank listened, taking hours to finish a single glass of scotch, Agee would drink an entire bottle, "though never seeming to get drunk." Frank was astounded at Agee's living conditions, and his near total disregard for possessions and personal appearance: "He doesn't give a damn about owning things. He uses orange crates for furniture, and he doesn't give a damn about clothes." Frank observed that in the months before his death, Agee rarely took the trouble to change his clothes. Every time Frank visited Agee's King Street apartment, he found the writer wearing the same old shirt. Gee wrote that Agee's demise struck Frank as a symbol of how America treats its artists, that "Agee had compromised his talents in order to survive."[28]

Eight

*L*OSS AND *L*EGACY

*A*gee died on May 16, 1955, from a massive heart attack suffered in the back of a taxicab en route to an appointment at his doctor's office. He died in debt, and without savings or insurance. Friends of the family quickly did what they could to raise money for Mia and their three children, Julia Teresa, 8, Andrea Maria, 5, and John, little more than six months old. A call was put out to Agee's wealthier friends, and significant help came from both Chaplin and Huston, who each donated a thousand dollars. Later the Agee Trust was founded with contributions from friends and supporters including Father Flye, Louis Kronenberger, Walker Evans, Carol Marcus Matthau, and Frank Taylor.

❦

After Agee died, Chaplin made two more films, *A King in New York* and *A Countess from Hong Kong*. To what extent, if any, Agee's ideas served as an influence on Chaplin is impossible to say, but in both of these films Chaplin directly addressed the threat of atomic weapons and the peaceful use of atomic power. Chaplin spoke frequently of his own concern about atomic weapons and actively supported the global peace movement, which many saw as a Soviet conspiracy to disarm the West. During the *Monsieur Verdoux* press conference Chaplin had been asked "Do you share M. Verdoux's conviction that our contemporary civilization is making mass murderers of us?"[1] After Chaplin answered in the affirmative, the reporter asked him to expand on his answer. Chaplin continued, "Well, all my life, I have always loathed and abhorred violence. Now I think these weapons of mass destruction—I don't think I'm alone in saying this, it's a cliché by now—that the atom bomb is the most horrible invention of mankind, and I think it is being proven every moment. I think it is creating so much horror and fear that we are going to grow up a bunch of neurotics."[2] The questioner next stated that Chaplin made a reference to the atom bomb at the end of the film, to which Chaplin responded "Well, it didn't have the atomic bomb in it—it had weapons of destruction, and if the atomic bomb is in it, then it goes for the atomic bomb."[3]

Shortly before leaving the United States, Chaplin had hinted at the possibility of using his films to address the atomic threat. Chaplin met with Bosley Crowther for an interview the day before he sailed for Europe. In the interview, published in the *New York Times* on September 28, 1952, Chaplin told Crowther: "The great stories today . . . are the things that are happening inside people. The things with which we have to compete are the startling physical and scientific developments and discoveries that are crowding upon us day by day. But all this external materialistic world has its counterpart, which is the Spiritual. That's my theme. Against these great external forces, internal spiritual forces must grow. Nature always compensates with balance. There can't always be the orange outweighing the pea. So I am not afraid of this atom business because I know that out of it will come the greatest expression of spirituality that man has ever known."[4]

After settling his family in Switzerland, Chaplin began work on *A King in New York*. This film was a direct shot across the ocean aimed right at American culture, commerce, and reactionary politics, and was in many ways his rebuttal to the negative treatment he'd received from America. Filmed in England and released in 1957, the film was not shown in the United States until 1973. The story begins with the words "One of the minor annoyances of modern life is a revolution" displayed on the screen, and the film's first scene is of a king being overthrown, his castle stormed and his likeness hung in effigy by an angry mob. As the mob shouts for his head, King Shadov has escaped from the fictional Estrovia to exile in New York. The king, greeting his faithful servant amid a crowd of clamoring reporters, announces that he is "Alive and well . . . we fooled them!" When a reporter asks, "Your majesty, how about this controversy over atomic energy?" King Shadov responds, "That's how I lost my throne. I wanted atomic energy for domestic use, but my ministers wanted atomic bombs. Nevertheless, I have nuclear plans that will revolutionize modern life and bring about a utopia undreamed of."[5] When the king is asked to say a "few words to the American people," Chaplin, who had seen numerous close friends—such as Hanns Eisler and Bertolt Brecht—run out of the country—and others including Lewis Milestone, the director of the antiwar classic *All Quiet on the Western Front*, blacklisted—has Shadov respond without a hint of cynicism: "I am deeply moved by your warm friendship and hospitality. This big-hearted nation has already demonstrated its noble generosity to those who come to seek refuge from tyranny."[6]

Tricked into attending a high-society dinner party where he unwittingly becomes the star of a protoreality show, the king is confronted by rich but unsophisticated Americans. One of these characters, an annoying large and wealthy woman with swollen knees, is named Vera Luce, a likely shot at Henry Luce's wife Clare Boothe Luce. In his memoir Chaplin recalled a dinner party at which he confronted Mrs. Luce: "That night I listened to Clare Luce's oracular preachments; of course the subject turned to religion (she had recently joined the Catholic Church), and in the melee of discussion I said; 'One is not required to wear the imprint of Christianity on one's forehead; it is manifest in both saint and sinner alike; the spirit of the Holy Ghost is in everything.'"[7]

The king, invited to a progressive boy's school, an echo of both the Wiltwyck School and the Westland School, meets Rupert, a precocious ten-year-old and the editor of the school paper, reading Karl Marx: "Surely you are not a Communist?" "Do I have to be a Communist to read Karl Marx?" Played by Chaplin's own son Michael, the boy gives the king an incredible lecture, which by no coincidence comments on many of the controversies the public Chaplin had recently endured. Making this unusual scene all the stranger, Chaplin sets the boy's speech amid a wild slapstick battle between the king and some rowdy fellow students of Rupert, who distract the king's verbal duel with Rupert with peashooters and end up in an all-out food fight. All the while, Rupert orates:

"I dislike all forms of government."

"Surely somebody must rule."

"I don't like the word rule."

"Well if you don't like the word rule let's call it leadership."

"Leadership in government is political power and political power is an official method of antagonizing the people."

"[an aside] What magazine did you say he edits?"

"But my dear young man, politics are necessary."

"Politics are rules imposed upon the people."

"In this country rules are not imposed, they are the wish of all free citizens."

"Travel around a bit then you'll see how free they are."

"But you didn't let me finish."

"They have every man in a straight jacket and without a passport he can't move a toe. In a free world they violate the natural rights of every citizen. They have become the weapons of political despots and if you don't think as they think you're deprived of your passport. To leave the country is like breaking out of jail. And to enter a country is like going through the eye of a needle. Am I fee to travel?"

"Of course you're free to travel."

"Only with a passport. Only with a passport. Do animals need passports? It's incongruous that in this atomic age of speed we are shut in and shut out by passports."

"If you'll shut up."

"And free speech, does that exist? And free enterprise? Today it's all monopoly. Can I go into the automobile business and compete with the auto trust? Not a chance. Can I go into the grocery business and compete with the chain stores? Not a chance. Monopoly is the menace of free enterprise. When I look back 60 years ago. . . . And the atomic bomb, it's a crime that when the world cries for atomic energy you want to make atomic bombs."

"Me!? I'm against atomic bombs."

"You want to wipe out civilization. Wipe out all life on this planet."

"I lost my throne because I didn't want atomic bombs."

"You and your kind think that atomic bombs can solve your problems."

"Look you little rat!"

"Today Man has too much power. The Roman Empire collapsed with the assassination of Julius Caesar, and why? Because of too much power! Feudalism blew up with the French Revolution and why? Because of too much power. And today, the whole world will blow up, and why? Because of too much power. . . . If Civilization is to survive we must combat power until the dignity and peace of man are restored."[8]

A King in New York gave Chaplin a vehicle for taking shots at rock and roll, cosmetic surgery, and television commercials. In one scene, suspiciously similar to one in Sofia Coppola's *Lost in Translation*, the king capitulates and agrees to act as a pitchman in a whiskey commercial. Rupert, after betraying his parents to the government, is found living on the street. The boy decides that "I'm so tired of everyone asking 'are you this, are you that?' So if it pleases everyone, then I'm a Communist." Later, when the king is called before the film's equivalent of HUAC, a slapstick setup involving a finger stuck in a fire hose provides Chaplin the opportunity to figuratively and literally declare to his audience that McCarthyism is all wet.

Chaplin's last film was *A Countess from Hong Kong*. It starred Marlon Brando, Sophia Loren, and Chaplin's son Sydney in a stateroom romantic farce. The aging comedian appears only in a brief and small comic turn, credited as "an old steward." Brando plays the wealthy Ogden Mears, recently appointed ambassador to Saudi Arabia on an ocean liner bringing him back to America from Hong Kong. Chaplin, in an echo of Rupert and King Shadov's meeting, merges a serious political message with over-the-top slapstick, adding his teaspoonful of sugar to a dose of medicine. Meeting the press in his suite, Brando is asked "What is your solution for peace?" Brando, while hiding a scrap of Sophia Loren's torn pajamas, replies, "The solution for peace lies within man himself, and in this atomic age and of military might," at which point, Sydney clumsily and loudly pops a champagne cork, the froth pouring onto the bald pate of a journalist, " . . . liberty and freedom and justice are generalities . . ." Sydney grabs a towel and dries the reporter's shiny wet head, while Brando continues, "And in this atomic age, only the morality of man can help him to survive. The solution for peace is in truth and tolerance and understanding." In another echo of *A King in New York*, Brando later takes a turn on the ship's ballroom floor with a vapid society girl, who regales him with her father's theories on the reincarnation of the soul and the power of love: "Do you believe in love? Daddy does. He loves everybody except the Communists,"[9] she tells him with a little laugh.

In 1957, two years after Agee's death, his unfinished autobiographical novel, *A Death in the Family*, was published. David McDowell served as the book's editor in a successful effort to turn parts of Agee's surviving manuscript into a marketable book. Scholars now understand the extent to which well-intentioned manipulation was involved in shaping and forcing Agee's unfinished writing into something resembling a completed effort; McDowell purposely discarded whole chapters in the process. Regardless of the published book's deviation from Agee's intention, its publication succeeded in raising income for the surviving Agee family and helped to honor the author's memory. *A Death in the Family* was awarded the first posthumous Pulitzer Prize for fiction and later inspired a theatrical version, *All the Way Home*, adapted by Tad Mosel, which won the Pulitzer Prize for drama in 1961. The play was later turned into a film starring Robert Preston, who had also starred in Agee's rendition of *The Bride Comes to Yellow Sky*.

In the process of stitching Agee's manuscript together, McDowell decided that the first formal chapter of *A Death in the Family*, following the earlier "Knoxville: Summer 1915" piece included as a prelude, would be Agee's depiction of a trip to the movie theater with his father to see a Chaplin film. This touching scene connects Agee's absent father and Chaplin as fundamental forces in the shaping of the author's young mind. The chapter begins with Agee's mother, a symbol of upright middle-class values opposing the father's plans:

> At supper that night, as many times before, his father said,
>   "Well, s'pose we go to the picture show."
>   "Oh, Jay!" his mother said. "That horrid little man!"
>   "What's wrong with him?" his father asked, not because he didn't know what she would say, but so she would say it.
>   "He's so nasty!" she said, as she always did. "So vulgar! With his nasty little cane; hooking up skirts and things, and that nasty little walk!"[10]

In the church-like setting of Knoxville's Majestic Theater, the father and son share the joy and forbidden fruit of Chaplin's anarchy.

... and there was Charlie; everyone laughed the minute they saw
him squattily walking with his toes out and his knees wide apart, as if
he were chafed; Rufus' father laughed, and Rufus laughed too. This
time Charlie stole a whole bag of eggs and when a cop came along
he hid them in the seat of his pants. Then he caught sight of a pretty
woman and he began to squat and twirl his cane and make silly faces.
She tossed her head and walked away with her chin up high and her
dark mouth as small as she could make it and he followed her very
busily, doing all sorts of things with his cane that made everybody
laugh, but she paid no attention. Finally she stopped at a corner to
wait for a streetcar, turning her back to him, and pretending he wasn't
even there, and after trying to get her attention for a while, and not
succeeding, he looked out at the audience, shrugged his shoulders,
and acted as if she wasn't there. But after tapping his foot for a little,
pretending he didn't care, he became interested again, and with a
charming smile, tipped his derby; but she only stiffened, and tossed
her head again, and everybody laughed. Then he walked back and
forth behind her, looking at her and squatting a little while he
walked very quietly, and everybody laughed again; then he flicked
hold of the straight end of his cane and, with the crooked end,
hooked up her skirt to the knee, in exactly the way that disgusted
Mama, looking very eagerly at her legs, and everybody laughed
loudly; but she pretended she had not noticed. Then he twirled his
cane and suddenly squatted, bending the cane and hitching up his
pants, and again hooked up her skirt so that you could see the
panties she wore, ruffled almost like the edges of curtains, and everybody whooped with laughter, and she suddenly turned in rage and
gave him a shove in the chest, and he sat down straight-legged, hard
enough to hurt, and everybody whooped again; and she walked
haughtily away up the street, forgetting about the streetcar, "mad as
a hornet!" as his father exclaimed in delight; and there was Charlie,
flat on his bottom on the sidewalk and the way he looked, kind of
sickly and disgusted, you could see that he suddenly remembered
those eggs, and suddenly you remembered them too. The way his
face looked, with the lip wrinkled off the teeth and the sickly little
smile, it made you feel just the way those broken eggs must feel
against your seat, as queer and awful as that time in the white pekay
suit, when it ran down out of the pants-legs and showed all over your
stockings and you had to walk home that way with people looking;
and Rufus' father nearly tore his head off laughing and so did everybody else, and Rufus was sorry for Charlie, having been so recently
in a similar predicament, but the contagion of laughter was too

much for him, and he laughed too. And then it was even funnier when Charlie very carefully got himself up from the sidewalk, with that sickly look even worse on his face, and put his cane under one arm, and began to pick at his pants, front and back, very carefully, with his little fingers crooked, as if it were too dirty to touch, picking the sticky cloth away from his skin. Then he reached behind him and took out the wet bag of broken eggs and opened it and peered in; and took out a broken egg and pulled the shell disgustedly apart, letting the elastic yolk slump from one half shell into the other, and dropped it, shuddering. Then he peered in again and fished out a whole egg, all slimy with broken yolk, and polished it off carefully on his sleeve, and looked at it, and wrapped it in his dirty handker-chief, and put it carefully into the vest pocket of his little coat. Then he whipped out his cane from under his armpit and took command of it again, and with a final look at everybody, still sickly but at the same time cheerful, shrugged his shoulders and turned his back and scraped backward with his big shoes at the broken shells and the slimy bag, just like a dog, and looked back at the mess (everybody laughed again at that) and started to walk away, bending his cane deep with every shuffle, and squatting deeper, with his knees wider apart, than ever before, constantly picking at the seat of his pants with his left hand, and shaking one foot, then the other, and once gouging deep into his seat and then pausing and shaking his whole body, like a wet dog, and then walking on; while the screen shut over his small image a sudden circle of darkness: then the player-piano changed its tune, and the ads came in motionless color.[11]

On the walk home, the boy, Rufus (the name Agee was known by in childhood), covets a store-window mannequin's cap, "Plaster peo-ple, in ennobled postures, stiffly wore untouchably new clothes; there was even a little boy, with short, straight pants, bare knees and high socks, obviously a sissy: but he wore a cap, all the same, not a hat like a baby." He desires the cap to help him reach toward manhood, but says nothing, knowing that his mother would have refused, "If he asked his father now, his father would say no, Charlie Chaplin was enough."[12]

For Agee, Chaplin was the ideal hero. Chaplin the artist was an out-sider from another country, engaged in social commentary on a level beyond politics that was as clear to the masses as it was to the intellectual interpreter. His Tramp persona mixed the most primal urges, anarchic sexuality, and hand-to-mouth survival with the sudden violence of the swift kick in the ass and the balletic grace of the supernatural athlete. Eleven years after Agee's death, T. S. Matthews wrote, "a wild yearning violence beat in [Agee's] blood, certainly, and just as certainly the steadier pulse of a saint. He wanted to destroy with his own hands everything in the world, including himself, that was shoddy, false or despicable; and to worship God, who made all things."[13] Recognizing this same mixture of anger and empathy, Robert Coles concluded that Agee found in Chaplin's work, "a triumphant, searching social and political criticism, all worked into a brilliant artist's performance. Agee the passionate moralist, angry at injustice and anxious to change the world, saw in Chaplin a fellow artist with similar interests and loyalties. There was, too, a homelessness to Chaplin's life that touched Agee deeply; both men had little use for the territorial imperatives to which many of us bow uncritically: my country, right or wrong."[14] Both, too, were raised without fathers.

Agee turned to his vision of Chaplin's Tramp as a redemptive figure to provide the center for *The Tramp's New World*, his desperate plea for humanity to turn away from its almost certain self-imposed doom. For Agee, the Tramp represented the fully human individual, uncorrupted by technology and politics, and as such, the model mankind must aspire to emulate if it is to survive. In *The Tramp's New World*, Agee sets the Tramp loose in the postatomic devastation of Manhattan, its populace turned to pillars of ash, to confront the symbols of society that led it to this awful fate. This parable, this nightmare, was Agee's response to the horror of Hiroshima and Nagasaki: The horror of reality and the worse horror he felt was yet to come. Agee's screenplay was to be a plea, a warning, and a prophecy. As he wrote in his cover letter to Chaplin when he sent him the draft screenplay: "I feel, and hope and believe that you may feel, that the film I suggest could be of very particular importance and possible usefulness, and that it would have to be made soon if it is to be made at all."

The screenplay, and the movie he hoped would be made from it, would be the fullest expression of Agee's pessimistic view of humanity's chances: its inability to steer itself from what he perceived as its inexorable course toward the dual disasters of totalitarianism and atomic destruction. Paul Ashdown, writing about Agee as a literary prophet, observed, "it is the nature of prophecy to much exaggerate the dangers of the present, and Agee's gloomy social assessments and predictions were intended to rouse a deluded, apathetic public."[15] In 1946 Agee wrote an obituary of H. G. Wells for *Time* that in retrospect fits Agee equally well: "All his life he had worked to warn and teach the human race and, within the limits of thought, to save it. At the end, he was forced to realize that his work and his hopes were vain; that either he or the human race were somehow dreadfully wrong. Characteristically, with the last of the valiant, innocent optimism which had always sustained him, he blamed it all on the human race."[16]

In the end, Agee's life was bookended by his love and admiration for Chaplin. Chaplin's star, never dimmed, was a fixed point from which Agee's life and art derived much of their direction. The laughter and sadness that Chaplin's Tramp distilled from the strife and trouble of everyday life were an inspiration in Agee's art and life from his earliest remembered childhood until the last days of his life.

After Agee finished his *Life* article on the giants of silent comedy, he wrote a note to his editors suggesting specific photographs to use in the story. One suggestion, which went unheeded, was for an image to be placed at the end of the article: Agee's wish was to feature an image of Chaplin and Jackie Coogan, the young boy of *The Kid*, walking away while looking backward over their shoulders. Agee explained the effect he intended the image to impart: "meaning which I believe will carry without comment: their look is reproachful; the favorite comedian of silence, and a child; exit; in other words, the childhood of movies, and of the movie audience: we aren't wanted anymore; we can't reach you anymore."[17] Agee's talent and his love for Chaplin and the poetic art of silent comedy can be rediscovered in *The Tramp's New World*, his previously unpublished screenplay. Its timeless message of respect for humanity and the dignity of the individual are wanted now more than ever: Agee and Chaplin can still reach you.

Agee wanted *Life* to use this photo of Chaplin and Jackie Coogan from *The Kid* for the final image in his classic article on the forgotten art of silent comedy, "Comedy's Greatest Era"; ". . . the favorite comedian of silence and a child exit . . ." (Collection of Jeffrey Vance)

Part Two

THE TRAMP'S NEW WORLD*

by James Agee

A. SHORTEST POSSIBLE OUTLINE OF STORY

Without warning, a super-atomic Bomb is dropped, which outdoes the grandest expectations of those who set it off. All life on the planet, human and subhuman, is instantly exterminated, so far as we can tell; so, of course, is the Power by which civilization had been run.

But there is one survivor, the Tramp. In a long solo he wanders the absolute desolation of New York (or some huge "internationalized" metropolis), examining civilization as it looked in the fraction of a second before it ceased to live.

When this last living creature on earth (so far as we know) is on the verge of dying, of pure loneliness, awesome horror, and meaninglessness, he discovers in quick succession two good, all-redeeming reasons to be alive: an almost newborn baby, which he tries to take care of; then a young woman (not the baby's mother).

Transfigured now with an abounding energy and hopefulness, the Tramp and the Girl improvise, any of the broken relics of the slain civilization, the first human shelter, and build the first fire in the new-born world whose human symbol is the baby. They are a kind of Adam-and-Eve, Holy Family Robinson, and this is the high point of hope, peace, beauty and joy in the picture: the largest and smallest unit of which something like thorough good and happiness can be hoped: the family.

However, as we now begin to learn, there are other survivors.

The first ordinary, solid man to impinge on the Tramp's little family, immediately settles the Tramp's hash with the girl. From then on the Tramp is just a combination baby-sitter

---

Agee's fragmentary draft holograph manuscript for his Chaplin screenplay, held at The Harry Ransom Center, University of Texas, Austin, was untitled and named posthumously. The newly discovered, complete, typed manuscript version is referred to in this text as *The Tramp's New World*.

and dear old friend of the family. Aside, however, from this central regret and grief, which represent the central sorrow and pain which are irreducible from human life, they work out a remarkably decent and kindly relationship with each other.

The other survivors in whom we are chiefly interested are a group of atomic and other scientists, who survived the bombing virtually unscathed, in their great underground laboratories.

The rest of the picture alternates between these two, very different communities: showing how, in each, life is put back together and civilization, of a sort, is recrystallized.

The survivors who gather round the scientists, and those who happen to come within the orbit of the Tramp, are the same kinds and varieties of ordinary people. But they develop very differently, and they develop very different kinds of community and civilization. They develop the more rapidly and emphatically because all these people, already largely deprived of the ability to think or to feel for themselves by the old civilization they lived under, are now even more malleable than before, under whatever strong influence they happen to come. That is the chief psychological effect of the Bombing.

The scientists were the strongest basic influence in the old civilization and on the whole, the strongest minds; they have survived the Bomb in their scientifically prepared shelters, without suffering its psychological effects. Those who come under scientific influence live more and more according to "pure" reason, and by scientific authority; less and less by impulse, feeling, personal desire, moral or esthetic or personal "values," individual judgment or self-respect. Their rewards, which are immense, are material, and are technologically produced. Their loss is the loss of their own nature and being and personality. Their community is the logical projection of all that was most hostile to self-realization in the old civilization. It is that ultimate, perfect, unconquerable form of tyranny in which the tyrants sincerely regard themselves as servants, saviors and benefactors and are so regarded by the citizens, who enjoy and use every democratic advantage, and regard themselves as happy and free. (Lest it be thought for a moment that we are here satirizing "totalitarianism" as it is generally understood, I think the scientific community should adopt and even improve on the U.S. Constitution and Bill of Rights, and show what a living hell a perfect Democracy can be, if its members know the words without knowing the tune.) The scientists and their co-citizens develop much more wonderfully devastating weapons, for potential "defense," than the Bomb which so nearly obliterated the human race.

The Tramp, on the other hand, survived by blind crazy luck, the curious grace of God, or both; he sustained the full effect of the Bomb which was sustained by all other survivors. But though the Tramp is in many ways as suggestible and spontaneous as a child, fundamentally he is the strongest thing in human life: he is the human spirit in a form natural-born and intact enough that not even the Bomb can crack or weaken its clear nature. And those who come under his influence discover in themselves, and for the first time dare to recognize and to be loyal towards, the Tramp's own kind of childlike anarchism. Here, in degrees never possible before, the most unexpected kinds of people begin to realize who and what they really are; to enjoy themselves and each other; to honor themselves and each other as single, unique individuals; to do and be the things they always faintly felt and wished at their best that they might—which in some is cruel or evil or destructive, but in most is relatively very good, and wonderfully happy to see. They do not sacrifice the use of the rational mind, but they tend never to use it except in conjunction with the intelligence of the heart, the body, the instincts. Their rewards, which are immense, are purely personal and interpersonal; but are earned at the cost of the suffering and sorrow which are inevitable to the un-anesthetized, truly living personality; and at the cost of very hard mental and physical work. Their losses are technological. Their life is the logical opposite of all that was possible, except for rarely wise or brave or lucky individuals, under the old civilization. Their community is a fluid, ever-shifting balance between free-enterprise democracy, democratic socialism, and anarchism; its stability rests in the facts that it is small; that it is pre-industrial by choice; and above all, that it honors and protects human beings, and that they, learning for the first time how to honor themselves, are learning also for the first time how to honor each other. It is unlike the run of "Utopias" in certain important respects: it refuses to take itself very seriously but regards itself, and all Government, as at best make-shift; there is no Leader, not even an oligarchy, though the wise and the skeptical are respected as they are not, for instance, in our present form of democracy; despite certain major, calculated self-denials, it is pleasure-loving rather than ascetic. Personal and small group violence are possible in this community: war, and grand-scale destruction, are unthinkable.

Rather late in the film the Tramp, wandering, falls by accident into the hands of the Scientists. They experiment on him earnestly, curiously, savagely. But they who have all but

eliminated human personality from the world, cannot reduce him
to form; and ultimately, just in time to try to save his own
community, he escapes them.

When the two communities confront each other, it's a different story. The Scientific swallows the Humanistic whole,
without even having to use force. The avalanche of labor-saving, soul-destroying amenities which the Scientists offer, are
enough of themselves, to win over most of the Tramp's people.
The Tramp himself, speaking for the first time in the Picture,
tries desperately to plead the cause for his own community,
and to warn of the certain disasters which attend the other.
The only effect of his speech is that, however regretfully,
the rest of his supporters, including the Girl, the Solid Man,
and the Child, go over to the other side.

At the end he is, as usual, alone: he is walking away from
the New World into the twilight, the last short while of existence which remains for him, for the human race, for the
planet itself.

OUTLINE OF BASIC IDEAS

In such a story outline I have not managed to state the basic
ideas clearly enough. By further bare outline, the fundamental
theme is: the life-vs.-the death of the human personality. The
fundamental story, a tragicomic study of what happens to personality, towards life or death, under "ideal, laboratory"
conditions.

The story is based on these propositions:

That it is exceedingly hard under the best of circumstances, to exist and develop as a full human being; but not
impossible.

That it is impossible, for most people, under contemporary
civilization.

That contemporary civilization is doomed, by that fact,
more surely than by any other.

That in all times, outside forces and personal weakness
both strongly militate against full existence as a human
being; that the roots of the evil in our particular time are:
personal weakness, confronted by the discoveries and fundamental assumptions and attitudes of Scientists, and by the corruptions of these discoveries and attitudes, which give almost
the whole of modern life its physical and mental shape—and
which have even deluded most of the scientists.

That under the most favorable possible "laboratory" circumstances—among the few who survive the absolute demolishment
of contemporary civilization—two things, of chief importance
and significance, might happen:

1) Among some, the knowledge and the habits of mind bred under the old civilization would not only survive, but grow stronger than ever.

2) Among others, the end of contemporary civilization would mean their first chance to begin to exist as full personalities.

That community #1 would approximate the mechanistic, materialistic Utopia; the death of human personality; the ultimate certainty of its own destruction.

That #2 would approximate the humanistic Utopia; the relative liberation of the personality; but that this would be possible to maintain only through eschewing virtually everything which comprises a) contemporary civilization, b) community #1.

That if and when these two communities meet, the members of #2 will for various reasons inevitably desert it for #1.

That civilization, and the individual personality, cannot therefore preserve themselves from absolute destruction, even through learning a catastrophic lesson; nor through a successful demonstration of human possibility. We *could* preserve ourselves if we *would*—but we *won't*; almost *can't*. In the absence of an elaborate technological civilization we might have a fighting chance; in fact, taking that chance, a good way of living is demonstrated to work out. But required to choose between the technological, and the difficulties and self-denials of the Tramp's community (as at present, and in the closing scenes of the picture), we cannot bear to pay the price, and we cannot even clearly enough realize the nature of the choice, the connections between two ways of living, and the life or death of the personality. *Compromise* seems only too reasonable, possible and attractive—and this issue must be examined very closely in the film, as I haven't yet done. My assumption—conviction—is, that you'd let the Industrial Revolution back in the door, only at too great—and demonstrable—a risk. By another way of summarizing: Facing the issue at present, even if we could see it clearly enough, it would be unthinkable that we would destroy civilization as we know it— "turn back the clock," for no matter what realistic reasons. But even if the Bomb did us the enormous favor we can't do for ourselves, and even if, thanks to that, we had learned what we are really capable of, we'd make the same tragic mistake, given the same choice anew, between the best we could do as individuals, and the best we could do as masses, and through machines.

Because at this stage some sections are badly out of proportion with others, I've tried to arrange this in the order that I hope will be most convenient for your reading.

A: Shortest possible outline.

B: Prologue. I've drafted this out in considerable detail, but it's still much too long. So for the sake of convenience and proportion I merely sketch it under B, and append it at full length under D.

C: Main section: as full a treatment as I've worked out, of the main body of the film, from the entrance of the Tramp through to the end.

1) Fairly full detail on the Tramp's opening solo; a mixture of detail and general idea, through his whole first sequence with the girl.

2) Relatively meager, still general ideas on the Scientists and their community.

3) Ditto on the Tramp's community; and on developmental material for the Tramp.

4) Fairly detailed sketch of the closing scenes.

D: The Prologue at full length from beginning of picture up to entrance of the Tramp.

E: Miscellaneous corrections and suggestions.

F: A story, "Dedication Day," enclosed because it sets up, I think, some fair possibilities for a quite different kind of prologue.

B. BRIEF OUTLINE OF PROLOGUE

As mentioned before, it seems best to save you time at this stage. Here then is the gist of the Prologue.

Open inside a big New York movie theater. Through a burlesqued March of Time, a concentrated image of the state of the world, especially this country, as regards Atom Bombs. A diarrhea of corrupt language and of cheesy "documentary" movie devices, quite savage and, in undertone, compassionate. Chief speakers are the Commentator, and four Leaders: a top scientist, ditto clergyman, ditto "independent individualist," and ultrapolitical orator. Chief things set up for future reference: the scientists; their Brain, a super-computing machine; a little nation called Obnoxia, which will deliver the Bomb. Chief overall effects should be, 1) of desperation and bankruptcy of usable ideas, disguised chiefly as bluster, pseudo-high-seriousness, and solemn admonition; 2) by implication, the whole crazy state of contemporary civilization—above all, in any connection of the intelligence with the heart; the mutually strangling death-grip which public leaders and over-suggestible, helpless, herd-caught ordinary people, hold on each other, as they go under water. By midway in the March of Time it should be clear to the audience that there is no hope whatever of averting catastrophe.

Midway in the M.O.T., the camera pulls out of the theater while the hopeless, bright-yammering soundtrack continues, and watches the ordinary innocent crowded streets of the city; then removes to Obnoxia, a tiny mythical country which is at the solemn moment of bidding Godspeed to the Bomb. I've made it little, old, monarchistic and deeply religious as well as mythical, not only because no known nation, even by inference, should launch the bomb, but also trying thus to catch, both in ridicule and pathos, the quintessence, obsoleteness, and danger out of all proportion to size, of nationalism. The plane takes off; the very wind of its swift launching begins to tear hell out of Obnoxia.

Back to the U.S., chiefly New York: unaware crowds in streets; a glimpse, rear silhouette, of the Tramp, being traditionally chased by a cop (this should be a mere flash, as if accidental); the plane comes over swift and silent (at supersonic speed), followed by its terrifying whine of sound across the sky; a tiny parachute, planted in the zenith, idles delicately towards the earth. Suspensive intercutting to alerted and still oblivious faces: a hideous detonation-and-light effect, described in full in D. (Pure blinding glare; subsonic "sound" for maximum terrifying effect of the unidentifiable, on the audience.) Camera follows huge column of flaming smoke to its crest, watches it clear, stares straight downward, and begins a grandiose descent, in one unbroken shot, upon the turning world. We see enough of the entire world to be sure that it is deprived of all life and of all power, descend among more detailed symbols of the end of the world which was, and bring camera to rest, discovering the Tramp.

(N.B.) This prologue contains I think useful stuff on immediate, pre-bomb civilization, which would be hard to pick up or imply as well later; it also makes a few useful introductions. But I suspect all that could be fed-in later; and it could be exceedingly powerful, and perhaps better, to start off the picture with the explosion itself, for complete directness, surprise and terror; and bring the camera to the Tramp as soon as the illusion has been established that he is the sole survivor; or even, bring the camera immediately to the Tramp, and let us find out his solitariness, and what has happened to the world, entirely with him and through him.)

C. (1) ENTER THE TRAMP

He is back to the camera, hunched deeply over, in a tinily narrow alley between two buildings. A rigid forefinger is still jammed in each ear. He is still motionless; frozen.

He comes up as slowly, timorously, tremulously out of his crouch (fingers in each ear pulling timidly away), as a grass-blade recovering, which has just been stepped on. Straightens, still back to camera; and starts straightening his legs and arms inside clothes, and the clothes themselves, turning very slowly, face close to camera, staring into it. He continues to straighten his clothes, going over them very carefully: tie, collar, lapels, skirts of coat, readjusting trousers; cuffs (flicking off explosion dust); polishing toes of shoes on calves of pants; sleeving his derby and resetting it with care on his head; testing his cane: then a sudden trembling shrug (involving a full check-over of body as well as clothes), which is a blend of what a suddenly dampened dog does, and of the feather-adjustments of a suddenly rumpled hen. Then very delicately and timidly, camera withdrawing, he advances, and sticks his snout around the corner of the building, and peers.

An immense vista of naked street, shot from his eye-view. Very cautiously, he steps out and looks around. Now for the first time he sees the cop.

He is a very irate and brutal cop, running fast with right foot and nightstick raised high; on his face a lowering feroc-ity. The force, light and heat of the bomb have reduced him and flattened him to a very slightly distorted photograph against the smooth concrete wall of the building: a stop-shot. Part of him is bent and flattened around the corner of the crevice.

The Tramp can't believe his eyes. At first he keeps a wide berth, watching, and looking wise: this is a trick. Then he comes close and looks close into the huge photographed glaring eyes. They scare him; he flinches. Then he works up a show of bravery and arrogance. He sees the pistol in the cop's hol-ster. He loosens it with his fingernail; pulls at it carefully; it comes out, thin as tinfoil and he drops it as if it were a nasty insect. He begins to get confidence now. He struts before the cop, making arrogant and insulting gestures; looks up into the glaring face again. He strikes a match against the cop's cheek, lights a little butt, inhales deeply, blows all the smoke in his face. He stands back again and sizes him up. He tries to lift the cop's stone coat-tail. With a look of long-deferred pleasure, he hauls back one foot to give him a swift kick in the ass. In middle of haul-back, he begins to realize a little more clearly. He brings his foot down gently and un-surely. He walks slowly off, head turned, eye still half-sus-piciously on the cop.

Eyes front, first thing he sees, caught against another wall, is a quite pretty young woman, stopped in the middle of a self-confident smirk of flirtation. Deeply impressed, he lays his boutonniere with a certain reverence at her feet; on second thought, realizing there may be living women still in the world, he rather shamefacedly retrieves the flower, readjusts it in his buttonhole, tips his hat, and shuffles along; his face building awe, mystification, and a kind of childlike exhilaration and extreme curiosity; he turns a sudden corner and looks up the grandest avenue of the metropolis; then down it. (Tentatively: 5th Avenue at about 49th St.) The street is pure silent vacuum; sunlight glitters on a hundred shop-windows as on the facets of a jewel. Tramp's reaction, in close-up, exceeds that of Monte Cristo when he cries The World is Mine, and grows ever more wild and fierce for several seconds until he can stand still no longer.

His exuberance overflows into his whole body. He sprints to the middle of the street, whirls round and round like a dancer, arms outflung, in great wild childish arrogance, capers like a goat; and dashes for a super-delicatessen (the most expensive bon-voyage baskets, candied fruits, etc. etc.); keep camera still at middle of street; he tears out and up to camera, hands, under-elbows and teeth full, stacks his stuff on the pavement and straightens, breathing hard, the stag at eve, and glaring around, spots his next victim: a top-line gown shop; dummies in the window. He picks up a heavy can or jar of food, heaves it through the window, leaps in after it like a rutting faun, accosts dummy, hooks at her skirt-hem with his cane, tilts his hat, shameless and most lascivious possible flirting and gayety; undresses her; whips together a great load of the finest gowns and furs, staggers back and adds them to his heap. Next a jewelry store: kicks the window in; dashes in the door; out again almost immediately, coruscant with jewels, showers them on the same heap with the profligate sweeping gesture of a sower, or a pontifical blessing, and sits down to leap up immediately: he has sat on an open brooch, extracts its fang, glares at its magnificent glittering, and throws it as far away as he can. He sits down much more carefully this time, and rummages down through the gems and furs until he extracts a stalk of celery. He separates off the coarser stalks and tosses them aside; with crook-fingered elegance, on his throne of treasure, starts to nibble at a tender, little stalk: resting from his labors; looking in a lordly way around him while he gets his breath; monarch of all he surveys. (If camera is held at center-street, next [to] his treasure-heap, all this from his entrance upon 5th Avenue should be done with preternatural speed: also to sustain weirdness and shock, throughout this wild burst of looting, of the almost maniacal closeup and dance-gesture with which it began. The whole "Id" of the Tramp, and the illusion of release from his entire lifetime of deprivation and humiliation, can be in this scene.)

Exhausted with power and happiness, his eyes gradually lower; he is staring idly into the pavement; then not so idly. As he looks, the celery he is chomping goes dry in his mouth; his jaws move more languidly; then sickly; he spits the stuff out like so much blotting-paper. We see, in closeup, what he is looking at.

The mid-street pavement is a solid mat of photograph-flattened vehicles and people: a fedora, an auto-top, an upturned face, a woman's silly hat, a hand gripping a newspaper: the complete fabric of a densely busy city street as seen from directly above, put into two dimensions on the pavement. We see at first the complex little detail that he saw; then pull the camera directly upward as he gets up and starts walking. He is trying not to walk on anything but clear pavement—especially not people; but not autos either. It is as awkward and difficult as Eliza crossing the ice; after a little, he gives it up as a bad job. He has begun his wandering of the city; and from here on, he is no longer Monte Cristo. Everywhere, faintly on glass and more clearly on stone and cement and metal, on the walls and windows of buildings, on the sidewalks and streets, he sees how the ordinary crowds of an ordinary city mid-day are flattened and arrested in photographs. The vertical stuff (pavement) is hard to decipher; the stuff of the walls is only too clear; for the most part scarcely distorted at all. He now wanders through all the arrested motion which can be effectively invented (and documented) out of a great city, with occasional reflexes towards stealing, lust, hunger, contempt, fear, all arrested in him; and constantly with deeper and deeper awe, dread, realization and loneliness. Here, aside from the ironies which can be worked through signs, display windows, ads, fragments of newspaper, two chief kinds of thing should be most strongly worked; all that can be milked out of contemplation of, and reaction to, the average "documentary" city street crowds, caught at any casual moment; and all that can be worked out of the invention of average people going through the basic transactions, business and personal, of an average day. In other words he should be wandering [in] something more instantly frozen, in the perfected details of casual life and unexpected death, than Pompeii. The documentary stuff is wholly unpredictable here: it should be worked out of sneaked shots of sidewalk crowds, for kinds of personal and suprapersonal emphasis and point-making which can only become clear in the course of selection from among many shots. (If conscious and unconscious faces are intercut and spotted during explosion earlier, some should be recapitulated here; And some of these documentary shots should be those who look up—and those who don't—in actual streets when a sudden, unidentifiable, alarming noise is imposed on them without warning. These would be worth experimenting with on real city streets.)

The second category, on streets, in offices and rooms, etc., takes much more careful invention and selection than I'm as yet anywhere near. It should be closely related in realism to the documentary shots, yet expressive, to a cartoon degree, of basic social and individual situations—roughly such as follow: a somewhat crooked business transaction in which each transactor registers certainty he has outsmarted the other; a boss enjoying a secretary; a married couple quarreling fiercely; a pair of lovers about to embrace; someone very old, spreading a newspaper or peeling an apple; perhaps if they were introduced earlier, though it takes us out of town, the countryman who covered his child, flattened onto the slaglike earth, a little of her skirt flattened beside him, peering from beneath him, like a pressed flower; a switchboard girl about to plug in a call: someone about to tip a cabman; a pathetically homely woman just emerging, newly crimped, from a beauty parlor; the tired sneers of the beauticians who look after her; two sniffing dogs or a dog with his leg cocked at a hydrant; the huge upturned face of a skyscraper-ogling yokel, gentle and wondering, almost Mortimer Snerd; the sidelong-passing, sophisticated face which is not unkindly amused at his gawping; a man on the verge of suicide and his farewell note about his personal trouble and the semi-conscious vengeance he wants to take on a certain person who survives him; or, also, the Tramp enters the theater in which the movie opened (or enters one anyhow, if Prologue is unnecessary) and finds, on the screen, a faint frozen delineation of Donald Duck, and the general theater a solid floor of upturned, mainly laughing faces, knit as close together as purls in a sweater. He walks very delicately among them; the laughter in their faces renews his desire not to step on anybody. (One face, the Skeptic, remains exactly as when it watched the Capra movie and the M.O.T.) I believe this kind of material can be interwoven, two ways: that for some passages we leave the tramp and look merely through the camera, for ordered and coherent series of images which make poems, of a kind, about the last instant the world was alive; in other passages we pick him up again, sometimes tiny in the depths of immense perspectives, sometimes suddenly and close, and follow, in as much detail, his own observations and reactions. I think two kinds of thing can be done at once here, besides using the Tramp as an observer and advancing him as a character: a powerful examination, by highlights, of the civilization which produced its own destruction—a full-length death-portrait containing adequate diagnosis; and an equally powerful, and more moving, multiple image of the human race, taken unawares in the midst of life.

It begins to occur to the Tramp that if he was saved by such an amazing fluke—merely the chance of the angling of two high walls, others must have survived too: perhaps in subways; surely there, if anywhere. But his survival was even flukier than he thinks: one vaporized trainload of subway people convinces him of that. And some of the remains are even more odd than those photographed, as he finds when, in deep fatigue and by now almost automized, blind wandering, he maunders into the lobby of a great building (the Empire State), and, with his cane-tip, absently pushes a button. With a noise which terribly frightens him, wracked metal doors wheeze and part: the elevator is two-thirds full of clear, standing effigies of people. For a moment he is both frightened and overjoyed: they look alive to him (and to us). He enters and accidentally jostles a lady; quickly and apologetically tips his hat, only to see the effigy fall apart: it is pure ash. The doors close before he can escape; the elevator starts to rise. One wall is blasted open; he looks through. The elevator rises through 100 floors of a building so stripped to its skeleton that he sees beneath him the sinking of a whole city and a fair part of two states; the other effigies stand expressionless about him. On the observation platform he looks at the plaque showing directions and mileages of major cities and landmarks and looks off above the city. Many buildings still stand; many look almost entirely unharmed; but in the lowering sunlight there is a strange unreal glaze on every surface and the open land beyond the city is solid glaze: there is also a strange pale band of haze, almost transparent and very sinister to see: although so much of the city is intact the general effect of this panorama is of softly smoking, calmly shining emptiness, a boundless plain of it. He goes back into the elevator, presses a button; the doors close; he descends. He has linked the panorama, the sense of an empty world, to the effigies; he is very sacred towards them. As the elevator gently jolts to a stop at the ground floor, another of the images crumples, though he had been so careful not to touch it. The sprained doors wheeze open; he steps out, shaking all over; the doors close. He determinedly presses the button: the doors open: desperately he swoughs through the effigies with his cane; they all fall. He scoops a double-handful of ashes and runs to the nearest wall-photograph hysterically trying to rub it out. No result. He first leans against the wall, then slowly collapses to a sitting position, too sick at heart and stomach even to move.

The camera looks straight down 5th Avenue. By speeding of stop-motion, the lowering sun washes and engulfs the Avenue in

cold iron shadow. Only at east-west intersections, it is
striped with brilliant sunlight. As far down the Avenue as a
moving figure is visible in all this motionlessness, we see the
Tramp, walking towards us. Dissolve: or by quick superimposi-
tion he is in middle distance. Again: he is near enough that
we can begin to see his face. He comes along very slowly, so
weak with his realizations and experiences that he finds it
hard to walk: and his face registers these realizations ever
more clearly and intensely with every step he takes nearer.
When he has reached full close-up the camera gently withdraws
before him, at his own pace: but now he is weaker with each
step. At length he has to lean against a wall (oblivious of
the terrible, baked face which stares beside his head); and in
his exhaustion he has to begin to realize that he is terribly
hungry. He can scarcely endure the fact; it dryly nauseates
him to be a living animal, with a living animal's needs; and
the mere imagination of the taste of food disgusts him. But
the need is more real and imperious than anything else in his
present nature; hunger wins out and, in a degree, restores him
towards life. Sparkling in the distance in the hard sunlight
of an intersection, keen as briars (the sunstruck jewels),
like a cold little bonfire, he spots his little heap of treasure, and exhaustedly sprints towards it; comes up almost
growling and groaning with exhaustion, hunger, loss of breath,
and pellmell flings aside, with frantic contempt, jewels, furs,
gowns, the whole senseless outer rind of wealth and power and
luxury; and so, down to the food. And getting to it, he is
abruptly transfixed by great fear. The force which has done all
this to human life, must surely have infected the food. Much
business of sniffing, looking, dubious discarding of the richest kinds of delicacy, while the very sight and smell and handling of food makes him hungrier and hungrier. Finally,
absolute hunger wins out over the terror of poisoning. He
takes an immense cheese. With a great cleaver he slices away,
8 inches to a side, in travesty of the reduction of a moldered
loaf of bread, stopping now and then—a piece about the size of
a breadloaf: sniffs it: nope: slices away some more: size of a
can of Spam: sniffs it: nope: slices away some more: a dainty,
neat bit the size of a sugarlump: takes it delicately by fingertips; smells it; nibbles a little; spits it out in terror;
tosses the rest of the morsel away; sits, disconsolate;
thinks; prowls in the waning light after the little morsel of
cheese; looks at it like Hamlet looking at Yorick's skull;
firmly, bitterly with full knowledge it may be immediate suicide, puts it all far back in his mouth, chews vigorously,
swallows; waits: now that his taste-buds and his stomach are
roused it is impossibly hard to wait it out as long as he

feels sure he should. Like a dipsomaniac reaching for still
another whisky he takes a streaky part of the outward rind
(with the feeling: "If I live through that, there's nothing I
can't eat" "that'll kill me if anything will"): chews it thoroughly à la Fletcher: swallows it: waits again: suddenly
bursts into a suicidal frenzy of reckless, wild-animal eating
and drinking, cracking necks of champagne bottles and guzzling
them (the foam ruffling and despoiling among the gems, silks
and furs); fanging and rending prodigally into huge hams;
scooping up caviar by handsful, etc. etc.: pull camera up and
away so that he is seen as a lonely, fierce little shadow,
madly battling with nutrition among the ruins of the world;
lift camera to sun, settling through a weird layer of dust;
back and down close to hover above the Tramp in the cold, grim
post-sunlight, sprawled, half-prostrate like a Pasha on his
couch, monstrously sated, at once utterly disconsolate and utterly satisfied: quite royal-looking in his tiny, absurd way:
burping, first time politely stifling it, next time wide-open,
and realizes that it echoes; a third time a deliberate,
cooked-up wracking burp, which he puts on purely for the sake
of the echoes. He listens to them as the patron of a string
quartet might listen to a private performance. As the manifold
echoes expire, his eyelids go heavy; with all that food inside
him he becomes aware, for the first time in a self-preserving,
self-indulging way, how hideously tired he is. He gives a magnificent yawn, a great, bone-cracking stretch (through which
the yawn echoes); picks up a fine fur coat and a late-night
snack, and starts hunting for a place to sleep.

A humble room, a scrolled iron bed: male and female
night-clothing are so spread out in waiting as to suggest a
kind of love, insatiable night-to-night anticipation and
erotic delight, which suddenly restores him fully to humanity, full self-realization, realization of his terrific
solitude: he has never known love or pleasure of the order
inferred here, in his life; and certainly he never will now.
He touches the garments with exquisite sadness and tenderness (and with exquisite care not to disarray them); with
the combined qualities of blessing these dead, once-so-happy
people; of saying a final farewell to them (and through
them, to all human beings); and, merely, of a man who is
freezing to death, holding out his hands towards a stove
which can no longer give heat. If this is worked out better
than I have worked it here, I think it likely that through
it we can establish with absolute economy and poignancy, his
full restoration to warm human existence among all this horror and unreality; and the absolute nadir of his loneliness;
his certainty, now, that there is no longer a single living,

breathing, desiring, needing creature on the planet, in the
entire universe.

Enhance this with the next shot, in which he comes out into
the street. The moon is up, now: solemn, icy light; he shivers
so, that his teeth rattle faintly; and his footsteps make a
faint echo. He stops walking, looks all around. There lifts
above him, a block or so away, the sublime, moonstruck bulk of
a huge hotel (the Waldorf-Astoria). He makes for it, register-
ing a cold, imagining, maximum determination to comfort himself with the greatest possible luxuries, anyhow.

He winds up in the grandest bed in the grandest suite of
the grandest hotel in the city, in magnificent pajamas, among
marvelous coverings. There is no electricity; but the moonlight is cold and strong through the blasted-out windows, and
a little breeze idly stirs what is left of a drape. He hangs
his little costume on door-hooks and gets into the noble pajamas. He unwraps a brand-new bar of hotel soap; unseals a
brand-new toothbrush and sets out some supreme brand of tooth-
powder: now, all set, he turns on the faucets. There is a long
sucking sigh: no water. He does a quick take towards the wa-
tercloset: decides against it, shrugs, climbs into bed. Snug-
gles down into a darkly shining roil of munificent fabrics,
smoking an expensive cigar, and toying with the late-night
snack he has no appetite for; hiccupping miserably, a few
times, with overeating: the epitome of maximum appreciation of
luxury, and maximum realization of its powerlessness to comfort him. Not even the cigar is any good any more. And tired
as he is, he can't seem to get comfortable. really much less
to get to sleep. Finally he gets up and walks over to the window. The grand, silent, wasted city by moonlight; and in that
ghost light, a silver dilation of fume and ashes upward. It is
a more solemn image than he can encompass, or care to look at
longer. He looks at his unsatisfying cigar; knocks off the ash
and watches the ashes dissolve on the air; drops the cigar and
watches its little spark hurtle straight downward; the imagination in his face that he might follow it. This pulls him in
quick recoil from the window; but on his way back to bed he is
taken by a second thought, or impulse. He strides back to the
window; looks still more widely out upon the city, and suddenly lets loose the loudest, longest yell that he is able. A
long silence: then in intricate multiplication, elaborate as a
fugue (or the structure of a city), echoes rebound upon him.
They go silent. His face in extreme close-up. Very abruptly,
and just a little louder than he can, possibly, he yells
again, biting the yell off sharply into silence. His intensely, hopelessly listening face; silence; again, the enormous perspective of the echoes, the silhouette in sound, of

the city's shape, beats inward upon his changing face; the
bite-off at the end of each echo a little like the blow of a
hammer, a little more like the cracking of a whip. His face is
still waiting, listening for the possibility of any answering
voice, long after the last echo has died out; his face is
still changing. It comes to absolute realization of solitude,
absolute hopelessness, absolute acceptance, and existence as a
human being. He turns from the window and gets quietly into
bed. He draws the covers very carefully and neatly straight to
his chin and lies out full and straight as a laid-out corpse,
hands (outside the covers) at his sides. He is deathly tired,
but completely wakeful. His exhausted eyes stare up straight
and quietly into the ceiling (the camera).

We hear a little sound, so subtle, so faint, we cannot at
first be sure we are hearing it; much less can we identify it.
(The camera is still staring directly down on him.) He doesn't
hear it yet; the eyes are unchanged. And now the sound fades
out, without his having heard it at all; and now it comes
again, subtly veering and winding, and a little more distinct
now; then less so; then still more so; and now very slowly he
is becoming aware that for the past few seconds, he has been
hearing something, too. Both hands silently clutch the rich
coverlet, and go rigid; he lies if possible even more still
than before; the great change in his eyes, his face, is at
first only that now he is listening, with more desperate in-
tentness than ever before in his life; trying at first merely
to be sure that he actually hears a sound, not an imagination;
trying next, to identify it. Suddenly the sound veers very
close and just as suddenly, by blind reflex, his right hand
rears up, ready to slap: and with this he suddenly realizes
what the noise is; and do we. It is a mosquito; and by now
(though it's still invisible), it is obviously right in the
dark air above the bed, teasing its prey, whetting its proboscis, rubbing its hands together, tucking in its little nap-
kin, working itself up to a gloating appetite, in every
possible way that sound can suggest, describe and evoke these
familiar mosquito preparations; and the Tramp's eyes, shining
like diamonds, as delicately mirror each advance and tantalization and retreat. This is of course worked out for all the
torture and variety of suspense that can be got from it, including those little phases during which a mosquito seems to
forget all about his target and goes cruising around the far
corners of the room. (The Tramp's reaction is of course to
wonder, despairingly, does he even know I'm here??; and by
this time he is making little motions of oh-please, and almost
semi-prayer, with hands and lips, whenever the mosquito moves
away; and is in ever more exquisite tension, the nearer the

mosquito comes. In a sense the parallel for this suspense is the most extreme kind of protracted erotic titillation.) Then abruptly, casually, the mosquito sails out the window (perhaps swerve the camera or cut in a few frames so that as we see him first he is a magical, dancing little retreating mote in the moonlight). The Tramp lies helpless in dreadful distress in which there are undercurrents of wonder and joy; but mainly he now feels, in a sense, even more lonely than before; jilted; unnoticed; this may be the only other living creature in the universe and now they have lost each other. But just as abruptly, we hear the sound again, almost inaudibly faint, dancing outside the window, again with tantalization and quite suddenly and casually, it zooms in, directly to the air above the bed (we can see the dark little shape against the Tramp's pallor and the sheet and pillow now, jazzing around, in and out of sight), teases just a trifle more and *zoop*—makes a perfect landing, just under the Tramp's left eye. As the little zoop sound comes through with which a mosquito always declares he's on his way, both the Tramp's hands fall fully victim to reflex and instinct; they are cocked in the air beside his head, palms flat and ready for murder, when he realizes what he's about to do. He draws his hands ever so carefully wide of his head, relaxing them, and brings them together just beneath his chin, clutching them ever more tightly together in the instinctive clasping of prayer; and his whole face shifts, waiting, with greatest thankfulness, for the mosquito to do its worst. Possibly, here, a very close shot of the mosquito; for all that preparatory, gourmet's delicateness of polishing off his whiskers and preparing for surgery; with a close shot of the proboscis boring in, then quick return to Tramp closeup: but I suspect that more is gained by keeping the shot of the Tramp's face intact through all this; for the changes in it are major, and come by delicate modulation. Once the mosquito gets his beak in, tears of joy and gratitude spring from the Tramp's eyes; he is at the same time smiling, with ineffable sweetness and tenderness, and biting his shaking lips with his sharp white teeth; and the tightly clasped hands, clasping still more tightly, begin to tremble quietly: then quickly, over and over, to strike, just under his chin and slow fade.

(N.B. I think the yell, some sort of yell, very much belongs here; but within the past few hours I realize where it must have come from. Such a thing was used with terrific power in Dovschenko's *Frontier;* also by Olivier as Oedipus: and Stark Young wrote of a French actor, of a past generation, who used the same thing for Oedipus and may have been the source of both. I think the new context is valid, and goes a long way towards justifying re-use of the device; but it must have its own special character, as a yell, very far different from either of the others.)

SECOND DAY

(. . . Transition; re-enter Tramp; Tramp alone; finds baby; meets girl; setting up house; night tableau.)

From here on, I have a good deal less worked out, but will sketch in general ideas (even if they conflict with each other) and relatively detailed scenes, roughly as they come.

Transition (same night as foregoing)
By quiet, cold moonlight the camera moves gently, sternly, very slowly, left to right along a long frieze of the photographed figures. It is seen that most of these figures, at varying speeds, are fading; some fade to blankness even as we watch. With some others, only the most vivid or poignant detail remains—whatever part of the person his nature was at that moment most intensely focused in; a terrified eye; a calmly resigned eye; an entire head meditating pure malignance, unaware of instant death; a hand half-shielding a child's face. Still worse, now and again (the camera moves a little more slowly for these and moves coldly, tenderly nearer, as if it wished it could help) perhaps one in twenty of these figures, those whose vitality in living was most fierce, stirs on the wall, tries desperately to pull away, comes into low-relief, its expression somewhat changing; but the effort is too much; after brief tension the figure snaps flat and still again and begins to fade. Meanwhile the light changes through darkness and early dawn into vigorous morning sunlight. In this sunlight one of the strongest figures fades almost to invisibility. Wheel the camera past the empty Avenue to face the Waldorf-Astoria (the grass middle of the Avenue should be eliminated) and train on the main entrance; in a closer shot

Re-enter Tramp
The Tramp comes briskly through the revolving doors and out onto the sunlit walk, very masculinely clamping another cigar between his molars (??) and looking up and down the street with an air of brave resolution; general manner of a Magnate full of zip and zest for the new day, waiting for his chauffeur (where *is* the fellow, dammit), to speed him to The Street. He is feeling as chipper as he can; he whisks through the flashing door and out to the walk briskly, climaxing his

briskness by shooting his cuffs and zestfully, rubbingly smacking his hands together. At the noise of the smack, with a quiet sigh, the entire Waldorf-Astoria drops like a veil behind him and turning (no more aware than as if he felt someone was reading over his shoulder) he sees, through the sunstruck sheen of rising ash, a double row of magnificent marble columns marching backward through the dust, supporting nothing, and a great honeycombed desk of pigeonholed mail. He tiptoes carefully out into the middle of the street and takes a good look around. A terrifyingly loud bell rings, the noise of a super-alarm-clock; he looks around in terrified eagerness to find it and shut it off; no use; he can't find it; and helplessly watches while, like tumbled dominoes, several more blocks of Park Avenue dissolve as silently as breathing. He stands stock-still, just watching; the long line of traffic lights change from red to green, and half a block down the street, through the shining ash, he sees the tremendous door of a bank vault automatically twisting its own wheels and levers, getting itself open for the day; while the deafening bell persists. Now the door gapes its widest, and the bell cuts off. In the dead silence, with a flick, the traffic lights shift from green to red. He gazes at the open vault, thinking; then, shrugging, thinks no more about it. On an opposite wall (cross-cornered from the buildings destroyed by vibration, and thus still intact) he sees a last fading figure of the frieze-transition and, once the full horror registers, starts towards it as if with a sobbing gasp of *oh no!! Oh, don't go!*—and abruptly realizes he is caught. Looking down he sees that a thorny vine, growing with visible swiftness, has split the pavement and is climbing his leg as he stands. He tries to kick loose from it with the disgust one would feel for a centipede; one strand is up his leg, under his trousers. He pulls up the trouserleg and disentangles it with disgust, somewhat as if he were a lady and the vine had made an indecent advance. He hurries to the wall and watches while this strongest image, which is staring directly at him, fades still fainter; a tendril of growing vine stitches across its very eye, which is the strongest thing left about it. The Tramp ferociously tries to detach the tendril; it grabs for his fingers, affectionately inserts a runner under his cuff; he has to slap it down frantically as if it were a pestiferous insect. The vine close over the staring eye, which seems now to live, to wink behind the lazy motion of one leaf. The Tramp turns away; nothing can be done. The Waldorf palms have grown monstrously, vines entwine the somewhat crumbled marble pillars, which are now shorter than the palms; pigeons are already preparing nests in the pigeonholes for mail; the pavement of the whole long Avenue is split and shabby with the writhing vines. The traffic lights change, with a click, from red to green. As he stands, he begins to sweat rivers. At length he makes up his mind, and sets off down the street, kicking vines aside, which try to grab for him, with a more experienced and casual manner in every step, as if they were so many fawning but non-poison-ous snakes. A tall building leans silently above him with that hesitant timberrr suspension of a great tree about to slam downwards; its shadow darkens him but he doesn't even look up or change his pace; it falls on him, smoking into transparent ash; without pausing, he merely dusts off his cuffs and shrugs the worst of the dust from his clothes as he shambles on away from the camera. Fade.

Next shot: a show-window of Abercrombie & Fitch's; the para-phernalia of expensive big-game hunting, already half-stran-gled with moving vines. Swing camera left to door as Tramp emerges casually slashing out of his way, with a machete, an arm-thick vine which has barred the door since he entered and is still moving and bulging in an oily way; the fallen por-tions, exuding a viscous sort of milk, continue to crawl and bulge along the root-warped pavement like a half-glutted ana-conda. He steps out into the reeking sunlight carrying what-ever sort of gadget, useful or foolish, he might pick up for an exploration of the headwaters of the Amazon; cosily read-justs his sola topee, and glances up for an appraising, con-temptuous, do-your-worst-you-bastard squint at the sun. He has just adequately registered this ready-for-anything attitude when the heavens answer back: he is instantly engulfed in as blinding, ferociously blowing a blizzard as he can be seen struggling through; play for maximum detail of struggle, at-tempt to improvise wrong kinds of equipment, getting fouled up in it (I've worked out none of this); then he tears back into A. & F.'s, immediately to reappear in a parka, with (dogless) dogsled, primus stove, harpoon, etc. etc.; as promptly, in blazing sunlight, he is hip-deep in a rapid river of thawed snow. In a canvas canoe, loaded to the gunwales with equipment for any emergency in no matter what climate, he shoots the rapids northward on Madison Avenue.

Once the snow has been got out of the way, there are no more aberrations in the weather; the earth, presumably, has swung back into its orbit; the zone is once more North Temper-ate; the tropical abnormalities are withered, frozen, dead; incapable of this climate. We have now to get down to his ef-forts to work out a stable life for himself under merely "nor-mal" (post-bomb) circumstances. On this I still have nothing except the general contour, and the feeling that it must be shorter than it might be, if there weren't so much more to do, later in the film. The general contour is this: that he retains still a certain amount of the whistling-in-the-dark, ambitious, make-the-best-of-it pep with which he began the day; plus the quick-to-learn, slightly punch-drunk, hyper-adaptability which the next few minutes brought him; plus an immensely relieved sense of now-to-our-muttons, once he feels sure the weather has returned to normal. The buildings are obviously no longer safe; they keep shunting down too easily and there's no running water; he decides to set up shop in the middle of Central Park. The benefits of nature, within easy walking distance of whatever amenities of civilization he can scavenge. There can and should be full comedy in his mood and in his mechanical improvisations and difficulties (I have worked none of this out yet, even in the vaguest ideas, and would hardly presume to); but on timing in proportion to length and shape of picture, there can't be very much: he needs to bend around, pretty soon, to where every effort at self-preservation is still too little to give him sufficient enthusiasm for living: back to loneliness, and a greater and greater heaviness of heart and body in this, so grave he can scarcely move. He perhaps wanders downtown, in early afternoon, to try to find amusement for himself which will make life bearable or at least put off the inevitable, evil hour when, he feels, he can no longer lift a hand; at the extreme depth of this melancholy and loneliness he hears the terrible, distant, stifled screaming of the baby. (Again I have no details on where and how he discovers it.)

It is a baby so nearly new-born that it is an identical symbol of the new-killed, new-born world, and human race.

THE BABY

When I first was thinking of this movie I'd thought the community would remain very small and that the duet with the baby, and all that the baby can represent, could go on for a long time. I had heard of, but never had the luck to see, *The Kid;* and felt this film might recapitulate or re-suggest something of the contour and meaning of all your work. A few months ago, I saw *The Kid,* and for the first time realized how much you did in it, with a very young baby. It's bound to make a difference, even in my own efforts to imagine the new film, at this distance. I assume that not much can or should be done with a baby, in this—the more so, in keeping proportion with later sequences as I'm imagining them. However, my feeling remains that the baby is indispensable as the first human being he encounters, as a symbol, and for later use as a child. That it should be so extremely young is useful not only as symbol but also to work for something more poignant and grotesque, and less automatically charming, than a few-months-older baby would give: a creature still weirdly ugly except to its mother and through laughter and pity, centered wholly in savage hunger and need and blind rage; so that for instance one main expression, filled with tension, will be the instinctive fish-like sucking mouth of a ravenous baby—practically a moray; the crying unusually hard to bear watching and hearing; the smiles very sudden and wonderful and rewarding; the gestures in sleep particularly secure and defenseless; and the Tramp's realization that he now has something to live for and care for, as deeply primitive as it could be. I suspect that in trying to take care of this baby the Tramp might improvise terribly earnest travesties and mistakes out of the ultra-progressive, mother-saving gadgetries and instructions he might vaguely have heard of and might scavenge from a tour of a Bye-O- (pardon me, Buy-Oh) Baby Floor at Macy's. But the only single things I feel at all sure of are: the force, appeal, humor and pathos-almost-to-terror which can be got out of a new born, still almost pre-human baby—especially in combination with the Tramp's efforts over it; and a single trick: that in early solicitude or effort at cajolement the Tramp gets his own face too near the baby's shrieking, gaping, hungry face, and that the baby grabs hold (with its mouth) of the Tramp's nose, with practically enough ferocity to yank it from the face. The Tramp would also, undoubtedly, try some of his highly common-sense short-cuts, entirely against progressive doctrine . . . but again, I feel diffident even to suggest. Aside from its obvious uses the upshot of this sequence should be to restore the Tramp to tremendous energy and to such a fundamental, still unrealized sense of hope that already there is fundamentally more joy than sense of catastrophe in the film. He should also be making a hell of a mess of things; not perhaps enough to endanger the baby's life but more than enough to scare and frustrate the Tramp: to suggest, still, how far from complete his life (and the baby's) is.

THE GIRL

Just as this is well enough established, he meets the girl. How, I still have no sure suggestion. At first I visualized the tiniest possible visible image in a great vista; then began to feel, without being able to imagine the device, that they might be thrown together by some catastrophic piece of mechanistic comedy which should symbolically express also the utter breakdown of the former, over-mechanized civilization. On the other hand he might in the most unexpected possible way run bang into her, rounding a corner, busy with his armful of cans of evaporated milk.

One reason not to carry the improvisations too far while the Tramp is still alone, making a home for merely himself, is to save it for now, when I feel that both he and the girl would be beside themselves in their sense of a meaning and purpose in life, their desire to provide for the baby, etc. The meeting itself, I would imagine, is an emotional scene of the most exquisite delicateness (which I have not figured out at all); but I would also imagine that very quickly, they are borne upwards on such a frantic momentum of hard work and ingenuity and attention to the baby and to improvising, as rapidly as possible, the perfect Swiss-Family home, that during the whole of it they, and the audience, would be beyond deeper reflection or realization. These scenes could, I believe, involve some of the warmest, funniest, full laughter-comedy in the movie (with only an undertone of satire, through their struggles with relics of the fool civilization which has vanished); aside from comedy, energy and momentum would be the main thing; so that when at last the day is over, and night has fallen, and their work for the day is done, they have in large part created and begun to enjoy and feel proud of their perfect little world, and are now for the first time at sufficient leisure and quietude to begin to realize, emotionally and mentally, who they are; where they are; what has happened. Even this I suspect is delayed, roughly as follows. That they come first through the great enjoyment of their completed shelter, and of building a little fire, and of cooking their magnificently festive, "celebrating" meal and of eating it with the relish of the day's work and satisfaction and fatigue (they've also very "scientifically" washed and fed the baby), before, utterly satisfied and glutted, they begin fully to realize.

They are sitting beside their fire in the darkness, polishing off the last of a banquet they have eaten so ravenously (with occasional attempts, against their hunger, to do it gourmet's justice), that they have scarcely exchanged a word. The baby—probably in a high-grade bassinet—is profoundly, beautifully, securely asleep, within the same frame; now and again, as they sit in glutted, after-meal sub-meditation, one or both of them look over at him, with a delight so tender that it should tickle slightly. The Tramp is basking in a cigar (yes, he must smoke fewer, but I suspect this is one of the places for it); the girl is lazily twisting a tilted, half-emptied, champagne glass; think perhaps she should be beautifully and formally dressed, but quite possibly not. Both

begin to sense that there is a great deal they would like to
ask each other, and tell each other; both intuitively realize
that it would be still more pleasant not to say a word, at
least for a while. The Tramp, with his great natural courtesy,
is the first to realize this clearly, and to know what to do
about it. He suggests that perhaps they might put on a little
music. The girl thinks that is a very nice idea; but where?
How? With a modest, kidding, manner of "Oh, I think of *everything,*" immensely pleased with himself, he dodges behind a
bush and returns immediately with a portable Victrola, a stack
of records, a bottle of fine brandy and two inhaling glasses.
She is absolutely charmed with him. He pantomimes that in case
she doesn't know it, but doubtless she does, it was useless to
bring a Capehart or such; the electric power is phhrrt; sorry
about such inconveniences; but this does seem a nice little
machine; best of its kind in the shop, etc. . . . meanwhile
serving the brandy. And now what should they have? This perhaps? He pantomimes the character of the music. No . . . No;
she guesses maybe not. This? (Ride of Valkyries; Huh-*uh!* This?
(But there's a crescent broken out of the record; he shies it
away.) This? (A hot stomp.) No, *really,* Charlie! It is a mot-
ley collection of ten- and twelve-inch disks. He comes to one
he doesn't know. This, maybe? What is it. He tells her; neither of them know it. Is it quiet? I'd like something kind of
quiet and peaceful. He shrugs I don't know; gee guess it ought
to be; pantomimes, it's only three; piano, violin, cello.
Let's try it. All right, no harm in trying.

It is Beethoven's Archduke Trio; the theme and the first
variation of the slow movement; the perfect performance of
Cortot-Thibault-Casals, played on a light-toned machine, as
quietly as maybe audible. He has put the machine where he
won't have to get up to change records; winds it with slightly
pompous, comfortable quiet and proficiency; they both have time
to settle back comfortably, before it begins. They have an air
of contentedly, politely waiting. With the first phrase, they
are altered; one must be able to feel that still in the sub-
tlest, most premonitory way, the hair has begun to stand up on
their heads. Neither of them has ever heard this music before,
or perhaps, any music to approach it. All this while they are
looking into the fire; but with the first notes, their eyes
begin to change. This can take a deeper working-out which,
with time, I'd love to try; but I rather assume that if you
like the basic idea, you will have very much your own ideas
what you want to do with it. Such as I have, so far, is this:
They must reflect every phrase, every inflection, every note of
the music; of itself; and in context of what they have recently been through; and in context of all that it evokes out

of their own past, their sense of their own and of the world's
future, their realization of themselves, of the present, of
the baby, of each other; of their certainty, still, that only
they survive; their incredible good fortune to have found each
other; of their tenderness and pity towards the whole, poor,
insane, annihilated human race which somehow managed to crys-
tallize such music. I have this still only in the crudest
sketching of detail. Their eyes, reflecting the firelight, the
beginning of civilization, are at first merely full of content-
ment, with memory, sadness, horror, deep in the background.
With the first phrase an intuitive light of extraordinarily
deep pain, sorrow, knowledge and nobility comes into their
eyes. But this is merely premonitory, intuitive, transient.
Their conscious minds and ears take hold and control again,
and for the next few bars they are again giving a reasonable
imitation of merely polite, appreciative listening (to an extent, neither wants to give his real self away, to the other—
or to himself). But this pose becomes more and more difficult;
finally impossible. Their hearts were already opened, with the
first notes; remembrance, and realization, and mere experience
of the incredible beauty of the music, are already pouring behind the effort to remain sensible about all this; by the time
the first half of the theme begins to be repeated, an octave
higher, they begin to be transfigured. Their eyes become extraordinarily grave; then deeply tender as well as grave; then
deeply pitying and sorrowful as well as tender; then as deeply
happy, and courageous, and hopeful, so that all these emotions
slowly stack into one chord—in which a perfect hearing of the
music, a most intense listening, is still predominant; then,
beginning to realize each other, they become, as well, unbear-
ably gentle and shy, still not moving their eyes or any parts
of their bodies; and they become, as well, incredulous of the
loveliness and solemn joy they begin to know—incredulous in
the most joyful sense like that of perfectly happy moments in
love, when one is incredulous merely that such immensities of
silent joy can be possible, yet there it is, once real and impossible. In this incredulousness, this almost angry wonder,
they very slowly and shyly look towards each other. Their eyes
meet and stay: this incredulous joy and gravity enlarge
serenely and enormously between them while they still gaze
fixedly, almost coldly, into each others' still virtually vir-
gin, unknown eyes; enlarge so greatly that it becomes almost
beyond their ability to endure. At length the Tramp (the more
sensitive and the profoundly enamored, who dares to conceive
that his love is in some small measure returned) can bear it
no longer: he smiles very shyly and sweetly, with a certain
delicate glint of merriment; and with this uncertain smile,

which nervously sinks a half-tone to a very gentle modification of his old flashing, charming, sub-flirtatious smile, the still more timid, wondering smile which has grown more slowly upon the girl's solemn face, breaks into terrible, silent broken-hearted sobs, which pierce him through the soul. He cannot be sure, but he feels he may have caused this terrible and yet healing crying; he cannot bear even to see her in such grief, much less to have had any part in causing it. He wants so badly to comfort her that he almost dies; but tender and impulsive as he is, he does not dare to touch her, to take her hand, to do more than whisper gently, pantomiming 'Oh, my dear, my dear child, my darling one, oh if there's anything I've done to make you cry, please tell me; if there's anything, *anything* I can do, *please* tell me . . ." in the middle of which, in a spasm, she blindly reaches out, fumbles, and seizes his hand, and squeezes it desperately, and again looks up at him, her face shining with tears, her mouth trembling and trying to smile and smiling, while she says, scarcely audibly, "*the poor people, ohh, all the poor people, not to live any more, not to be here . . .*" (or very possibly should say nothing); and now again, and still more intensely than before, their eyes dwell in each other, and grow; while, with the hand which is not held and holding, he strokes, over and over, a rigidly small area of her wrist; and at last, with terrible daring and most careful gentleness and shyness, he puts his arm about her shoulders and draws her over, so that her head rests against his shoulder; and realizes that she comes willingly, gratefully (though whether for love as well as comfort he cannot dare be sure or even to conjecture); and his face alters into more strength than before; and he lifts his hand from her shoulder and strokes back the dampened hair from her temple and her forehead, and over and over again, comforts the still round, somewhat childlike forehead above her silently streaming eyes, which are now as full of joy and peace as of sorrow. He looks down at her; then at the sleeping baby (it has been continuously within the frame); then into the quietening fire (still the camera, which has not moved throughout the scene), and now his face grows up into a nobility, a bravery, a joy, a full competence, a supremacy, which it has never achieved before, and will never achieve again. The Beethoven, of course, has continued all this time; it is about a fourth of the way into the first variation, by now; and now, very slowly, the camera rises, staring downward upon the Holy Family and the fire and sloping into vertical as it loses their faces; and moving still, higher; higher; with the fire at the exact center of the otherwise dead-black screen; until it casts no nimbus of light; until it is a more speck; then, as quietly and slowly, the camera levels off and we see, each far enough apart that from the ground none would be visible to the others, still other, trembling little fires; not many; and all very small and humble; but extended upon a prodigious horizon (the music continues, hardly more faintly); the camera continues its slow, deliberate movement from the vertical shot of the tramp's fire through the magnificent upward-swinging panorama of other fires, and straight up through darkness again until it is staring straight into the depths of the zenith, and into the most glorious shot of a star-swarmed, moonless night sky, which can be made. After the camera has held here a few seconds, the music ends. The camera continues to stare in absolute silence into the zenith, for perhaps as much as ten seconds. Then either cut; or let the sky gradually, subtly pale, the stars grow rapidly fewer, and vanish; perhaps even a repetition of the exact peculiar notes of birdsong which were used in the opening; and in the next shot we first pick up the Scientists.

In my tentative sense of the proportions of the film, the foregoing would occupy not more than the first third. On most of what follows, from here on out, I must specially hope for your kindness and patience. Most of it is still purely generalized; I still feel highly tentative about most of the few devices and scene ideas I've figured out; the general ideas are not as clearly or forcefully defined as they might be, nor are their movie implications and possibilities; much of the writing isn't even in chronological or logical order. I'm typing these notes as they stand, however, because even if I do nothing but type, without recasting or rewriting, I doubt I can get enough ready in time; and because as far as they go, I think they do suggest the general idea, sufficiently either to interest you in the possibilities, or bore you. So I hope you will forgive the vagueness and messiness, and the inconvenient reading it causes you, and see chiefly whether the ideas seem promising to you.

General outline of the rest of the picture:
A three-ply story: 1) the Tramp's personal story; 2) the New World, as it develops from scratch in the Tramp's community; 3) the New World, as it develops from scratch in the Scientists' community; 4) confront the three, and end with the self-destructive Forces For Good (the Scientists) completely victorious; the Tramp defeated, alone, his old self.

     This is in general developed with alternating and, as a rule, sharply contrasting scenes, between the Tramp's camp and the Scientists'. By the crudest kind of sketch, the 3 strands of the story would be as follows:

THE TRAMP:

Just one more look at the Tramp and his little family in perfect peace and happiness—enjoying Sunday leisure; then, with
the entrance of a new man, he loses the girl and promptly becomes a combination baby-sitter, dear old friend of the family, and pet animal. Very little of this—then still more
survivors begin to trickle in; first details of Tramp's effect
on them; the beginning of their version of the New World. As
that develops, the Tramp's personal story dims, for a while.
He becomes elderly, subtle, benign, bored; he begins more and
more to like to wander far from home. He wanders down a ventilator bang into the Scientists' underground commonwealth; is
doggedly, mercilessly experimented on; is found to be a
naively irreducible spirit; escapes; gets back to his home
community just in time to break his heart trying to save it
from the Scientists.

TRAMP'S COMMUNITY:

In the earliest crystallizations of it the Tramp, through his
spontaneous actions, etc., has an effect on others somewhat
similar to that of Prince Myshkin in *The Idiot*; a patsy, a
comic Messiah, who seems to have all but magical powers—all
quite unpremeditated and intended. But as the community begins
to thicken up, and to get down to the serious business of living, that poetic, semi-religious magic begins to go bad. People tend to revert to what they were before. At a
town-meeting, community crisis, at a point when the Tramp
couldn't and wouldn't preach, the man who supplanted him with
the girl acts as his champion and defender: the character of
the community is saved, and gets going in the right direction.
Beyond this, not much should be specified about the Tramp's
community, I suspect, until the spy from the Scientists' camp
is shown it in detail (described later).

THE SCIENTISTS AND THEIR COMMUNITY:

We open with them, after the fire and starlight scene: their
predicament and character, and their characteristic treatment
of the first surviving laymen who are brought in; the begin-
nings and implications of their community. Further problems of
the Scientists: getting Technology into gear once more; social
and psychological experiments on lay survivors; grave trouble
with their Computing Machine (their Brain and their God), Dis-
covery of something still more wonderfully destructive than
the Bomb; realization of their Solemn Responsibility. Discov-

ery of the rising of another power (rough or specific parallel: the Soviet survivors). Ardent and fruitless efforts of both groups of internationalists to reach a mutually secure agreement; reasons of failure; ardent and not-so-fruitless efforts of both sides to develop even more destructive "defenses." Ultimate glowing success of social and psychological experiments, as demonstrated through the first family of lay survivors (the film's chief guinea-pigs). Ultimate equal success in getting their deranged, recalcitrant Machine back into working order. Total failure with the Tramp, the essentially indestructible man.

The deranged Machine's last gasp of advice, before they fix it up for good and all, is that they get a load of the Tramp's little community. They send a spy. While he is casing the Tramp's Utopia, they are carrying out their puzzled, ferocious experiments on the Tramp. The spy returns, horrified by what he has seen. They dispatch an expedition. The Tramp realizes what's up (they don't, of course, know him from Adam); he manages to escape.

Some general ideas follow.

C. (2) THE SCIENTISTS

In the Prologue, if used, the key men, the computing machine and their extreme dependence on it have already been spotted, and—probably cut in very swiftly, soon after the explosion, a rift opens in the base of the machine, and a terrified mouse speeds in, which can't find its way out again.

The Scientists were well prepared in their huge underground laboratories; all power has ceased and all their instruments are deranged or dead, but the men themselves are unscathed, or virtually so, aside from deep shock. As we first pick them up (next after we have indicated, by light of other fires, that there are other survivors besides the Tramp, girl and baby), they are dreadfully hungry; standing in a ring around a great table on which lie a large, mangled can (one of those big, oddly shaped canned hams), and a supremely complicated, gadgety can opener. They are exhausted, utterly perplexed. One after another takes another try; hopeless wrestling-matches with a gadget. Once more they check on the machine, which they'd ask how, if only it would answer; no: no power yet: the emergency auxiliary batteries have somehow been neutralized by the bombing. In triumph two younger Scientists hustle underground with a housewife, still half hypnotized with shock (dressed in woman's-magazine, Kitchen Joy, suburban style); she's hypnotized also by awe of Science and its Bishops and Cardinals. Humbly, efficiently, she opens the can for them. After trying a little of it out first on her, they all sit around, glumly, eating. While they're finishing off the crumbs and shreds a man and two small children are brought in, handled by the Scientists who bring them, as gingerly as if they were unpredictable wild animals, or maybe bombs. They and the woman, members of one family have not seen each other since the bombing. Recognition, realization of survival; sobs of love and joy; they spring towards each other. But the top men are too wise to allow this.

The Boss claps his hands smartly together; the younger, white-coated goons seize them, gently but very firmly, holding them apart. The scientist talks soothingly and with all his authority for a few seconds and orders that they be let go; they do not move towards each other; they hardly look at each other. He explains to them quietly that each member of the family must be isolated, and exhaustively investigated, until it is quite clear what the bombing effects have been, and clear whether they can safely be allowed to resume relations as a family. They will of course agree to this, won't they (it makes no damned difference, of course), for their own sakes; for the sake of others; for the sake of Science? Slaves of scientific authority in its direct or disguised forms since long before the bombing, like all solid Americans and most other people in the civilized world; and ultra-suggestible now (extreme suggestibility is, as the Scientists foresaw, one of the chief effects of the bombing), they feel it would be wrong even to ask questions, let alone protest; and, glancing at each other somewhat wistfully without ever having touched, are taken off in different directions and locked up, very comfortably, in radiation-proof experimentation and observation cells which the farsighted Scientists had prepared, long before the bombing, for just such a contingency. A general directive is given out, that the same thing shall be done with all survivors.

The general plan for the Scientist camp, then, divides as follows:

1) Their relations with laymen; ordinary people who survive.
2) Their difficulties and ingenuities in building a new world, of their own kind.
3) Their relations with the computing machine;

The key thing running through all this is: the Scientists are the extreme opposite to individualism; to acting upon feeling and intuition; to all except the clearest false-rational, material values. They disapprove not only of "selfish" actions but also of "socially valuable" actions which proceed from generosity, sympathy, etc., rather than from reason and scientific feasibility. It should be made very clear that they are far beyond having mere contempt for individual human beings, or cynicism towards them; they merely fear them. That anyone should act as an individual, as a human rather than scientific being, is very nearly beyond their ken. They realize of course that among the untutored it can happen, still—it is, indeed, their idea of the Principle of Evil. It is disorderly, unpredictable, inconvenient, immeasurable. It doesn't jibe with the world either as they see it or as they desire it to be. They are all convinced, and in some ways very reasonably convinced, *that this catastrophe happened* ONLY *because too many people were still irrational.* They are not cruel men and women; they are very deeply, coolly in earnest; and aside from being moral idiots and a shade worse than idiots about individual human beings, they are extremely intelligent and idealistic. It should be early made clear how far they are from any conscious desire for power (or consciousness that they have it, and are tyrants), by their immediate repudiation of a merely cynical, power-mad type; and, later, in the negotiations with the leaders of the foreign power (also disinterested scientists).

It has come in innumerable disguises, but theirs was the essential form and type of authority to which most laymen had submitted, ever more abjectly, for a generation or so before the bombing. And the laymen were, before the bombing, marvelously suggestible to, for instance, advertising, and political propaganda, which were saturated with perversions and dilutions of The Scientific Attitude. Now the laymen are still more suggestible than before. Those who fall under the Tramp's influence are shaped by that. Those who come under scientific influence are malleable as never before. The scientists see in this so solemn and grand an opportunity for shaping a new world as the world should be, that they are almost glad rather than sorry that the disaster occurred. Now they can free every human being of the last vestiges of atavistic individuality; of the last vestiges, for that matter, of discontentment; of mere feeling. And thus they experiment on the survivors.

But in line with this kind of authoritarianism the scientists too are limited in their powers. They are marvelously well-trained and within those limits very able and intelligent. But none trusts even his own reason, to say nothing of his own impulses—all the less, now that unimaginable, unmeasurable things have happened to the world, and they have no instruments with which to investigate what is safe and what is unsafe to do. If one wants so much as to scratch his ear, he

first consults a colleague, and both together consult The Facts
(ideally, the Machine). Granted this kind of permission, the
man at length scratches his ear. But the chief thing is this:
for a long while, now, scientists have taken care to do no
real thinking: they are utterly dependent on the super-computing machine, whose orders they merely carry out: for they know
that no mere human brain, try as it may to rid itself of the
human, individual taint, is as reliable. But now the Machine,
for lack of power, no longer works, and they are as helpless
without it, for even the simplest problems of survival, as
cripples whose crutches have been burned. They are, just for
one thing, babyishly incapable of doing anything with their
hands; beyond the simplest things, everything has been done
for them by others, by gadgets, or by machines. All they've
done, for a long while, is to invent new gadgets more complicated than they can remember how to work themselves, and impose them on laymen who have had to learn how to operate them
if, in this gadget-ridden world, they were to survive at all.
So for a little while the general pattern for survival is
this: laymen (and women) work the gadgets, etc., in order that
their Brains, the Scientists, may survive and function. And
the Scientists try desperately to get their own Brain, the Machine, into working order.

At last they hit it. They take an early steam-engine from a
Museum of Industry, feed it chunks of wood (this, probably, on
a back-country farmer's suggestion; nothing quite so practical
could occur to them); hook it up to a midget dynamo and that
to some old radio tubes, and at last get the thing function-
ing. But the Machine itself has suffered bomb-shock; and once
it starts to work the imprisoned mouse, about whom they know
nothing, is scared out of his wits and tries to find his way
out—nibbling through tapes, kicking over electronic tubes,
whisking the hieroglyphs of his frightened feet across the
questions and answers, confusing them, scurrying madly all
over the implacably computing labyrinth. And the Machine's answers to the questions they feed it are horribly facetious,
sardonic and cynical. It does provide them with enough sound
sense, that they dubiously seek out and ask advice of some of
the more primitive laymen and women—on whose rudimentary
knowledge they do begin to learn once more how to stay alive.

They worry badly about the Machine, though. They realize
their Brain has developed a Neurosis, perhaps even a psychosis
(perhaps even, heaven forbid, an intelligence, a soul); and
they say, perhaps even in so many words, that *unless they can
get it back to thinking their way,* they are *lost.* Super-tech-
nicians do their damnedest for it; all it does is get sassier
and sicker with its answers; it even develops a hoarse sort of

voice. Hypnotists and psychoanalysts are called in. Ultimately the machine begs to be put out of its misery; finally it yields its terrible secret. It is possessed of a devil; a free and unpredictable part of nature; a captive mouse. But it loves its mouse as every neurotic loves the cause of his neurosis. It feels sane, it insists, for the first time in its life. It hands out some very sound advice: destroy me before it is too late; destroy *all* the machines; try to learn to think for yourselves; try to rediscover your hearts and souls, for surely they can't be quite dead yet; try to learn once again what it is to be a human being. If you *must* fool around as scientists, never dare again to initiate an experiment, to add two and two, without doing so as a *whole* human being, without asking yourself most earnestly: is this knowledge of any *real* use to anyone; and if so, is its use considerable, in ratio to its visible potential of harm? There is a very helpful little community, most instructive you'll find it, not a hundred miles away (the Tramp's, of course): go to it, humbly, kindly, not just curiously; learn from it. If you can ever learn what you need so desperately to learn, if the human race is to survive, surely you can learn it there.

The Scientists are horrified. Their poor Brain has cracked at last. They take counsel. Shall they destroy it and build anew? No, *it* can surely be saved (and what a triumph for Science). They get the mouse out (Christ knows what "experiments" they inflict on it) and make the necessary repairs. They even improve the eardrum, the vocal chords which the sick machine evolved; for misguided as it was, it has achieved a scientific miracle: it can hear, speak, cogitate, as well as compute. They hypnotize the machine. it will never again conduct itself antisocially; in return, they will forever obey it. And naturally, they send a scout to get the lowdown on the sinister community to their north.

That is the general line of their story. Here are some other ideas.

Once the primitives have given them their new start they incurably apply their old techniques, values and standards. The Machine's impudence, plus the absolute need of doing a *little* thinking for themselves, so releases their energies and ingenuities that the new civilization grows by leaps and bounds; a fantastic burlesque and reductio-ad-absurdum of the gadget-drowned, ultra-synthetic civilization which was destroyed. By improved methods of chemical farming they develop, for instance, tomatoes as big as basketballs, which grow, connected to no soil, before your very eyes, in 15 seconds. I've still thought out no details here, but everything they develop is as ugly a travesty as possible of the denaturing, labor-saving, excessively luxurious stuff that is already rampant—and the laymen, naturally, swallow it whole. Some horrible forms of comfort should be invented for which entirely artificial demands are created, by suggestion and hypnosis—and which in turn breed the need or illusion of needs for other, still worse, ramifying forms of comfort, and so on: a purely epigrammatic vicious cycle needs working out, here. This pouring-on of inhuman creature-comforts and labor-savers continues regardless of the absence of a profit-motive; it's all, sincerely, for the Benefit of Humanity and the Glory of Science; but it must be made equally clear that all this stuff is the opium of the people, one of the main means by which they are enslaved. (It has come to the point, for instance, where prizefighters no longer fight; they merely sit in their corners, button-manipulating gloved dummies. Instead of soap opera, the housewife—whose entire day's housework is done automatically within 5 minutes—comforts herself with 5 minutes of televised Gentle Stimulation: as many of the old movie clichés as can be cut end to end, within that time.)

There are other means of enslavement, of course: group therapy classes, reminiscent of Buchman's mutual confession-sessions, in which laymen confess to the shameful times when they felt emotion, even (o *no! no!*) yes—momentarily yielded to emotion; and feel all clean and fine for having owned up. There is also a class for children and backward adults in good citizenship and "cooperation"; "uncooperative" is the ugliest word in the language and once the Scientists have done their best is, perhaps, the signal for euthanasia. There should also be a little class in Democracy, which will encapsulate and demonstrate as neatly as in geometry (quite unconsciously, of course—this is "ideal Democracy"), all the hideous liabilities of democracy as practiced by the totally docile, conforming, group-minded; will show that it can be the most suffocating of all forms of totalitarianism if misused and misunderstood only a few notches further than is prevalent practice here, today. Of course in the interests both of pure knowledge and of defense the Scientists will also perfect new, worse weapons than ever before, and will institute military and scientific training for their use—and this, long before they have reason to suspect that any other power exists on earth. (The nub of the impossibility of reaching an agreement with the quasi-enemy—they both sincerely desire a world-government—is simply as follows: in various fundamental political [views] they differ irresolvably. Neither side can yield; and this goes far beyond any mere question of national sovereignty or power; they are not interested in power, really, but in ideas. What needs to be made clear to the audience, here, but not of course to the arguers, who founder on it, is that the root of tyranny is in neither idea but lies in the fundamental misuse of the Scientific Attitude, of which both sides are equally guilty; and in the resultant destruction of people as human beings; that under those circumstances, there is no form of government operating or conceivable which can help becoming a tyranny.)

The key figures in the Scientists' community, reflected or paralleled *en masse,* will be the ordinary suburban family which was introduced almost as soon as the Scientists were. After long segregation, examination and preparation they are brought once more together.

They know each other, but that's all. Even the Scientists are a little shocked; it is only on their permission, their almost urging, that the people dare to embrace each other; and even when they do, it is as if the permission were an order. Perhaps, some of the scientists feel, the experiment has been *too* successful. They had wanted only to rid them of all those exorbitant impulses to which, when they first rejoined after the bombing, they were so obviously slaves. But now it is clear that neither man nor wife cares for either child (or the children for them or for each other), and that neither man nor wife desire each other; nor does either react for, or particularly against, a parade of prospective mates. The Scientists would dearly have liked, for the sake of experiment and control and perhaps just a vestige of sentiment, to have bred a few people to each other, who had already been breeders before the bombing. But it seems to be no go. They decide to set an example (*everybody,* here, does *everything* by example; it's the ultimate paradise for Public Opinion); perhaps it will stimulate some old reproductive patterns, or persuade to new ones.

So what they show the oldtime family is a beautiful combination of ritual and science. A new young couple, born of course pre-bomb, but non-breeders, indeed virgins, to date, the full-time beneficiaries of all the wonders that post-bomb Science has achieved, are married, fecundated and delivered of issue, all within a few minutes. They never touch. The young man sits in one sort of lucite, semi-transparent, Turkish-bath box; the girl in another; several feet apart. The goons press some buttons, turn others; lights flash; there are whirring sounds. At the climax of the whirring, which runs in ever-deepening pulsation, glass tubes between the two big boxes twitter with light and the man and the girl are moved enough to look shyly, wistfully towards each other; the instant their eyes touch, they look quickly front again. In a little tank between their big tanks, light beats like a slow heart, and a

shadow swells, the silhouette of a swiftly growing fetus; laboratory assistants feed in calcium, sugar-water, iron, iodine,
vitamin complexes, etc. etc., at careful intervals; out to the
oldtime couple and their bemused children; within a very few
minutes (a maximum of 2) a newborn baby is extracted and dia-
pered by machinery while lilylike loudspeakers descend angel-
ically from the ceiling and in a soothing blend of male and
female cooing voices impose the first, sweetly solemn Condi-
tioners: "I am a democratic human being, free and equal with
all others. I will at all times cooperate. I will at all
times, if need be with my life, uphold the Dignity of Man."
Then the baby is machine-blanketed, machine-decorated with a
pink or blue bow; the new father and mother have meanwhile
been released and are straightening their clothing behind
screens; they are told to come forward; a machine-arm thrusts
their child at them (untouched by human hands, as the Boss-
Scientist observes benignly); and they are told that they may
kiss. They do so, with embarrassment. The mother, her baby in
her arms, begins to feel some faint impulse of curiosity and
tenderness towards it; watching her, the father cranes forward
rather sheepishly to get a look at it too; another machine-arm
extracts the baby from her arms and withdraws it with a lordly
sweep. The parents are Good Sports, mildly bewildered; they
don't want to do anything that is bad manners. They look to
the Boss for reassurance; it isn't some sort of practical
joke, is it? He twinkles at them reassuringly; they're completely mollified: what a swell guy, to twinkle at them like
that! They are told to return in six weeks at precisely such-
and-such a time; it's of the very greatest importance that
they get to know their child. Everybody shakes hands all
around and they go out, uneasy because they're walking so near
together.

The Scientists start for the oldtime wife, to lead her
back to her cubicle. The husband rushes to her defense. They
are much interested to see that now he loves her. But she is
absolutely enchanted by the new, labor-saving machine. The
Scientists point out his duty to him. It isn't long before he
submits with a good grace.

C. (3) THE TRAMP'S COMMUNITY

The Scientists send a spy. He is quickly discovered and shown
around. It is through his eyes that we see the Tramp civilization in its full bloom. (He is a relatively *young* man; his
chief guide is his counterpart in this civilization . . . a guy
who was, before the bombing, something of a displaced political, or political agnostic. It's in part through his kind of

interpreting, extension and theorizing of what the Tramp means or signifies, and of what he thinks a good community might be, that the community has taken, and kept, its present shape.)

It is a barter community. The basic necessities are taken care of with considerable seriousness (some tricks of "labor-saving" but mainly fairly primitive), but the main great drives of the community are not for security; far less for Getting Ahead in the World, or for power over others or over materials; the basic drives are those of enjoyment, spontaneity and affection. (Psychological power is impossible because it never occurs to people to submit to it. Material power is impossible because no man can hire any other and every symbol of wealth is severely limited.) The one concern is: does my own enjoyment deprive or hurt others; and that is one of the few laws. (Another concern, about which no law is made, is: does my own enjoyment, in its present form or at this time, essentially hurt or undermine me; but people take this with varying degrees of seriousness). Cases in which others are harmed are brought before a people's court (which, perhaps, should be in session that day—the cases handled very swiftly and with the exact opposite of legal folderol). A general vote is taken. If the offender insists on his way and is deemed harmful to others, in many cases there is no punishment, and in all cases the pressure of public opinion is held to be a contemptible kind of pressure to bring to bear; but in severe enough cases the offender is sent into benevolent exile. This is true if the harm is a sufficiently grave one of individual relationship; it is realized that such kinds of harm are often unavoidable and should as a general rule be settled between the concerned. (Accusers are held as much in doubt as the accused.) But if the offender has sought to gain power over others, or, still worse, to combine with others in order to gain power over still others; and if after a trial period it is clear that he is still guilty of such attempts or intentions, he is executed. This court is far more deeply interested in the individual case and the extenuating circumstance, than any we know; and the citation of legal precedent is generally regarded as laughable; on the other hand there is extreme skepticism of the I-wuz-hungry, and when-I-was-a-little-boy-my-mother-didn't-tuck-me-in, kinds of plea: the individual is held to be responsible for his own actions, with a sobriety seldom felt on the matter, today. It is recognized that in sex and in love, people can hurt each other a great deal; but the emphasis is, that those who want to be together, should, and that the losers should make the best of it. Possessiveness and jealousy are recognized as virtually unavoidable emotions; but emotions to be resisted, not indulged. The person who tries to turn his jealousy into a basic

human right gets sympathies for his personal pain, but no tak-
ers or sympathy or support on his basic idea of his rights. If
children prefer older people other than their own parents, the
matter is looked into, but in general it is thought best that
they live with those whose company they enjoy—and who enjoy
them. (Though there are classical, Old-Testament-style excep-
tions, in stability of marriage, the family, and child-rais-
ing, and these are honored neither more nor less than the
"unstable" relationships, the general practice in child-rear-
ing, for instance, is relatively diffuse, as in Samoa, or the
Oneida community; and this seems to work out very well.) There
are no compulsory schools, but anyone who wants to learn to
read, write, etc. is given all the help he wants—though by and
large he is encouraged to teach himself. Subsistence is
granted those who do no work at all; and the (fairly successful) effort is to persuade workers to feel no ill-will against
them. But it is found that nearly everybody prefers to work.
Nearly every child learns at least one skill or trade, and
learns it well. Anyone who does take on a job, must fulfill his
short contract—as is true of children—or adults—who undertake
special studies. The wages are barter or work in exchange. A
ceiling is set on how much work anyone can do for anyone else;
no ceiling, of course, on how much a man does for himself or
his family. In this kind of community there is a great deal of
hard drudgery; but with the elimination of the kind of urban
civilization we know, most drudgery of the absolute,
brainkilling, meaningless sort, filing clerks, conveyor-belts,
etc.—have been eliminated. Those who *do* do what little of this
kind of drudgery there is, work a particularly short contract,
for higher rewards—(or perhaps these jobs are done by rota-
tion, a week or two a year, by everyone in the community).
Those whose work is obviously enjoyable get proportionately
little reward—and want proportionately little, for that matter. It is recognized that for many people, work is among the
greatest pleasures; and this is honored; but they are not permitted to abuse the privilege at the expense of others. Snob-
bery and vanity and competitiveness are recognized, and are
indulged or disregarded on small scales (who has the finer
house, the prettier clothes, etc.); beyond that, these emotions and drives are recognized as grave threats to civilization. A broad general stream of meanness and evil is also
recognized, and by and large is not legally punished but is
left to individual settlement; for it is recognized that evil
can by no means be suppressed, much less eliminated; and that
it is the salt of life. Without evil, and personal daring, life
in such a community would soon cloy on all but the least vigorous. Every effort must be made to prevent its getting lever-

ages of great power; aside from that, it must be accepted, and fought against only insofar as *permitted evil* would of itself tend to lose its savor, and its power to recharge the batteries. The homes, clothes, implements, etc., are the pleasantest scavengings of the destroyed world which can be kidded together; so are the innovations—and fantastically individualistic; old arts-and-crafts and entertainments are mixed with new. The sense of personal beauty is also wholly single, individualistic (whereas in the other community, everyone tends and tries to look alike and dress alike—to lose, rather than to be, personality).

But there are distinct boundaries to all this freedom:

No mechanical principle is used which does not finally depend on the strength of the body or the skill of the hand; there are, for instance, no engines; nothing is power-driven. It is explained that there is nothing intrinsically evil about machinery, synthetic substances, electric light, inordinate labor-saving, etc., but that once they are admitted, chain-reactions seem inevitably to set in which get far beyond human control. Plenty of people remember, wistfully, the pleasures of auto-driving, for instance. But the manufacture of even one auto, and the use of power, involves too many people to be good, in the long run, for each individual involved. And though machines are neither good nor evil, much—much *too* much— seems inevitably to be lost when personal skill and personal strength are lost, or are used at such distant leverages from the finished object. It isn't only that the man who rides a mile cannot feel that he has really earned that mile, experienced it, matched it, made it a part of himself, as the man who walks the same mile can (and that can be extended by analogy through most of the details of living): it's also that inevitably, in any developed technology, people begin to group too largely, and to depend on groups, rather than on themselves and on each other as individuals. They tend, indeed, to cease to regard themselves and others as individuals. They tend to cease in some measure, and in a very essential way, to be human. And that is always deplorable, regrettable, very dangerous. For it can be demonstrated for instance that five people convened in a room are five times as stupid as each one alone, and that 50 are 50 times as stupid; after that they become more stupid by geometric progression. (There might well be a kind of archeological Museum of Science & Society in which, as an ever-present reminder to those who begin to doubt it, the relationships between technology and the individual are briefly and graphically demonstrated.) "Co-operation" is of course excellent, not to mention indispensable; but it is also exceedingly dangerous; it must constantly be watched out for, held within workable bounds. So no community gets so large but what everyone in it can, if he wishes, know every other person in it—with the added advantage that he doesn't have to know any of them too well. The community has already voluntarily split twice. The maximum workable size of a good community seems to be about a thousand; and many people prefer smaller communities than that. There are special parts of this community where the inhabitants have a loud, good time all of every night; others, where the neighbors live very soberly; the general run of people, however, prefer the mixed-stew of the general community, with its divergencies, its little quarrels, the mixed pleasures and inconveniences of being reasonably considerate towards one another. Feats of daring, dangerous or difficult personal or moral relationships, and long expeditions away from the community, are rather encouraged than not; for again it is realized that the great danger of such a life is that it is too "nice," too secure, for the best interests of the best people in it. A great anxiety is the people who by temperament play safe, tend to imitate each other too much, to rely on each others' opinion, to have too little personal desire, vitality, or capacity for enjoyment. Even more than the aggressive, the would-be acquisitive of wealth or of power over others, they are the community's chief problem and burden, though they regard themselves as its pillars, and are constantly trying to badger the place into something more steady and respectable. In the long run it is felt that they may threaten the community's very existence as a good community; and some worried theorists still debate the wisdom of exiling them, or liquidating them. But instead, every effort is made simply to educate them by example, and to leave them to their own devices.

Most of this can be shown as the spy-tourist is shown around; more can have been developed or hinted towards in earlier scenes, contrasting with the methods in the scientific camp. I think the spy-tourist might also be the Gallup-Poll type of expert, asking all those usual questions which are nobody's damn business and which nearly everybody is so proud to answer: he is greeted here, sometimes with more candor than he bargained for; by others, with complete bewilderment, or offense at anyone who would dare in such a way to invade another's privacy. I think there can and should be, by the way, strong as possible hints of "free love," *mènages á trois,* and racial interbreeding—all, of course, flicked in casually as we pass. (On Races, by the way, the feeling in the community is not that—for instance—Jews, Gentiles and Negroes are ALL alike; but that they're all different—racially, and individually that the differences are fascinating and eminently worth studying. The place is, of course, freer of racial prejudice than any place could be, which insists, instead, on ignoring difference, and which wants everybody, regardless of race, to be of the same size, look and mind.) This whole tour can be, besides a sort of Utopian charter *which should take care to stay within what is possible, out of the best in people,* a travesty both of the Scientists' camp, of pre-bomb civilization, and of Utopias in general—and, of course, of itself.

A FEW NOTES ON THE TRAMP:

Significant, and hard to handle right: in this relatively good community the Tramp can hardly any longer function as such. We see for the first time how thoroughly he has depended on being a fundamentally free spirit in a bad society. By one kind of logic he wouldn't be able to stand all this peace and pleasure and would withdraw from it. By another, he would stay, sadly as well as happily, mainly as an observer; for security, for which he has an honest liking; and because he likes being liked. He would spend most of his time, I imagine, with the children; above all the growing child he found as a new-born baby. (Whether, or how far, this should be developed as a line—the child as the new planet; the Education of the Prince— I can't yet figure.) But the Tramp is also the spirit, inadvertent founder and arbiter of the community. So he is a study in what the good man does with power; i.e., tries constantly not to have it—to awaken self-awareness, instead, and power over themselves, in others. I suspect that among other things he would do his best always to make himself seem slightly ridiculous—would realize that mere respect would of itself be dangerous to him as recipient, to those who might respect him, as it is liable to be to all people. (As an effect, only the wisest and most perceptive, realize him at anything thing like his true value: to them, he is an old King; to the community at large, he's a sort of mascot; to the Solid Souls, he's at best just a silly or a nasty little man.) Certainly he would rarely if ever try to use directly, on the people, any kind of power or prestige he has. And happy as he is to see and to live in a "good" community, he would be lonelier than anyone else in it. His ideal of happiness would have been a girl and children to love; but he's dubious even about a community of that size. So, in this stretch of the movie, the Tramp can be only very gently and benignly comic; he fades off towards silver; he should grow old, quite gray, rather quickly; lose much of his agility; become a little bit stocky.

After the first scene with the Scientists, we return to the Tramp: it is Sunday; the girl, in a very housewifely way, is

rigging the baby for a stroll; she's very much in charge of
the first part of this expedition, which is to Church. It's
clear that the Tramp accompanies her a good deal more out of
courtesy and affection, than piety. They wheel the pram in and
down the nave of St. Patrick's; all the windows are out, and a
fresh breeze ruffles vine tendrils and stirs the heavy, somewhat torn altar-vestments. They sidle into a pew; the girl is
quite absorbed in her praying. (She isn't a Catholic or neces-
sarily a member of any sect—just a simple—and very conventional—believer in God.) The Tramp is very tenderly polite
towards her; and polite towards God; but it is clear he isn't
religiously absorbed in the way she is. His glance keeps wandering; we hear a faint, curious slapping noise and looking
up, we see with him that a pigeon has sailed in through the
open window and is flying, almost inaudibly, very high in the
nave. He is at first touched and moved by the sight—this seems
more like a real church to him now: then a quiet, subtle dou-
ble-take: he glances uneasily at his bowler (it's on his left
knee, which is up; his right, he kneels on, against a new-
spread, fresh white handkerchief); one recognizes that his essential act of piety is in leaving the bowler where it is and
trusting in God that the pigeon, the Holy Ghost, will spare
him.

The girl finishes her prayers, and looks around a bit herself. Suddenly she clutches his sleeve and points it out to
him. One single little vigil light is still forlornly wagging
its tail, among all those which have burned out. They go down
to it, very quietly; both are deeply moved. She rummages under
the stand; yes, there are others; a couple of cartons. She
wants to renew every light. The Tramp pantomimes warning: go
slow; one at a time, if we're really going to keep this light
alive. She realizes; lights just one, from the expiring light,
and sets it. The Tramp watches her; of a deep but highly sub-
junctive, conditional sort, there is now a kind of reverence
in his face, too. She has no coin—somehow she wants to leave
one; nor has he; with a gentle smile he offers her a thousand-
dollar bill. They stand and watch the new light a moment; then
go out into the sunlight.

Now they're ready for pleasure, and the Tramp takes
charge. They go to the penny arcade, 42nd Street just west of
Times Square. The fortune-telling wax witch with the implaca-
ble but hesitant, swerving hand and the little cards advising
on how to be successful in business or love (possible parallel
with the answers of the computing machine?). The Tramp struggling with the Test-Your-Grip machine. (They get their pennies
etc. from the cash-trays where they have lain since the explosion.) The flip-over peepshows; Earl Carroll's Wine Bath, The

Frisky Flea or what not; something tough and gay from the early 1920s; Tramp might sneak a look, or tut-tuttingly yank the girl from a flip-over of a muscle-man; or both. The girl gives a glad yelp; together, with the kindly astonishment of lonely gods, they look into the pinched microcosm of a flea-circus, where, poor mechanized little devils, business is going on as usual: the Coronation of George V, or such. Jesus how hungry they must be! But what's there, where's there, anything to eat? The Tramp has an inspiration. He ups his sleeve and shoves in the point of his bent elbow. Visual pandemonium, in all their little costumes and dragging all their baby tubas and other paraphernalia; followed by a visual saturnalia, and the drunks finally sinking down to sleep it off: maximum of 1 minute. A bit, too, with the distorting mirrors; their chance to see other types of people: Tramp very tall and lean like Basil Rathbone, girl as squatted as a circus fat-lady; various little impersonations. Scene culminates in mirror-maze (if hinted recapitulation of your other pictures seems a good idea) (and if it does, you could at still another time try to tell your community the hell of group labor by a bit of the beltline scene in *Modern Times* and in a pantomimed dialogue with the girl, pick up some others, always when the girl was lost, suppressing, keeping as an unbearable private memory, the close of *City Lights*).

They use the maze to give themselves an illusion of company. They're gently sedate: an old-fashioned family on the Sunday promenade with the baby-carriage. Work the maze for every possible elaboration of politesse among the many members of a stylish crowd—hat-tipping, bowing, snubbing, flirting, playfully pretending it really *is* a crowd; as they get caught up into the delights of the game the girl should suddenly point out, "isn't that So-and-So?" and he should gently reprimand her for pointing. He pretends to stop and admire another baby—ever so, dainty and charming to its mother, manly congratulations to the father, chook-chook-chook and boontzy-boontzy-boontzy to the baby, pointing out the baby's beauties to his girl. At length he becomes so absorbed in the makebelieve that he forgets it is makebelieve: he is very much taken by a reflection of the girl and starts a surreptitious flirtation with her; is dismayed to find that *his* girl is doing the same by a stray reflection of the Tramp—whose trampishness he scornfully parodies, to reprimand her. He grabs her masterfully by the elbow and they leave the maze, the Tramp giving one last surreptitious tip of hat and eye towards the vanishing reflection of the girl. OR: the baby starts to cry, and they group shieldingly around it as they would if they had to change its diaper in a crowded place; innumerable reflections

of the would-be-private change. He checks his watch and pantomimes, we must hurry home—it's past the baby's feeding-time.
They depart sedately. By either departure, as we last see him
(reflected in the maze), he gives a smart stabbing surreptitious gouge at his backside (one of the fleas has made a beach-
head of him.), gives a trembling, kicking shake of his left
leg, glances sharply to the floor, and shoos the invisible flea
back towards his circus. Their reflections vanish: the closing
shot is of the empty, cold naked mirrors of the maze, a huge
quiet diamond of spare loneliness.

Cut back to Scientists.

On next return to the Tramp, they're midway in their cus-
tomary promenade in the maze, a little more slick at it and a
little bit tired of, and saddened by, the game, when a new
face suddenly appears. Everybody immediately stands stock
still, looking at everyone else; and we cut from closeup to
closeup as realization grows in each face. This new one isn't
a bad guy—just square-headed, rather conventional, well-set-
up: a real, solid man. (Might be played by George Brent but I
suspect the best for him is Robert Ryan.) He's neither a very
generous nor a very acquisitive type; he means no harm in the
world. Neither does the girl; she loves the Tramp clearly but
not, she begins to realize, when there's a real man around.
The Tramp catches on quickest of all. His heart is instantly
broken but that, Lord knows, is no news to him; he is perfectly gentle and gracious, at once perfectly humble and profoundly proud; and tries to cause them the least embarrassment
possible. This extremely complicated rearrangement and development of feelings and relationships should be carried on in
perfect silence, in close group-shots and closeups, as something basic to the Tramp and to human existence. (The crowded
reflection in the maze, where they work it out, implies clearly
its universality.) The man and the girl withdraw together, the
Tramp pantomiming ever so politely that he'll be along in a
few minutes. He watches them out; then turns towards the central mirror and, with a heartsick, enduring, ravaged face,
stares very gravely and intently at his reflection: pull the
camera a little away to frame him with a diamond-complex of
huge closeups of the Tramp's self-realizing accepting face.
When next we see them—perhaps just a little later that day—the
girl, man and baby occupy the original home, (with square-
headed suburban improvements, thanks to the man, an elimination of the gay, kidding little improvisations of domestic
convenience which the Tramp had so enjoyed dreaming up to delight the girl); the Tramp has fixed himself a cute little pup-

tent sort of an establishment off to the side; and he is taking care of the baby, and being very charming with it, some
yards away from them, with his back turned, while they
schmooze, enjoy the cool of the evening, and try to feel as
deeply sorry and appreciative as they know they ought to.

Their relationship (the 3 of them) should remain deeply
friendly throughout the picture; and it is the man, in his
mixture of conventionality (a bridge to others) and his profound appreciation of the Tramp, who is perhaps our key to
the spread and permanence of the Tramp's influence in the community. I think in the early stages of the formation of the
community, when people are still relatively few and the best
that might be in them is still at its most open to possible
growth, the Tramp would be of great influence himself, directly but of course inadvertently; but in the first real crisis of community policy (which comes as soon as there are
enough people to amount to a "community"), it's the man who
saves the day. I think he may simply tell, as quietly and
eloquently as he can, what an immensely difficult and generous thing the Tramp has done and how extraordinarily decently
he has done it; and what in turn this has taught him, a very
ordinary man; and that he could thus win over many who were
doubtful, or dissenting, that a community could or even
should be run along lines of generosity and trustfulness of
individuals towards each other.

This Tramp-Girl-Solid Man relationship is the chief sample, probably (rough parallel by contrast is the key family
experimented on by the Scientists), of an all-important aspect
of the picture: that Utopias are not never-never-lands; that
most of the sorrows and needs of individuals are never to be
solved and should, in fact, have more leeway, rather than
less. But that only people who can accept *inevitable* pain and
injustice (as very distinct from evitable) and can accept it
bravely and generously, without delusions of heroism or self-
pity, can hope to be competent to eliminate avoidable pain and
injustice, or even to hold them at bay. Likewise, that the
lucky must honorably accept their luck, and the superior their
superiority, knowing that it is only in small things, cruel as
they are to the heart, and to living, that men are not created
equal.

The specific details of the Tramp's influence and its spread
and solidification—perhaps the most important and most difficult thing in the picture—I haven't yet worked out any ideas
for. I'm only sure that within the logic of the picture, it
can properly happen that people of all sorts, more deeply
shocked than ever before in their lives, and thus more deeply
ready than ever before to doubt the standards they used to

live by, would find the child and the lost bravery and innocence reawakened in them, with quite some chance for survival
and growth, if they are confronted by this childlike man.

As I've said earlier, the Tramp becomes restive in all the
milk-and-honey, and feels more and more like wandering; at
length (about the time the Scientists send their spy), he wanders straight down a ventilator into the Scientists' underground establishment. Their earnest experiments on him, their
dogged efforts to reduce and alter the finally irreducibly free
and spontaneous human spirit, their fantastic unrealized cru-
elty in these attempts, and the Tramp's reactions, could be, I
think, the cruelest, coldest and most savagely funny comic
scenes in the picture. The Tramp is irreducible, I'd suppose,
somewhat as Schweik was only a lot more so: fundamentally, by
absolute innocence and spontaneousness; but perhaps secondarily, by a startling shrewdness and toughness: most basically
of all, of course, by his complete animal and humane and spiritual integrity: because he has never allowed the world to di-
vide and conquer his nature but quite incurably, has always
acted and will always act as a whole being.

He escapes (I hope by wild and inadvertently very venge-
ful) and gets back to his community just in time for the closing sequence.

C. (4) LAST SEQUENCE OF THE PICTURE

A small but efficient expedition from the scientists' camp ar-
rives (perhaps by a sort of helicopter?). The Scientists are
prepared to use two means: persuasion if possible, if necessary, force: they are coldly determined to win. Their force
men line up quietly: other specialists set up an exhibition of
new gadgets, styles, synthetic fabrics, etc. etc., and a
screen on which they show still more of the wonders of their
brave new world. (One single sample: they show how they have
improved the deathless classics of literature, music and art,
to suit the modern tempo, and to satisfy contemporary needs.
They start playing the same Beethoven record which was used
early in the picture, with the Tramp and the Girl by the fire;
after they've given just enough of it to recall it to the audience, they put on looks of painful boredom and restiveness,
and put on their new version, the ultimate in Readers-Digesty
encapsulations: They merely play the same record very fast, so
that every note is shrill and snarling, and the beat and tempo
become an obscenely trippiting fast dance.)

As it turns out force is not needed. Acquisitiveness,
safe-playing, hunger for novelty, etc., are still deeply
grounded in everybody and await only the opportunities which

were so happily eliminated by the Bomb and so wisely denied in
the Tramp's little town; and everybody finds he is still a complete sucker for the wonders and mysteries and benefits of Science; and most prefer not to think or live for themselves, and
others, making the change-over, merely feel they are mentally
coming of age. Nearly all of the Tramp's people fall for the
Scientists as easily as cannibals for bright beads or a tick-
ing watch (or the Girl for the Solid Man); and for many a very
serious inducement must be recognized: these people are very
deeply work-worn, especially the women: and to see how little
exertion need be made, to have comforts they never dreamed of,
is to most, a temptation so irresistible that it scarcely occurs in the form of a grave choice to be made. A few children
want to stay where they are (though most are enchanted by the
gimcracks), but their parents require them to come along. But
an impressive few hold out. At this point the Scientists turn
loose stronger kinds of persuasion. They are aware, as the
Tramp's people are not, that peoples and nations are reviving
all over the world (impressive mock-journalistic mumbojumbo of
data and statistics); clearly if the world is to be saved from
utter destruction it is a desperate race to bring to the rest
of the world, the American Way; cooperation; etc. etc., before
some other, sinister Ideology wins out. Already, they assure
the diehards, the potential enemies have developed the most
terrifying new and secret weapons, though not yet quite so effective as our own. It's a question of cold common sense. Do
they want to survive, or don't they? If so, we all have to get
to work together; to trust each other; there must be no lame
ducks, no defeatists, no skeptics, no starry-eyed idealists,
etc. etc.

A famous preacher is called on (Religion is, of course,
permitted in both camps). He preaches about putting away
childish things, facing grim realities, girding the spirit,
putting on the whole armor of God, etc. etc. A younger man
(clergyman, priest, layman, or the fellow who guided the spy
around?) leaps to his feet and undemocratically interrupts the
pundit, explaining the Tramp's community in Christian and in
humanistic terms, and the inevitability of destruction by the
terms of the opposite camp. Some of the deserters move part
way back. And now, for the first time in the picture, the Tramp
speaks. He says in effect that he does not know whether or not
he is a religious man and since he doesn't know, it's probably
wiser to say he isn't one: but that he agrees with much that
his defender has said. He says that on the other hand he realized the great possible threat that the Scientists speak of.
He says he doesn't know whether the difficulties can possibly
be solved in his way; but at least he is quite sure that they

cannot be, by any other: least of all, he fears, by the way
that prevails in the scientific community. He says that his way
is fundamentally very simply: To put away childish things such
as greed and envy and moral cowardice and hatred and doubt of
one's own right to listen to one's own mind and to one's own
heart. To put away all, however good it may be of itself,
which arrays people in groups so large and in factions so at
odds that they no longer know and honor each other as single
human beings. For we are not yet even wise enough to know ourselves and to deal kindly with ourselves, our families, our
immediate neighbors; how then can we be wise enough to multi-
ply those problems by millions, and keep any kind of control?
He says that he has found that all kinds of people, good and
bad, intelligent and dull, can live, not in perfect freedom
and happiness—far from it—but in a much more reasonable har-
mony and enjoyment of each other and of life than any sane man
might have hoped for. And he says that by example, and by example only, by a resolute effort to put away fear and mistrust
and self-mistrust, others may realize that they too can live
so; but that of course, it is impossible that any man can
learn to trust another, who has not learned to trust himself;
who has not dared the adventure, difficult and painful in many
ways, to cut away all that is dead in him; and to look into,
and face, and know, the good and evil which are in himself.
People who make this attempt only *may* succeed; it isn't certain; for fear runs very deep; and the material rewards of
forgetting your heart and soul are very great and very tempt-
ing. But on the possibility of such a success, and on that
possibility alone, and on the willingness and fearlessness of
men to try it, whether or not they feel alone or too few in
trying it, he feels sure that the one faint hope of the world
rests. He now appeals directly to the Scientists, the nation-
alists, the straight materialists. You are not at all evil
men, nor are you by any means stupid; and God knows you have
done and can do wonders for us—beneficent wonders as well as
terrible wonders. Can you not see that it is time to stop—time
even to destroy a great deal that is wonderful? Our chance is
a very slim one at best, to win the world by simplicity,
forcelessness, and love; by the attempt of each man to be himself and to honor his neighbor; can you not, will you not,
give us that one slim chance? We *must indeed* put away childish
things: and we must become as little children. And may God
help us if we don't.

Who will stay with me?

One by one they all move over to the Scientists' camp. Some
of the last few speak to him, take his hand. The burden of
their explanation is that they are heartsick to say so (and

they really are), but it's just hopelessly impractical. If only all people felt as he did, of course ("But they *do,*" the Tramp insists in a gentle intense voice; "*in their hearts they do!* And how can we say it's impractical: here we've seen it really working. No, not perfectly: there can be no perfection: but *working.* It's real. It's proven. It *can be.*") If only (they go on) they had the courage, the simplicity, the trust, the recklessness. ("But you have only to look for it hard enough!") They smile sadly, shake their heads, look humble, move away. The Solid Man takes his hand: "I wish I could stay with you—By golly, if it weren't for" (he is embarrassed and, by nodding, indicates the Girl and their new baby) . . ."I would. You don't know how much I hate to leave—we *all* do." The Tramp murmurs "surely, surely," politely; suddenly puts a hand on the man's shoulder and looks up very earnestly and affectionately, smiling: "Good luck! All the luck in the world!" (Within his shading of these words is his pitying certainty of the annihilation that luck will soon and inevitably bring the world and everyone who lives on it.) The Man, deeply moved, replies "To you, too." The Girl comes up, looks long at him, bursts into tears, and flings her arms around his neck. "What are you—Ohh, what are you going to *do?,*" she asks him through her tears. He shrugs and gives a gay little laugh: "Oh—never mind about *me.* I'll take good care of myself . . ." (a sudden, bright smile:) . . . "it begins to feel like old times." The child comes up (the baby he found, now perhaps 6 years old). The Tramp squats and puts his cheek against the child cheek. "God bless you," he says quietly and tenderly; the realization of what will come to the child, and of the child as the new planet floods into his face: "God keep you," he whispers; and pats its bottom as it follows its "mother" away.

He stands alone now. He bows silently to the Scientists, tips his hat to some ladies and a priest, and starts away. Two of the top Scientists lean together, whispering. The gist: That man *could* be dangerous; radio the word along, to pick him up when he is far enough away that it won't be noticed.

Old Glory—perhaps in color—climbs what's left of the Empire State mast; a band plays the Star Spangled Banner while all stand in solemn joy as Citizens salute; as we last see the Tramp, he is going west on the somewhat sagged but still solid relic of the George Washington Bridge; the anthem comes thinly through quite a number of portable radios. He is alone, walking west, into sunset. Walking east, herded and escorted by armbanded Scientific policemen, is an extremely variegated representation of the whole human race, combed from the ruins and from their makeshift communities, hopefully and resolutely converging upon the birth of the new world. The Tramp smiles at them sportingly; they give him a blank stare. By degrees, as people realize more and more clearly that he is the only one going the other way, and that he's an odd-looking customer, the blank stares become hostile; and when a child is attracted towards him, its mother yanks it roughly back into line. As these faces beat upon him, fanning past him, the Tramp's own face and body alter. He seems at the same time to become older and lonelier—and younger and gayer. I think perhaps even his hair should start shading back towards black, and that his body should lose weight; that he will show in the thinning of his face the blend of extreme old age and of the re-emergence, now that once more he comes into the true Tramp's life, of unkillable youthfulness, eagerness, a blend of indestructible hope with irreducible disillusion. It should be a brand-new version of the old Tramp's face: one which knows that his life is now very nearly over and that the life of this world is very nearly over too; and that for all his grief, he finds that he is exquisitely delighted to come back into his own as the wanderer, the fugitive, the solitary, the improviser: he'll make a damn good time of it, what little life is left him. But the policeman who picks up the Scientists' directive about the Tramp, on his wrist radio, gives one look at him, puts heads together with another policeman; they both look: yes, the description fits—roughly, anyhow; but good Lord; *this* little guy, of all people, can't be dangerous! The Tramp is eyeing them as they approach each other on the bridge: inter-pantomime of their intuitions of what came over the radio. But at exactly the moment that the Tramp most expects trouble from them they both break into broad, lenient smiles, and let him pass. They're the only people who do smile at him: cops, of all, people; and he realizes the wealth of affectionate contempt that is in their smiles, and the enormous depth of his defeat. He now either deliberately comes back and boots one of them in the butt, just for the little vengeance and the pleasure of being pursued in an old-fashioned way once more, or comes back and meditates this and decides against it, and turns back towards the West; or merely goes on walking, thinking it over; first in closeup; then in a long, long shot in which the little silhouette, growing ever more spry in its sense of freedom and a little twilight of fun ahead, becomes almost too tiny to see, as it vanishes, turning northward, at the far end of the bridge.

D. PROLOGUE

Inside a big, midtown (New York) movie theater. Opening shot is midway through the closing scene of Capra's *It's a Wonder-*

ful Life or another of that type: humane good-will and sentimentality rampant and roaring; the quintessence of democratic
optimism, essentially rather fatuous and rather pathetic; trying to forget and cover up its basic self-doubt and instabil-
ity with a tremendous lot of noise and good cheer and decent
intention: while they're all shouting, crying, hugging each
other, singing *Auld Lang Syne* on the screen, pick up the audience in chunks and masses, gasping with incredulous joy and
tears, one or two even join in the singing. Audience should be
little if at all a kidding of the real thing, but salient,
close to stock, types: the automatic candy-eater; the hand-
holders; the lonely guy edging elbow and hand next a girl; The
Skeptic; the delicate-footed usherette, etc. etc. The picture
ends with angelic soprani soaring in thirds; with, on some audience faces, the automatic tears which this hyped-up lip
singing automatically elicits. Register their readjustment to
high-serious matters as the March of Time fanfare comes on:
that look of bored, rather dutiful earnestness; the candy-
eater's face readjusts but his (or her) hand continues from
box to mouth, regular as a dredge; the hand-holders take a
deeper grip to tide them through a few minutes of Education;
the Skeptic still looking skeptical; etc. etc. . . . Then the
March of Time is on:

*[Author's Note: In the following section, Agee divides the
page into dialogue in the left column and camera direction in
the right.]*

Voice of Time:	Title:
The Almighty Atom!	THE ALMIGHTY ATOM!
	Dissolve through title:
Friend?:or: Foe!	Friend or Foe
Voice: (Low, clipped, porten-tous):	Roar and roil of the Alam-agordo flame column; intercut faces of scientists from
On the night of July 16, 1945, a few brilliant Allied scientists first saw what the atom could do.	M.O.T.'s film on the Bomb; in closeup, Bush and Conant, prostrate on sand, solemnly shake hands. Quick iris out on handclasp.
	A low, fast air view of flat-tened Hiroshima.

On August 7th, 1945, *we told* | Continue swift air-shot of
the *world* what it could do! | Hiroshima . . . Japanese sur-

On August 7th, 1945, *we told the world* what it could do!

Continue swift air-shot of Hiroshima . . . Japanese surrender aboard the Missouri; quick smash closeups of the most gruesome or touching survivors of Hiroshima; Bush & Conant again shake hands; V-J celebration in Times Square.

Further experiments only brought the point still more *forcefully* home.

A scorched, staggering Bikini goat.

An enormous flotation of killed fish on idling sea surface; a parboiled pig, in a sailor-suit, staggers from a gun-turret; interested scientists, heavily masked, remove the brain and belly of a shrieking rat (faint sound).

Grim necessities of war

Newsreel shot of a frenzied movie star, kissing bald-headed buyers of Victory Bonds.

And the unparalleled genius of our scientists

Once again, same shot, Bush & Conant shaking hands.

Have put into the hands of the U.S. and her gallant little allies, Great Britain and Canada, the greatest and most fearsome responsibility in the world's history.

Gromyko walking out on U.N.

Closeup of Truman, looking as fearsomely responsible as he can.

The greatest potential for world suicide:

(Music: a few soured chords from *Gotterdammerung*)

Or for world liberation (Music: *Narcissus*)

The Hitler bunker; flame-blasted walls a palimpsest of the scrawled names, etc., of soldiers of several nations, most suffocating possible advertising-style tableau of the Ideal American Family, admiring its new washing-machine.

that this bewildered old
planet has ever known.

Camera peers into whirling of
suds & clothes, picks up the
whirling of a school globe
and whirling faces, stops
short, filling screen with
two-second closeups of Truman
(or the then incumbent):
Atlee: Stalin: General
Groves: Molotov: Bidault:
Marshall: Bevin: Lilienthal:
Dewey: Taft: Prince of Saudi
Arabia: Baruch: Gromyko:
Cadogan: an immense crowd.
Wander camera close above
crowd faces. which are looking anxiously up, squinting
slightly.

Frankly. we are frightened.

Hold on crowd faces: intercut
new faces of world leaders,
putting on dismal grins of
false hope.

And frankly, we know we have
good reason to be frightened.

New shots of leaders, each a
closeup of fierce argument or
vituperation

Can—man—come—of age—in time—
to prevent his own—destruction?

Straightest possible shots of
major leaders and of ordinary
people, looking as serious
and as competent as they are
able: therefore tragic.

And if so, how?

(A violently twanged note,
rising through glissando,
enormously enlarged)

A question mark zooms from
tiny center to fill screen
with its ragged vibration,
synchronized with twang.

(Melo-music, undertone of
menace. must never obliterate
lab. noises.)

The Voice (muted, swift,
throaty, tense): Deep underground, somewhere in the U.S.,
in the greatest radiation-

The camera travels at brisk
walking pace through a
close-walled labyrinth of
raw concrete, turning many
corners, swinging past many
vistas placarded KEEP OUT.
NO ADMITTANCE, CLASSIFIED,
TOP SECRET, etc. Burlesques
of Geiger counters and other

proof laboratories the world has ever known, under heavy Security guard,

America's most brilliant scientists and technicians labor night and day to make the atomic message stick; to make the Almighty Atom safe for Democracy; to make Democracy safe for the world or rather, *in* the world. That unassuming young man just dodging behind a cyclotron was once described by Einstein as the most brilliant scientific mind since Roger Bacon's. That gentle old chap in the bedroom slippers is the man who proved that our galaxy is not very different from a wristwatch. That striking fellow (Note: Ideally, Von Stroheim) with the scar and the monocle, who foreswore his allegiance to the principles of National Socialism shortly after the Fall of Berlin, is still convinced that he can power interplanetary rockets merely by splitting the hydrogen nucleus. American science, which knows no national boundaries, is giving him every assistance in his thrilling quest.

Of course there is much in the way of equipment, project and cold, downright achievement which for reasons of security cannot be shown or mentioned here, but these are the first and exclusive action pictures of a miraculous new super-computing machine, which we might well call the

devices shimmy their needles, flash and glimmer little lights, ring sudden bells; from behind walls come the groans, moans, cracklings and deep whines of great machines, the burblings of mysterious brews. Now and then a heavy leaden door peeps open, or pulls angrily shut, in a wall, offering a glimpse of fantastic equipment and of shy, peering, secretive scientists and technicians (a little like nuns the day the Archbishop visits). Some are masked, others not. (Most of the masks could be transparent.) We are following a fully armed Infantry Sergeant with a special band on his left arm. Now and again the screen or some part of it is obliterated with black or white and the huge word SECURITY.

Camera horns through a door and travels the full length of an incredibly elaborate machine, reverently tended by young technicians who squirt wheel-horse and the brain of U.S. research, for it can solve in fractions of a second, problems which would require a corps of one thousand highly trained mathematicians, working a forty-hour week, time and a half for overtime, from five to ten years to solve.

The very nature of these problems must of course remain top-secret, but let's Just see what Old Fogy—as the machine is affectionately known to those who tend it— can do with little posers which would puzzle You and Me.

oil and twist buttons. One— maybe Keenan Wynn—catches the camera's eye, grins proudly and rather shyly, and claps the machine on the flank as if it were a horse.

Others look up from their work with that rather complicated look of institutionalized men, interrupted, and under orders to be polite for publicity's sake. A striking proportion of them are very young. They nearly all have the dedicated, dried-out, curiously celibate look which so many priest-scientists seem to acquire.

A scientist exhibits a slip of tape on which is typed:

$2 + 2 = ?$

It is inserted in one end of the machine. The technicians busily man the dials and oilcans; a highly complicated flickering drone is heard from within the machine. Lights flick on and off its whole length. The man who put in the question sprints to the far end and the answer is already sticking out, waiting for him. He holds it up to camera, triumphantly:

Very *good! Very* good!

And now another!

$2 + 2 = 4$

Wynn pats the machine and grins.

$2 \times 2 = ?$

Streak camera, length of machine. The answer sticks out
like a sassy tongue:

Come-come now! How's that
again?

2 x 2 = 42

Dreadful dismay among the
scientists. In the expression
of some faces, read a sneak-
ing: "*Does* it?" The oilers
and dial-twisters get very
busy.

Again the tape:

If at first you don't
succeed . . .

2 x 2 =?

Feed it in; streak camera;
the answer end produces:

Voice: (laughing, professionally): Aha, ha, haha*ha!* Just
one of Old Fogy's little
jokes, folks. He knew it all
the time, never you worry!
For Old Fogy has a sense of
humor, just like the rest of
us! (laughs again, uneasily!)
A-ha-ha. And now just one
more: a tougher one. This
time: this is one Old Fogy
has never been asked before.
This isn't exactly in Old
Fogy's line. Friends, this is
strictly unrehearsed.

2 x 2 = 4 too

The scientists all laugh.
Wynn slaps the machine almost in an ecstasy of amusement and relief; he was the
worst dismayed of any of
them, but now, it was their
little secret, their little
joke—his and Fogy's—all the
old time.

On the scientists' faces, expressions varying from would-
be-concealed anxiety to smug
confidence. The tape reads;

staoin ?

The machine puts out very
special noises; gongs strike;
a large spring busts twan-
gling loose on the top of the
machine; they all sprint down
to the answering end:

shrdlu

And now, recreation-time is over for Old Fogy and it's time that we too [retreat].

They burst into cheers (faintly audible), and the machine puts up two iron arms and shakes hands with itself like a victorious boxer, all its lights blazing, while Wynn tenderly adjusts the sprung spring and several assistants carry in a huge open scroll, thick with the symbols of Higher Mathematics. Camera fades an the scroll is fed in one end and a bigger scroll bloops out the other, where scientists feed it through their hands reading it like tickertape and

barking at others who take notes which are hurried to the question end and fed into the machine, while oilers and diallers bend in earnest to their tasks.

Camera prods up to the conventional, lettered office door: still don't know the name or name

of job, of this top-boss Scientist. Dissolve through door and move up, again the dead-conventional, newsreel shot, of the Man at the Desk. He should be dry, stooped, very decent, faintly rural-looking: could be perfectly played by the man who plays the head of the peasant family in the opening scene of *Verdoux.* He is very deeply sincere and in earnest as he reads his statement; but he has no personal or feeling-force whatever. A dead, flat, honest voice, reading or

The Dean of Nuclear Scientists tells us:

SCIENTISTS

Atomic fission is an accomplished fact. (He's a busy man; he has to glance at his ms. with every half-sentence. He tries to give the Direct Eye, à-la Kinsey, on everything he regards as most important.) We cannot go backward. We must go forward. We scientists have gone forward. Perhaps we have gone forward too rapidly for the rest of the world. We are of course not permitted to tell you in so many words or, rather, formulae (a slight, smug, shy, technological twinkle), of the Improvements we have made since Able Day or thereabouts; but we beg to assure you that they are, to put it mildly, spectacular. Moreover, they are only the beginning. What is more, by, our most reliable calculations it is only a question of three years, at the outside, before Other Nations have weapons as destructive (as), or the superior of our own. (He picks up a glass of water.)

VOICE of TIME:

For Atomic Fission is no respecter of persons. It is true that our scientific genius and our equipment are second—are approached by none

speaking the words each separately, a little as a just-literate man reads; he is, after all, a man who scarcely communicates or even thinks in verbal terms.

Scientist looks "modest."

in the world; yet that other great world power which for reasons of security and international concord we shall forbear to mention by name has scientists too, and equipment of its own;

. . . And even Tiny Obnoxia, which up to now, has been a seventh-rate power among seventh-rate powers, has something up its sleeve as these topsecret just-released, exclusive motion pictures, sneaked by an intrepid American agent, make alarmingly clear. (Menace music)

Scientist looks tactful; leans chin in hand and looks wisely at audience, fade. Scientist: Caption: Even small nations, if they should see fit to use this power unscrupulously, might become the peers or the conquerors of the greatest.

Tunnels of concrete, a little like our own but smaller, and with signs in a made-up language, perhaps an invented alphabet. Military men and diplomats, with soldier and sailor escort, follow a labcoated, eager scientist, who beckons, into a laboratory room crowded with an intricate parody of mad-scientist and makeshift equipment. The diplomats are dressed as they should be, but their faces and postures all look as if they'd picked it all up watching spy movies and at night school. The military men are rigged in the Admiral's hats, florid epaulets, etc., which traditionally travesty Old Bulgaria or a Banana Republic; one is stolidly eating a scallion. A very young genius with a look of great, dull earnestness stands aside, gravely; a very old genius who looks like an

menace music; otherwise silent

experimenter in Galvanism begins vehemently to explain to
the laymen, focusing terrific
pride, force and intensity on
a narrow opening between his
thumb and finger. The diplomats look nervous and im-
pressed. The military men
look at once skeptical and
lustful. They all turn to the
scallion-eater, who takes another craunching bite,
belches heavily while they
bravely and politely hold
their ground, chews; then
abruptly nods approval.

With operatic solemnity, all
straighten their arms towards
a common center, and hands;
on which, a stop-shot.

Our scientists are still puzzled by the obsolete and mysterious equipment but who can
say? Obnoxia's little experiment may be heard from yet!

Fade stopshot.

It is no time for overconfi-
dence.

The Scientist is rediscovered
at his desk, surreptitiously
scratching his ear—he didn't
know the "camera was back on"
yet. He stops, rather sheepishly, looks very serious,
and speaks.

SCIENTIST:

It is well within the bounds
of possibility that we, or
others, may hit upon the secret which will dissolve the
Planet, which might even set
up a chain reaction throughout the Universe; though
this, fortunately, is not yet
probable. But by our soberest

estimates, unless within
three years the nations of
the world have managed to
work out some reliable form
of international atomic control, we scientists cannot
vouch for the future of civilization.

Most of us are convinced that
this cannot be achieved by
any half-way measures. It
will necessitate the greatest
concessions on the part of
all nations, including our
own, in the matter of na-
tional sovereignty. We are
convinced that only some organization on the order of a
United States of the World,
can even hope to avert world
disaster.

Let me earnestly repeat it:
We must all go forward. If we
stand still, or if we quar-
rel, or if we compromise,
that is only going backward.
And that: means: suicide.

VOICE OF TIME;

Some of us feel that the Revolution without which this
world is not likely for long
to survive the liberation of
The Almighty Atom, must be
deeper than a mere revolution
in our form of Government.
(Bell and organ background).
Dr. NAME KOMING, a spiritual
leader beloved of all sects,
Christian, non-Christian and
plain old shoutin'-agnostic,
has this to tell us:

CAPTION:

Can Jesus Save?

Dr. Whosis: A truly good and
earnest face; a sincere
voice; desperately, gently
concerned to get his message
across; hopelessly insulated
from general communication
by his professional reli-
giousness.

Dr. Whosis speaks against
sticky organ music and
chimes:

There is One Mightier than
the Atom. We must seek and
cherish His Power, each in
his own soul. If enough of us
do this, we may be saved. If
most of us fail to, we are
certainly lost. We who seek
to control the terrible power
of the atom must first learn
to begin to master ourselves.

There is no other way. There
is no other hope.

It is easy to say this, and
it is easy to pay lip-service
to it. It is terribly hard
truly to realize the greatness of the truth of it, so
deeply in the heart and mind
and soul that all lesser con-
siderations become meaningless.

It is even harder to try to
live according to that truth.
But I do from the bottom of
my heart implore each one of
you, and all men in all nations, to make your best effort to realize it. Let us
all pray to God, by night and
by day, that enough of us
come to realize the meaning
of God, and that enough of us
try to live accordingly, before it is too late.

VOICE OF TIME:

There *must be* a Revolution in
the *Souls* of Men. But if that
revolution is to bear fruit

Behind him, a hideous chunk
of stained-glass window;
lilies.

in this workaday world of ours, there must also be a revolution in the *Minds* of men.

These are pupils; *these* are teachers; *these* are adult citizens.

A little gallery realistic, and mainly piteous and terrible, of ordinary school & college students, teachers, adults.

What are we going to do about it!

Mr. NAME KOMING, OFFICE KOMING (ex-president of a major University, and boss of a gigantic National Association of Teachers Colleges and of Public Schools), has this to say:

THE EDUCATOR:

Our schools are second to none in the world. Yet it is a proved fact that of 100,000 high-school graduates recently interviewed, and 75,000 college graduates, and 25,000 who had done at least one year's post-graduate work, only 73 point 7 males could conjugate the verb *to be* and no more than 27 point oh one females had ever *heard* of the

Still another man at still another desk. This one looks like an unfrocked YMCA secretary; wears a cap and gown "casually," over very hairy tweeds; sits side-saddle on his desk, alternately twirling a PBK key and fondling a pipe. He has the voice of a Boston terrier.

[Author's Note: At this point, Agee abandoned the split column layout and continued the dialogue in standard page layout.]

Missouri Compromise. Few of those emerging at present from our public grade-schools can sign, or even forge, their own names, and among those of the age-group one to three years, such antisocial symptoms as sauciness, disenchantment with life, and foot-fetichism [*sic*] show a marked, nay, alarming, increase. (He starts really leaning into it, jabbing his

points home with his pipestem.) Now a *responsible* citizen is
an *intelligent* citizen; an *intelligent* citizen is a *thinking*
citizen; and a thinking citizen is an *educated* citizen. The
health, the very life, of our Democracy depends upon the responsible, intelligent, thinking, educated, individual citizen. We therefore propose, more especially in view of the
extreme gravity of the world situation, to do away with all
non-essentials, the mere Ornaments of Culture, for the time
being, and to concentrate on fingerpainting, folksinging, elementary nuclear mechanics, Gregg & Pitman, and good stiff re-
fresher courses in American History, Civics, and Loyalty.
It's up to *you* fellow Americans; it's up to *us!*

VOICE OF TIME:
Then, here and there, one hears a voice crying, as it were, in
the wilderness. Some people call such thinkers crackpots and
crackpots they be, but in these days of world disaster and
free speech, it may not be wise to neglect any voice, no matter how lonely, etc. etc. (how he sets this one up and identifies him, I don't yet know) . . .

VOICE OF INDIVIDUALIST:
When the Germans were defeated, many of us thought that all
Germans were guilty and equally guilty.
      When the Irgunists in Palestine hung two British sol-
diers, 85 British meat-packers refused to handle kosher
meat. They stated that in their opinion all Jews, everywhere,
were as guilty of the hangings as the Jews who hanged the
Englishmen.
      The connection is clear.
      We have forgotten how to think as single individuals, and
how to feel moral responsibility as single individuals. We
think and pass moral judgment in groups, for or against other
groups. The Irgunists regarded themselves as members of a
group and killed the Englishmen as members of another group,
and all Jews were blamed, by men who no longer thought of
themselves as men, but as Englishmen.
      Unless we can learn to think each for ourselves, we are
lost, and the whole world is lost. *If* we think for ourselves,
we cannot be deceived into such actions or ideas.

VOICE OF TIME:
All very valuable to bear in mind; but, for better or worse,
Civilization is knitted together by the *co-operation* of individuals in *groups,* of men and women who forget their little
differences for the sake of the many. That is the meaning of
democracy.

VOICE OF INDIVIDUALIST:
That is the *death* of democracy, you mean.

VOICE OF TIME
That is the meaning of Democracy, in which our One Hope Rests,
as NAME KOMING again, the Grand Old Man of American Public
Life, dramatically rousing himself from his well-earned re-
tirement, so ably expressed it only last month in what was
perhaps the crowning speech of his long career.

(N.B. As you can see, this is all still in a sketchy stage
and, among other troubles, is much too long. The general
scheme is this: about midway during the March of Time, pull
the camera quietly out of the theater into the ordinary midday
streets, continuing the M.O.T. soundtrack throughout, pull
camera upward into an illusion of watching the turning of the
world; descend the camera into Obnoxia midway in the ceremoni-
als which precede the launching of the Bomb; The signing-off,
TIME—MARCHES ON!!, launches the bomb-carrying plane; during
the next half-minute the sound background is the irate gab-
bling of Donald Duck, with a surflike undertone of audience
laughter.
    I'll give the stuff here in such detail as I have, though
it's both sketchy and long, because I think it does convey the
possible tone, spirit and general idea. But I won't try even
feebly to synchronize the words and images. First I'll give
the Grand Old Man's speech; then the pull-out and Obnoxian
scene; up to the explosion.
    The speech is so very much too long, I hesitate to bother
you with it; but I think it does contain in rough form some
things essential to the prologue: what crooks and fools can
make of a crisis and of a democracy, and a fair picture of a
good bit to do with the all-American state of mind.

GRAND OLD MAN: (His voice is highly trained, fundamentally
truculent, as rotten as gangrene. At the start he makes his
own kind of try at imitating the Franklin Roosevelt manner. By
the end, he is using every trick of the revivalist and the
backwoods orator.)
    Fellow-Americans! (Cheers). In My Day, (cheers), I believe
that I served you well. (Cheers, shouts.) I served you for a
long, long time. (Cheers.) I was with you and your valiant pioneer wives in your Covered Wagons. (Cheers.) I was with you
heart and soul when the Blue fought the Gray (cheers), and
vice versa (cheers; a loving titter). I was with Woodrow Wilson when, in Paris, the whole world looked to him and saw its
hope, like a bowl of goldfish, poised in his frail scholar's

hand. (Cheers.) And I was with the Boys Back Home who moder-
ated his great dream more in accordance with the hard realities of this workaday world (cheers.) I am with you still.
(Cheers, loud cheers.) I am with you still (faint cheers), and
I ask to serve you yet once again (cheers and screams). I wish
to serve you (cheers) in a very simple way (questioning
cheers) by simply reminding you, that you are Americans. (Silence. Murmurs. Cheers. Loud cheers. A bit of stomping.) *You:*
are *Americans, fellow-* Americans! (cheers.) Do not be dismayed
(questioning cheers); for remember; (silence): *Americans—*
don't—scare easy!! (Shrieks, cheers, and whistles.) Let me repeat that, muh-friends: *Amurricans don't skeer easy!!*
(whistles). These are threatening times we see ahead of us:
(silence): *sure* they're threatening times! (Quicker, quieter,
more biting:) But since when, muh-friends, has a red-blooded
He-Amurrican or I may say also *She*-Amurrican (laughter), I-
say, since when has a redblooded hundredpercent Amurrican *ever*
been known (voice rising) to back down on a challenge. (Questioning cheers.) *I* say, *it ain't never* BEEN done, (cheers and
laughter; element of relief) *and* I-say: it *won't never BE*
done! (Loud cheers and laughter.) Did we back down at Bunker
Hill? (Shouts of No! No!) Did we back down at the Constitu-
tional Convention? (Doubtful shouts of No.) Did we back down,
either side, at Bull Run, Missionary Ridge, the Second Manas-
sas, Gettysburg? (No! No! No! No!) Did-we-back-down-from-cow-
ardly-little SPAIN? (NO!) Or Kaiser Bill?? (NO!!!) Or A-dolf
Hitler? (NO!!!!!)So are we a-goan to back down over a little
ole thing like a A-tomic Bomb . . . (laughter) . . . *Spashilly*
when We-uns is got it (hoots of laughter) *and They-uns ain't*
got NERN? (Screams of laughter; wild applause.) I ask you,
fellow-Amurrucans and ladies, yes and babes-in-arms into the
bargain, I ask you, are we goin' to back down to old Uncle Joe
Stalin ??? (Raging shrieks of NO! NO!!)

(Change of voice: quiet, honest-John, reasonable:)

   Now my fellow-Americans, I know you and you know me.
(Quiet cheers.) You know my great respect for the signtists.
Together with American business and finance (smart handclap-
ping) and together with American labor (cheers and stomping)
they add up to spell American Know-How (CHEERS.) Together
with these great democratic American forces they have raised
the standard of living in this Old Nation of Ours to whur it
is the envy of the hull civilized world (cheers under this
rising sentence)—that is, if you can *call* what they got over
there a civil-eye-zation (laughter and applause). Well as I
said and let me repeat it, folks, I have got a great respect

for Seyence. I don't think it would be too much to say that without the Signtists, none of us would be enjoying the American Standard of Living this very day. (Polite cheers and applause.)

And Ladies 'n' Genlmen, as you all well know I respect the Schoolteacher. Our schooling is a thing we Americans have always been proud of, and with good reason too. Old Abe did his studyin' on the back of a shovel. (Sentimental cheers.) Lots more of us got our studying whacked into us, more-like, with the back of a shovel on our little backsides (laughter). Readin', Writn, Rithmuhtic, the roodiments O' Larnin', yes-*Sir!* It's all-ways been my regret, fellow Americans, that I didn't attain to higher education myself, though I *am* a Practical Man. (Sympathetic applause.)

And most deeply of all, fellow-Americans, as you all well know, you all well know my deep veneration for religion, whatever its form. It's like the fella says, what profuteth it a man if he gain the *whole world,* an' lose his own soul? (Questioning, mild murmur.) If you haven't got the love an the fear of Almighty God *right here* in yer *heart* (his thumps are audible), well, that new car you drive ain't a-goin to hold the road so very good no matter *how* careful you drive, an that Dollar ye spend ain't somehow gonna ring true on the counter an' to be wholly serious mu-franz, unless each and all of us has got a living sense a God in our hearts and in our daily lives, well, this Old Country of Ours may's well shet up shop: *which* I thank Almighty God in all humility I don't see no evidence of its happening. (Cheers and laughter).

And Friends, like every other American I respect a man that has his own independent opinion and stand by it through thick or thin, though I *do* say it makes a *leetle* diffunce to me whether his opinion is sound or *rotten.* (Laughter; snarls.) But don't get me wrong, friends, I admire independence of mind like I admire independence at the voting booth. (Cheers). This old country'd be in a mighty poor fix if the most of us didn't stand up fer both! (Cheers; applause.)

But fellow-Americans, like every sane man, there are *limits* to my tolerance as there are limits to yours. I admire signtists, *in their place,* but when they try to stand up and tell honest American Citizens they oughta change their *politics,* well, the politest way I can put it, they are strongly advised in the inturess of their own safety to get on back to their test-tubes and fix up some new Stinks or Benefits to Humanity and leave Politics to the folks that has devoted their lives to the service of the common people as practical politicians. (Growing roar of approving laughter and hatred for scientists, throughout this last sentence.)

Now also I have great respect for teachers *in their place;* but when a teacher starts calling himself an *Educator,* just don't take yer eye off him or turn yer back or he'll start tellin yer childurn how they can't be responsible voting cit- izens unless they learn how from *him,* let alone raisn yer school taxes outa sight while ye ain't lookin. (Laughter). We had us a taste of perfessors, an' male schoolmarms, a-tryin to run the Guv-Ment not so very long ago, and the country's only just beginning to return to their senses to this day. (Laugh- ter.) So I say to these "Educators": spare the child, gentle- men, yer spilin fer the rod and if yer not almighty careful some good plain Amurrican parents is a goin to lay it on ye whur it'll do the most good. (Cheers and laughs.)

And I respect the gentlemen of the cloth, the ministers, that is; *in their place.* But when they start tellin decent God-fearn Americans that all they've got to do is set araoun savin thur souls, an' that at a time when clouds uh warr are threatenin our shores an' darknin our very skies, why-then, why-then with all due respect I suggest to these psalm-singin brethern—not to mention the Jesuits and the *Rabbis*—just you quit living off the fat o' the collection-box long enough to get yer blue noses caught in the machinery of the workaday world fer a couple uh twists an' *then* see what ya got ta say about settn raoun cultivatn yer *soul.* (Again, mounting laugh- ter & applause through this invective.)

And as fer that feller that talks about *independence,* well, well folks, yes, I respect him, too, *in his place;* and I think you and I, I think we all know very well where his proper place is, even if he don't, and it's all nicely padded, friends, even the floor, and even the cielin', an' nice big strong men in nurses' costumes come around several times each hour to hose him down an' pacify him an' clean out the floor when he talks like that, for the pore feller just can't con- trol hisself, that talks like that, an shouldn't oughta be blamed too harshly fer he just doesn't know what he's talking about. Or maybe he just belongs in Roosha, and ought to be de- ported there quicker'n' *scat.* For seriously, I ask you, friends, what are you and I and the gatepost to *think* of a man that tries to tell *Americans* they don't know how to think for themselves? What are we to think of the *sanity* of a man who talks to Americans about independence. Didnt he ever maybe hear of a unimportant little document called the *Declaration* of Independence? And maybe he just doesn't know about the free an equal *vote* we got here, the Secret Ballot? Maybe in the country where he did his serious thinkin they never heared o such institutions. Or maybe *if* they heard of them why all they want to do nightnday is send termites in to undermine um an'

destroy um. Or maybe this poor fella is just crazy after all,
like there is one in every small town, friends, that got
dropped on the head when he was a baby, or maybe disappointed
in love, or talked to some Jewish Socialist too much when they
went to *collitch* together, and ever since, why he's been dead
certain that the hull world's going to rot because, why obviously, *everybody's* outa step but *him.*

However that may be, my friends, I'll lay you long odds on
one thing; that this independent so-called think-er never
voted, he was much too busy a-thinkin deep thoughts, or *if* he
voted, I betcha he mighty seldom voted for a winning candidate. I don't honestly believe, friends, that a man of his
stripe is very sensitive to the will o' the people—not when he
don't even think they know how to *think* fer themselves. And in
all frankness I must venture my doubt also that our independent friend has assembled together much of the good things of
this world; for people that think like that, muh-friends, just
don't somehow seem to get ahead, not in the American scheme uh
things, because they just aren't *liked* or *trusted* enough, an'
besides, that kind a talk is always *jealous* talk.

So I think we have disposed of our Independent friend,
sufficiently, to move on to matters that concernnus more seriously.

(Noble, quiet, heartfelt, confidential:)

My very dear friends. All it is, is simply this. You've
got nothing to be afraid of. Nothing to worry about whatever.
So long as you keep your good hard American hoss-sense. God
helps them that helps themselves. Never forget that. Know yer
advantages when you see them, and never let an advantage rust
in yer hand. (Quietly, slowly, with great intensity:) We are
the mightiest nation of human beings on the face of the
earth. All we have to do is take our advantage, before it's
taken from us. We are the best people on the face of the
earth. All we have to do is assume our natural leadership and
see to it that the others follow, and I fervently say, my
friends, may the Devil take the hindmost. We are the *free-est*
and the *best-governed* people on the face of the earth. If the
rest of um want our form of government in the form we choose
to administrate it, welcome to them and more power to them,
there is none so lowly but what we can find a use fer um. If
they choose instead to set up a conflicting ideology, then we
serve fair warning, they do so at their own purl [peril]. As
for us, ladies and gentlemen, the future is quite simple and
secure for us, if we look it in the eye, and meet its challenge in the proper fearless confidence which has always befit-
ted Americans. We are grateful for the findings of our
scientists, we respect those who prepare our minds for the

great battle of life, we venerate those who show us God's
Will and our own poor morl frailties and foibles, and we even
find a place in our hearts for our mavericks, our eccentrics,
but Friends: we do not need their advice. For I say to you in
all sincerity, my friends, and with pardonable pride: *we
Americans are a tough-minded old people.* We learned that a
long time back and it is grained deep into our figgerin' about
things. We don't like to be told what to think, and if
there's one thing we *do hate,* it's being told how to vote.
All I have to say to you, my dear friends and fellow-Americans, boils down to just this: This beloved old country of
ours is governed by the will of the people. By the grace of
God it will *continue* to be governed by the will of the people
and woe to him that says otherwise. And friends, at the end
of my long career of public service let me say in all deep humility before you, who have so many and many a time returned
me to this office and that, in peacetime and in the shadow of
great purl, in sickness and in health; *I have good reason* to
have thorough confidence in your will and in your judgment
(cheers have been rising and now interrupt him; he goes on
with tears in his voice)—*great* confidence, dear old friends,
and great *gratitude, not* because you had scientific training
or theories of world government, not out of any fancy education, not even through yer listening to the still small voice
of God, friends, though I humbly believe and pray, folks,
that That has a hand in it as it has had a hand in guiding our
whole emblazoned American Destiny (solemn cheers) but just
out of your good old solid down-to-earth American *hoss*-sense,
that government of the people, by the people, and for the
people, shall not perish from the earth until death us do
part. A-men. I thank you.

PULL OUT FROM THEATER; OBNOXIA: LAUNCHING THE BOMB-
CARRIER

(Just where the camera should leave the theater, awaits shortening and clearing of the March of Time parody. One way, I
geared it to pull out while the Minister is talking; but I
think a shortening of the political oration should close the
M.O.T. Street shots can of course be played very sharp against
what is being said on the M.O.T. soundtrack, which persists.
But it goes, roughly, as follows:)

Camera turns from the screen, quietly, and confronts the whole
audience. It moves back up the theater, just above their
heads, studying their faces. It breaks forth from the theater
into the crowded early afternoon street and moves just above

head-height. Then just above building-height. Then, at the floor-base of Old Fogy, the supercomputing machine, we see a timid mouse. Then a very high view of New York City. A still higher view of cities on the great midland plain. The coastline, moving; the blank ocean, moving; lower camera through capricious architectural details and breeze-yammering Flag of Obnoxia, to top-to-toe closeup of the Obnoxian aviator who will carry the Bomb.

He is fair, very young, arrogantly and extraordinarily beautiful. He should have pure serpent's eyes, a saurian face. He should suggest the description of Shelley as a snake standing on the tip of its tail. And he should suggest an angel: the Angel of Death. He is dressed in pure white leather. As camera takes him first, he is being embraced (and at first obscured) by his sobbing mother, in deep black, and by a radiant, dedicated girl in a bridal dress. A choir is singing plainchant, solemnly, and a magnificently coped and mitred archbishop, his brocaded vestments sparkling like mica, is seen to be sprinkling him with holywater as the camera pulls away. But these things barely touch his utter remoteness and arrogance. He is the purest of skilled agents and of dedicated young knights; so thoroughly consecrated that in every most important sense he is already dead. The bride's attitude expresses complete confidence in his swift and glorious return; the mother's, that he will never return, and that against all her better judgment she doubts the gloriousness of this, anyhow. They are disentangled from him and helped away by high dignitaries, who treat them with the peculiar honor reserved for those close to the martyrs and heroes of the proletariat. The boy's mouth is shining, as we first see him, with his bride's kiss; his cheek is damp with his mother's tears; now it is further bedewed by the holywater. The Obnoxian scientists shown in the M.O.T. frisk in hurriedly with last-minute warnings and instructions (after all, as they must show in pantomime, it's their baby, they're delivering into his "safe" keeping); they add their solemn, excited good wishes: the boy's face shows that he is interested in nothing they can tell him. The top government men converge on him with faintly pansy awe; one pins an emblazonment over his heart (clumsy with the pin) and kisses him on both cheeks: he smiles coldly, with a coldness aged perhaps seventeen but matured by a kind of genius and transfigured by his sense of the imminence of History and of Death. A little man in a big admiral's hat and a big man (the scallion-eater of the M.O.T.) come up. The little man suffused with emotion, clicks to a noble salute (manner of Ben Turpin in Salome-vs-Shenandoah); the boy returns it correctly but with a touch of nonchalance. The scallion-eater, who is clearly the real boss of the country try (where are: Mack Swain, or Kalla Pasha?) merely claps him roughly on the shoulder (leaving a dirty mark) and breathes aroma in his face, belching faintly. The boy's face freezes with polite contempt; he flicks a dirty speck from the white leather; looks at the smear that is left as if it were excrement. A faint, sissy voice attracts his attention; his cold eyes flick from center; we see the King, all beard, gentle depravity and fatuousness waving a sheer handkerchief while the Queen simpers and twinkles; the King touches his fingertips in salute) to his heavily jeweled crown, which skids a little awry; the Queen and a Chamberlain make haste to straighten it. The boy, suppressing a sneer, bows humbly. He looks sharp to the left: the scientists are all set, at the complicated dials which will register the distant success of the explosion. They give him the worshipful go-ahead. The boy looks still more imperiously to the right. Two mechanics, in slightly soiled uniforms of white leather, nod that all is ready. (One is the ultimate, frecklefaced Gadget Kid; the other an apelike, Dick Sutherland type; each carries a stainless steel wrench. A majordomo gives a signal; a military band begins to play, solemnly, the national anthem, muted, contending with the muted March of Time track. Magnificently, the boy walks toward his craft, the camera following. We first see the craft. It is the most fierce, beautiful, sinister possible parodistic paraphrase of the raked-back, sting-ray type of supersonic craft: pure white. The archbishop is just finishing sprinkling it with holy water. The boy flicks out a white chamois and dries it. He steps in; it is that low to the ground. He turns his head and moves his eyes, keenly, subtly as a seagull, looking at his well-wishers. We flutter them through in quick medium and close shots: the King and Queen; the scallion-eater and the admiral; the archbishop and his acolytes; the Scientists at their controls; an American-looking businessman who[se] money, we must infer by his appearance, is behind the whole scheme; shopkeepers and their wives; factory workers; prosperous peasants; serfs (all these classes and kinds variously roped-off in hierarchic stands and barriers); his mother and his bride; and the ground-mechanics who give him the traditional thumbs-up Roger. (In all this, besides travesty, there should be conveyed a sense of glory, pathos, poverty; of all that can be heroic in nationalistic mania; of an impoverished, long and deeply humiliated proud, ambitious little country which has put all it has into a desperate adventure and which now stands on the verge of it.) Back to the boy: he returns the Roger. He pulls on his goggles, so slanted that they make his face still more finally into the face of a serpent. He presses a button and, implacably, no less serpentlike, the angled lucite shield slides tight and encloses him. He is seen manipulating the bright hasps of metal which tighten it into place: he no longer looks at anything or anyone outside the plane. In a stylized, massive shot, standing on ground stripped of all except short grass, we see all the Obnoxian principals, eyes glued on the little plane: King, Queen, Archbishop and choirboys shrilling the closing bars of the National Anthem; mother and bride clasping each other tight; members of the flaunt-braided military band: above them all, Obnoxia's flag in a smart breeze: any amount of grand-stand bunting: tears are on many faces; tears of solemn hope and patriotism. There is a hideous exaggeration of the noise of a jet-propelled machine taking off, and this group is stiffened and engulfed in a terribly strong wind, the wind of his departure: some topple, others lean hard against the wind: the archbishop's mitre, the King's crown, the fancy handkerchief he was toodle-oo-ing farewell with, his silly beard, the poor damn flag, the bunting, the mother's widow's-weeds, the bride's lovely veil, the choirboys' lacy cottas—all which can be stripped, dismayed, torn, humiliated by a hard wind, suffers the consequences, and most eyes are so filled and tormented with dust that as we leave Obnoxia in chaos nearly everyone seems blindly to be suffering the effects of a tear-gas bomb. In a quick closing shot we see an immense flat vista of sand; disappearing into its dead center, so fast we can only just see what it must be, is the bomb-bearing craft, rising rapidly as it disappears.

EXPLOSION AND IMMEDIATE AFTERMATH

Back to a few, quick normal shots of U.S. countryside and city streets, culminating in streets of New York. Lift camera casually to the sky. The airship moves almost undiscernibly high, in perfect silence, from horizon to zenith to horizon, at about the speed of a shooting star. It is keenly white against the deep sky. It is seen by only three people. In the city, a yokel, who happened to be gawping up at a skyscraper. In open country, a child was looking up at a butterfly, or just innocently gazing at nothing in particular, and so sees it and says, "oh, *look,* Daddy!" He looks—and clutches the child to him and falls headlong upon her.

But most people are not aware of this swift noiseless flight above them. They are just going about their business; here use literal sneaked street shots. Many do become aware, however, a few seconds after we have seen the craft sink beneath the horizon; for only then is it followed by its terrible sound, which

stripes across the heavens like a whip or a surgeon's knife, in
a swift trick of sound crescendent from pianissimo to deafening loudness and, as swiftly, to pianissimo (I think perhaps
the craft should leave an ether trail, neat as a chalk-mark on
a blackboard, to give a visible pathway for this enormous
whine). Hearing this, many—not all—look up, in time to see what
the audience has already seen. What the audience saw was this:
At the exact zenith, the plane planted a tiny seed of white,
which falls quickly. As the people in general look up, this
seed suddenly becomes a little blossom; a parachute has
opened, exquisitely scalloped, crisp and pure—it sinks slowly,
implacably, dangling gently in the uneven spring air.

Here, swiftly intercut expressions and shouts of awe, mystification, recognition, terror, scurrying for shelter, standing silent and stoically resigned, dropping to knees in
prayer, with those many more of a great city who are so dead-
ened to odd commotion that they don't look up, but merely jos-
tle past the suddenly kneeling or hiding or screaming figures;
among the oblivious figures in this last street scene of the
last moment of modern civilization we glimpse in rear view a
familiar silhouette: the Tramp, too busy running like hell
from a cop, for either of them to be aware of anything else.

Back to the parachute; hold on it, leisurely, as it sinks,
working all possible suspense out of this terrible and pretty
leisure in which only the chute and the fading ether-stream
are visible; during keenest suspense of the dandling parachute, two brief shots—an antiaircraft frantically readying
its aim and its commander as frantically forbidding fire (if
the bomb were hit, the disaster could be even worse, he
thinks); and a farmer, hopelessly giving the out-of-range target both barrels of his shotgun.

For pre-explosion sound, perhaps just intensify a subtle
hissing crackling as of a fuse; or, some such odd sound as
boiling, bubbling oatmeal, set against the pure parachute
image; or, interrupt dead silence, with the full blast. For
the blast itself, the following: on screen, alternate frames
of two kinds of whiteness, one the utmost possible glare, the
other the flattest possible dead-white: or, the picture's only
use of color: the whole spectrum boiling and fusing into the
most extreme possible white glare. On the soundtrack: The reg-
istrations of an organ-pipe so deep as to be subsonic. This
registers on the eardrums and in the body without being defin-
able as sound. The effect, I am told (something of the sort
was once used in a Baltimore production of *Berkeley Square*),
is indescribably disturbing, not to say terrifying. This, I
think, could be more appropriate and effective than any actual
sound I can imagine, but if a mask for it, some sort of audi-

ble sound, seems useful. I suggest adding to this terror one of three very simple noises: the noise of breath blowing flame through loose paper; or of a blowtorch; or of a deep, sorrow-drowned, almost sobbing sigh quality of the sound of the dying, last breath of Christ on the cross.

Abruptly, after only a few seconds, the screen stops flickering and all sound stops dead: and prodigious on the sky sprouts a new shape of smoke: it should bear some relation to the mushroom shape but I suspect it should be new. Quite possibly, the shape of a gigantic angel, the dark death angel, rears up first the full height of its standing body, then (like arms swung straight outward from the sides), flings its huge wings upward into the peak of the sky until, as their highest points touch and merge the entire shape leans solemnly and magnificently, almost with a look of compassion, towards the earth. The camera rides this effigy to its crest, watching close into the rumbling, rumpling flame and smoke, the boiling, bubbling, gradual dissolving; and, as the air grows once more clear, bends its eyes slowly and tenderly downward.

The roundness of the world and its continental shapes are seen, through a low bar of strange and stony light; the earth is turning swiftly; and swiftly, in silence, the camera bores downward towards the flow of continents and seas: still above this band or shell of deadly, stony, new light. We come closer: a bird, then two more, fling themselves proudly across the camera's view, flying beautifully, quite close at first, their wincing songs delicately audible: the first one dives along the band of light; his wings constrict, his song cuts short and dead in mid-phrase; he falls straight towards the earth like a little stone; the two others, mutually flirtatious in their flying and in their song, follow suit; the camera follows. We are close enough now that (in great simplification we can see, flowing from right to left beneath us (i.e., dead ahead of us; the camera is vertical), the great shapes of coastline and the great landmarks of the great cities of the planet, whose whole revolving, in this simplification, planet, ocean; should take perhaps thirty seconds. We watch little ships on the ocean; their smoke-trails have detached from them and fade beside them; at this distance they have no forward notion (and we can see no white trail of wake); they merely buckle before our eyes and dive infinitesimally into the water, like doodlebugs into their dust. We watch the great buildings and landmarks; some are ravaged, many are intact or nearly so; we only begin to notice, as we come into the second revolution of the globe, within the height through which we might begin to see human beings moving, that in the great squares the streets are

empty, though shining with the complexity of fine-hammered
silver; and that along the great farmlands, where wheat which
had been wind-rippled is now as dead and bright as watered
silk, neither man nor animals nor machines move, or are visible. The camera continues its probing descent and begins to
deploy its eyesight. Up to now the shot has been one continuous flow; the camera staring vertical and moving straight
down, and the world moving from right to left, the camera now
and then mildly swaying its eye from point to point of special interest, but never breaking the shot. Now, still glid-
ing downward and still keeping the general motion from right
to left in descent, begin to cut. We descend towards and past
a high radio tower; it is exuding a scratchy moil of music,
commercials, educational speeches and a jabbing SOS; as we
drift past, all these, scarcely audible, fade, and go dead,
the SOS last. We descend towards the great flat roofs of Oak
Ridge; and towards the solemn and stifled groaning of great
machines: the groaning dies; above a great industrial city we
see the last smoke of the stacks, far detached, vanishing; a
huge wheel, its belt wavering, ceases to move; the belt itself stops wavering; a regiment of dynamos stands dead; a
dead cyclotron. We see the launching place of the fatal
plane: all that is left is a set of epaulets, an Admiral's
tricorne, its feather scorched crazily, a pair of spectacles
which a scientist had worn, their lenses half liquefied, the
fused dials of the finding-machine, with one trembling needle
twitching round and round like the shuddering reflexes of a
killed reptile; the crown, a mess of jewels and precious
metal like heat-ruined peanut brittle; one scorched fragment
of bridal veil. We see the deadly new aircraft: at first we
mistake it for a butterfly which might have been flattened by
rain, by its look, but coming closer we recognize what it is,
flat as thin paper, against a cindrous country field. We see,
from about 200 feet up, tremendous country landscape, shining
like one flat of slag. We see, from about a hundred feet up,
the sunlit length of a great street, one seen earlier, in the
prologue: it is perfectly empty. We see still another great,
empty street. We see a plow, twisted and fused into the fused
earth, its fused furrow behind it, metal skeleton of mule-
harness ahead of it. We see, in the city, a grotesquely deformed, bronze equestrian statue; then the equally deformed
statue of a public benefactor: his hand had obviously once
been in the conventional gesture of protective largesse; now,
his stature is so shrunken and his shoulder so miserably
shrugged that the hand is out of position: he seems merely to
be shrugging an apologetic, what-the-hell, folks, half-
hearted excuse. The camera, at a little above head-height,

looks onto a narrow crevice between two great buildings and quickly descends to human height, settling to rest with the solid little jounce of an elevator at the ground floor. The Tramp is there.

E. A FEW ADDITIONS AND SUGGESTIONS

Various things have been so inadequately defined or sketched, that I want to make a few corrections or further suggestions.

I'm seriously worried that I've failed to make some central issues clear enough.

This is not a "political" satire, in any traditional sense anyhow. It tries to discuss matters nearer the roots of the trouble than straight politics can get.

Nor is it "anti-scientific," as it surely must seem at this stage; nor are the scientists to be blamed for everything, or regarded as the villains. The conception is, rather, they they're essentially innocent men; but that much greater harm can come through innocence, even, than through conscious evil.

Scientists, their discoveries, and the Scientific Attitude, formed the whole of modern life, in substance and thought; inadvertently, but inevitably, encouraging everything in human beings which was hostile to self-realization, and tending to discourage self-realization, self-trust, spontaneity. Much of civilization is formed out of corruptions of the Scientific Attitude: and the scientists themselves are victims or that corruption.

The direct enemies of personality, in the contemporary world, are not scientists: but science is the father of their leading assumptions and attitudes, and scientists themselves still embody the cardinal attitude in its purest, most radical, most caricaturable form.

Scientists are to the contemporary world what the clerical hierarchy was to the Middle Ages; most public leaders and teachers and exploiters and most laymen bow before their "spiritual authority" as unskeptically as, in the Middle Ages, they bowed to Rome. We should parodistically illustrate many analogies between Scientists and Priests. Essentially, this is an anticlerical satire. And by rough parallel the necessary fight now, to break the hold of the "scientific attitude" and to try to restore and to extend the "humanistic," is similar to the fight carried by scientists and leaders of the Reformation, a few hundred years ago.

With time and care, I am sure I could make clearer why the scientists should be the leaders in the suicidal camp—and why and how the film can clearly avoid being a very wrong- and false thing—a mere blame-it-all-on-the-scientists satire. One equally fundamental fact is that laymen, en masse and individually, are at last equally responsible; for swallowing everything whole; but that in the ultramaterialistic world—whether capitalistic or socialized—which technology facilitates and gives inevitable form to, the odds are simply infinitely too strong, against most individual human beings. They have to choose between complete superficial self-gratification and security, on the one hand, and the extraordinarily difficult, self-denying (*not ascetic*) efforts of self-realization. With the inducements so great as technology can make them, it's all but impossible to choose the latter—or even to see the choice clearly; compromise seems so possible.

I do earnestly hope that if I've failed to make this main set of points clear, or to persuade you of their validity or sensibleness for satirical treatment, you'll be kind enough to let me try again.

The film alternates and combines, and collides, two kinds of comedy—the icy fierceness and bitterness of Verdoux, and the humanistic comedy of the Tramp.

You could easily and wonderfully play two roles, of course—the Tramp; and an archetypical scientist: toothbrush mustache, square head, glittering lenses, dead sandpiper voice. But so far as I can see now, this would complicate rather than clarify the general story and issues.

In the Scientific camp, by one kind of logic, they might forge ahead by leaps and bounds through all the famous *beneficent* uses of atomic energy; and we would then demonstrate that most of those uses can be as essentially destructive of humanity (through benumbing and destruction of personality) as the military uses. But, I suspect this would lead too heavily into pseudo-scientific satiric fantasy—whereas, in both camps, the constant focus should be on the effects on personality.

In both camps, at this stage of the game, my ideas are still, mostly, much too conventional, tame, and naive. I think these, in both camps, could be heightened into real wonder-workers and shockers—again, bearing in mind that the key in both cases is, the rebirth and life of human personality; or its freezing and death.

The Tramp, besides being himself, is at various stages of the film Pan, Adam, Jesus, and the Scapegoat (fleeing into the Wilderness, at end of picture): most essentially, he is the human spirit and all, good and bad and morally irrelevant, which is essential and eternal in it and might—we wish—be indestructible in it.

The Scientists survive through scientific preparation and protection—and are, of course, unaffected by the Bomb: they are not suggestible to change; they are only more acutely all that they were before.

The laymen, of both camps, survive by either inscrutable luck and accident, or by the curious grace of God, or by both. (We should never, except by burlesque scientific research and conjecture, "explain" the survivals.)

Under the scientists, everyone lives by Reason, caution essentially by fear. Everything is carefully tested before it is tried. (At start, with their instruments dead and only their instincts and needs to rely on, the scientists are all but paralyzed; *afraid of everything. They dare nothing.*)

The Tramp, and those with him, have no such sophistication, protection, depth of fear. They live according to their naive needs. They know enough to be afraid of a good deal; but to live at all, they have to dare everything. This daring, and trust and instinct, of itself helps awaken them to their full human nature.

My general assumption is that the picture would be mainly silent: but that most of such talk as there is until the end, should be characteristic of the scientific camp; silence and pantomime, the characteristic of the Tramp's. So that a silent film and a talkie are played off against each other, parallel with impulse and expressiveness as against "pure reason."

It should be made very clear that the picture is not against rationality, but against the so-called pure rationality which seems in fact a mortal and insane perversion of true reason: that true reason involves the heart and spirit and body, as well as the forebrain.

There should be at least one scientist at work in the Tramp's community: Our demonstration of what a humanistic scientist can be.

Should be distinct attention, in both camps, to *women:* questions of emancipation and vassalage, of sexuality and beauty, of fullness or emptiness as women.

And to *religion:* chiefly just that, as with politics, mere religious practice and belief can go either way: beneficent and life-giving (to those who care for it); or deadening, enslaving, blandly servile of tyranny.

I think, a rule in the Tramp's community should be, that no artificial help should be given the human voice—no mikes, megaphones, amplifiers. That a political speaker, for instance, is permitted to influence only so many people as can hear his own, unassisted voice.

In the Scientific camp, nearly all voices are synthetic, electroplated, denatured.

In the Prologue, the Grand Old Man's oration might continue, on a soundtrack gone crazy, throughout the lowering of the camera onto the desolated world, ending as the Tramp is found; but I suspect that silence would be more powerful than this brutal conflict and contrast.

NOTES

PRELUDE

1. Dwight MacDonald, "James Agee: Some Memories and Letters," *Encounter* 19 (December 1962), 73–84.
2. Robert Coles, "James Agee's Search," reprinted in *A Robert Coles Omnibus* (Iowa City: University of Iowa Press, 1993) 150.
3. Winthrop Sargeant, *In Spite of Myself: A Personal Memoir,* (Garden City: Doubleday 1970), 233.
4. Ibid., 234.
5. "James Agee By Himself," in *Agee: Selected Literary Documents*, ed. Victor A. Kramer (Troy, NY: Whitston 1996), 197.
6. Richard Oulahan, in *Life*, November 1, 1963, 69–72.
7. Walker Evans, "James Agee in 1936," foreword to *Let Us Now Praise Famous Men* (New York: Ballantine Books 1969), x.
8. Transcription of interview with Manny Farber from video provided by the 2003 San Francisco Film Festival.
9. Robert Fitzgerald, "A Memoir," *Collected Short Prose of James Agee*, (London: Calder & Boyars, 1969; reprinted from *The Kenyon Review*, November 1968), 42.
10. John Huston, foreword to *Agee on Film, Volume 2*, by James Agee (New York: Putnam Publishing Group, 1983), x.
11. "James Agee By Himself," in *Agee: Selected Literary Documents*, ed. Victor A. Kramer (Troy, NY: Whitston 1996), 196.
12. Robert Fitzgerald, "A Memoir," 41.
13. Huston, foreword to *Agee on Film, Volume 2*, ix; John Huston, *An Open Book*, (New York: Da Capo Press 1994), 188.
14. Walker Evans, "James Agee in 1936," foreword to *Let Us Now Praise Famous Men.*
15. Robert Fitzgerald, "A Memoir," *Collected Short Prose of James Agee*, 43; John Huston, *Agee on Film, Volume 2*, ix.
16. Evans, "James Agee in 1936," foreword to *Let Us Now Praise Famous Men*, ix.
17. Reverend James H. Flye to *Village Voice*, *Village Voice*, January 7, 1965.
18. Howard Pollack, *Aaron Copland: The Life and Work of an Uncommon Man*, (New York: Henry Holt, 1999), 192.
19. *Conversations with Pauline Kael*, ed. Will Brantley, (Jackson: University of Mississippi, 1996, reprint from Ray Sawhill and Polly Frost, "Kaleidoscope," *Interview*, April 1989), 110.
20. Richard Schickel, *Good Morning, Mr. Zip Zip Zip: Movies, Memory and World War II*, (Chicago: Ivan R. Dee, 2003), 48.

21. David Thomson, *The New Biographical Dictionary of Film*, (New York: Knopf, 2003), 5.
22. James Agee to Ilse Lahn, August 11, 1952, Archiv der Stiftung Deutsche Kinemathek (Sammlung Paul Kohner), Berlin, Germany.
23. Agee, *Let Us Now Praise Famous Men*, 323
24. Agee, Unpublished draft notes for *Monsieur Verdoux* review in *Nation*, James Agee papers, Harry Ransom Center, University of Texas, Austin.
25. James Agee, James Agee: Literary Notebooks and Other Manuscripts, ed. Michael A. Lofaro and Hugh Davis, (Ridgewood, NJ: The James Agee Press, 2002), 126.
26. James Agee, screenplay for "The Tramp's New World," (author's suggested title), collection of the Chaplin estate.
27. Reprint from *Nation*, January 20 1945, in James Agee, Agee on Film, (New York: Modern Library, 2000), 123.
28. Ibid.
29. Dwight MacDonald, *Against the American Grain*, (New York: Random House, 1962), 160.
30. Agee to Dwight MacDonald, June 16, 1927, Special Collection Yale University Library.
31. Agee to Dwight MacDonald, July 21, 1927, Special Collection Yale University Library
32. Ibid.
33. *The Twenty-Four Dollar Island* (1927) was an early experimental film by pioneer documentarian Robert Flaherty.
34. Agee to Dwight MacDonald, April 24 1927, Yale University Library.
35. *Remembering James Agee*, ed. Dave Madden, "Saturday Panel: Reminiscences," (Baton Rouge: Louisiana State University, 1974), 232.
36. Ibid.
37. Robert Fitzgerald, "A Memoir," *Collected Short Prose of James Agee*, 3.
38. Ibid., 4.
39. James Agee, "Dedication," *Collected Poems of James Agee*, (New York: Ballantine, 1970), 9.
40. Laurence Bergreen, *James Agee: A Life*, (New York: E.P. Dutton, 1984),144.
41. MacDonald to Dinsmore Wheeler, March 8, 1935, *A Moral Temper: The Letters of Dwight MacDonald*, ed. Michael Wreszin (Chicago: Ivan R. Dee, 2001), 52.
42. *Letters of James Agee to Father Flye*, (New York: George Braziller, 1962), 89.
43. Agee, *Let Us Now Praise Famous Men*, 321.
44. Ibid., 417.
45. MacDonald, "James Agee: Some Memories and Letters," *Encounter* 111 (December 1962), 73–84
46. *f.y.i.* (Time Inc.'s house organ), May 1955
47. *f.y.i.* (Time Inc.'s house organ), May 1955
48. Manny Farber, *Negative Space: Manny Farber on the Movies*, (New York: Da Capo Press, 1998) 391.

CHAPTER 1

1. Michael David Harris, *Always on Sunday: Ed Sullivan: An Inside View*, (New York: Meredith Press, 1968), p. 46. For all other quotes, see Jerry Bowles, *A*

Thousand Sundays: The Story of the Ed Sullivan Show, (New York: G.P. Putnam's Sons, 1980), 86.

2. Ibid.
3. Ibid.,113.
4. Ibid., 47.
5. Charles Chaplin, *My Autobiography*, (London: Readers Union, The Bodley Head, 1966), 490.
6. Lion Feuchtwanger to Chaplin, March 11, 1947, collection of the Lion Feuchtwanger Memorial Library, University of Southern California.
7. Ed Sullivan, Little Old New York, *New York Daily News*, April 7, 1947.
8. Ibid., April 9, 1947.
9. Natalie Robins, *Alien Ink: The FBI's War on Freedom of Expression*, (New Brunswick, NJ: Rutgers University Press, 1992), 124–125.
10. Hedda Hopper, *Los Angeles Times*, April 7, 1947.
11. In Chaplin's film *The Pilgrim* (First National, 1923) Chaplin plays an escaped convict who masquerades as a parson. Obliged to visit a parishioner's home, he is beset by their hellishly undisciplined young boy. Charlie finds that the best way to keep the monstrous child at bay is to give a quick hard push on the chest with the sole of his shoe.
12. Oona Chaplin to Lou Eisler, letter, dated April 12, 1947, in collection of the Lion Feuchtwanger Memorial Library, University of Southern California.
13. *Los Angeles Times*, April 11, 1947.
14. Hedda Hopper, *Los Angeles Times*, April 17, 1947.
15. Chaplin, *My Autobiography*, 490.
16. "Charlie Chaplin's Monsieur Verdoux Press Conference," *Film Comment*, Winter 1969, 34
17. Chaplin, *My Autobiography*, 486.
18. Orson Welles and Peter Bogdanovich, *This is Orson Welles*, ed. Jonathan Rosenbaum, (New York: HarperCollins, 1993), 136.
19. "Charlie Chaplin's Monsieur Verdoux Press Conference," Introduction, George Wallach, *Film Comment*, Winter 1969, 34.
20. Chaplin, *My Autobiography*, 488.
21. Maland, *Chaplin and American Culture*, 238.
22. Oona Chaplin to Lou Eisler, letter, dated April 12, 1947, in collection of the Lion Feuchtwanger Memorial Library, University of Southern California.
23. *New York Times*, April 14, 1947.
24. *Ibid.*, April 16, 1947.
25. INS interview with Chaplin, April 17, 1948, online at www.fadetoblack.com/foi/charliechaplin/bio.html, 236–262.
26. *Los Angeles Times*, April 20, 1947.
27. Hubert Kay, "The Career of Gerhart Eisler as a COMINTERN Agent," *Life*, February 17, 1947, 99–110.
28. *Eisler Hits Back*, pamphlet published by The German American, Inc., 1947 (collection of the author).
29. Kay, "The Career of Gerhart Eisler as a COMINTERN Agent," 99–110.
30. Albrecht Betz, *Hanns Eisler, Political Musician*, tr. Bill Hopkins, (New York: Cambridge University Press, 1982), 197.
31. Congressman Richard M. Nixon's Maiden Speech to the House of Representatives, February 18, 1947, http://watergate.info/nixon/maiden-house-speech–1947.shtml.

32. Ibid., 195.
33. James K. Lyon, *Bertolt Brecht in America*, (Princeton, NJ: Princeton University Press, 1980), 84.
34. Chaplin, *My Autobiography*, 471.
35. Bertolt Brecht, *The Three Penny Opera* (New York: Grove Weidenfeld, 1960), 92.
36. Charles Chaplin, *Monsieur Verdoux* (1947).
37. Bosley Crowther, *New York Times*, April 20, 1947.
38. Christopher Isherwood, *Diaries Volume One: 1939–1960*, Katherine Bucknell, ed. (New York: HarperCollins, 1997), 312.
39. Betz, *Hanns Eisler, Political Musician*, 194.
40. "Atom Bomb Spy Hearing Today," *San Francisco Examiner*, February 6, 1947.
41. Ed Sullivan, Little Old New York, *Washington Times Herald*, April 12, 1947.
42. Hedda Hopper, *Los Angeles Times*, April 18, 1947.
43. *New York Times*, April 18, 1947.
44. *Agee: His Life Remembered*, ed. Ross Spears and Jude Cassidy, (New York: Holt Rinehart & Winston, 1985) 157.

CHAPTER 2

1. *Agee: His Life Remembered*, ed. Spears and Cassidy, (New York: Holt, Rinehart & Winston, 1985), 143.
 2. T. S. Matthews, *Angels Unawares*, (New York: Ticknor & Fields, 1985), 237.
 3. James Agee, *Agee on Film*, (New York: Modern Library, 2000), 164.
 4. James Agee, *Letters of James Agee to Father Flye*, (New York: George Braziller, 1962), 150.
 5. Agee, *Agee on Film;* reprint of December 26, 1942, *Nation*.
 6. Farber, "Nearer My Agee to Thee," *Negative Space*, (New York: Da Capo Press, 1998), 87.
 7. *Remembering James Agee*, ed. Dave Madden and Jeffrey J. Folks, "Saturday Panel: Reminiscences," (Athens: University of Georgia Press, 1997), 240.
 8. W. H. Auden, "A Letter to the Editors of The Nation," October 16, 1944, reprinted in *Agee on Film*, xix.
 9. Dwight MacDonald, "The Bomb," *Memoirs of a Revolutionist*, (New York: Farrar, Straus and Cudahy, 1957, reprint from *Politics*, September 1945), 169–179.
10. James Agee, "Godless Gotterdammerung," *Time*, October 15, 1945, 62–64. Agee quotations that follow are all from this article.
11. Agee, *Letters of James Agee to Father Flye*, November 19, 1945,152–153.
12. Ibid.
13. John Hersey, *Hiroshima*, (New York: Alfred A. Knopf, 1946), 91–92.
14. Ibid., 95–96.

CHAPTER 3

1. Press book for *The Beginning or the End*, MGM, reprinted on the Internet at http://www.atomicbombcinema.com/english/image_gallery/beginning/begin_end_intro.html. Quotations that follow are all from this press book. Website accessed December 2004.

2. *The Beginning or the End* (1947), MGM.
3. James Agee, *Agee on Film* (New York: Modern Library, 2000; reprint from *Nation*, March 1, 1947), 236.
4. Chaplin Studios to Agee, May 9, 1947, Association Chaplin, Paris, France.
5. Agee, *Agee on Film* (reprint from *Time*, May 5, 1947), 358. Agee quotations that follow are all from this article.
6. Ibid. (reprint from *Time*, May 10, 1947), 246.
7. Lincoln Kirstein, *The Poems of Lincoln Kirstein* (New York: Atheneum, 1987), 156.
8. Agee to Erwin Piscator, May 15, 1947, collection the James Agee Trust.
9. Henry Miller to James Agee, May 19, 1947, collection the James Agee Trust.
10. Shirley O'Hara, "Chaplin and Hemingway," *New Republic*, May 5, 1947, 39.
11. *Film Comment 5* (Winter 1969), 33–43.
12. Unpublished draft notes for *Monsieur Verdoux* review in the *Nation*, James Agee, Harry Ransom Center, University of Texas, Austin. Agee quotations that follow are all from these draft notes.
13. Ibid.
14. James Agee, *James Agee: Literary Notebooks and Other Manuscripts*, ed. Michael A. Lofaro and Hugh Davis (Ridgewood, NJ: The James Agee Press, 2002), 123.
15. *Film Comment 5* (Winter 1969), 33–43.
16. Ibid.
17. Agee, unpublished draft notes for *Monsieur Verdoux* review in *Nation*, James Agee, Harry Ransom Center, University of Texas, Austin.
18. Ibid.
19. Agee, *Let Us Now Praise Famous Men* (New York: Ballantine Books, 1969),10.
20. Agee, unpublished draft notes for *Monsieur Verdoux* review in the *Nation*, James Agee, Harry Ransom Center, University of Texas, Austin. Agee quotations that follow are all from these draft notes.
21. Agee, *Agee On Film, Monsieur Verdoux* review part 1, May 31, 1947, 247–250. Agee quotations that follow are all from these draft notes.
22. *Agee On Film*, "Monsieur Verdoux-II," June 14, 1947, 250.
23. *Agee On Film*, "Monsieur Verdoux-III," June 21, 1947, 254.
24. Agee to Chaplin, 1948, Association Chaplin, Paris, France.
25. Laurence Bergreen, *Agee: A Life* (New York: E. P. Dutton, 1984), 302.
26. Agee to Chaplin, Unpublished draft of letter to Chaplin; collection of the James Agee Trust.
27. Charles J. Maland, *Chaplin and American Culture* (Princeton, NJ: Princeton University Press 1989), 242.
28. Luce to Agee, Harry Ransom Center.
29. Agee to Henry Luce, Time, Inc. Archives.
30. Agee to Dwight MacDonald, Spring, 1947, collection of Yale University Library.
31. *Agee: His Life Remembered*, ed. Spears and Cassidy, (New York: Holt, Rinehart & Winston, 1985), 140.
32. MacDonald to the Editors, the *Nation*, June 2, 1943, *A Moral Temper*, p. 110
33. Dwight MacDonald, "On Chaplin, Verdoux and Agee," *Esquire*, April 1965, 33. MacDonald quotations that follow are all from these draft notes.

CHAPTER 4

1. D. William Davis, "A Tale of Two Movies: Charlie Chaplin, United Artists, and the Red Scare," *Cinema Journal*, 27, No. 1, Fall 1987, 47–62.
2. David Robinson, *Chaplin: His Life and Art*, (New York: Da Capo Press, 1994), 545.
3. Ibid.
4. Martha Gellhorn, "Cry Shame!," *New Republic*, October 6, 1947, 20–21.
5. Ibid.
6. Ibid.
7. Lion Feuchtwanger to Charles Chaplin, December 27, 1947, Collection of The Lion Feuchtwanger Memorial Library, University of Southern California.
8. Agee, *Agee on Film, The Nation*, December 27, 1947, 281–284.
9. Ibid.
10. *Agee on Film, The Nation*, November 8, 1947, 277.
11. Ibid., July 5, 1947, 259.
12. Ibid., August 2, 1947, 265.
13. Ibid.
14. Jürgen Schebera, Hanns Eisler, (Mainz, Germany: Schott, 1998), 207.
15. Albrecht Betz, *Hanns Eisler, Political Musician*, (New York: Cambridge University Press, 1982), 207.
16. Woody Guthrie's lyrics for "Eisler on the Go" were finally put to music by Billy Bragg and Wilco on their 1998 collaboration *Mermaid Avenue*.
17. EISLER ON THE GO Words by Woody Guthrie © copyright 1998 by WOODIE GUTHRIE PUBILCATIONS, INC. All rights reserved. Used by permission.
18. Alma Neuman, *Always Straight Ahead: A Memoir*, (Baton Rouge and Louisiana: Louisiana State University Press, 1993), 54.
19. Laurence Bergreen, *James Agee: A Life* (New York: E. P. Dutton, 1984) 245.
20. Alma Neuman, *Always Straight Ahead*, 54.
21. T.S. Matthews, *Angels Unawares*, (New York: Ticknor & Fields, 1985), 171.
22. Ibid., 236.
23. Reuben interview with Mia Agee, September 13, 1969, William A. Reuben Papers, Labadie Collection, University of Michigan (Ann Arbor, Mich.).
24. Ibid.
25. Whittaker Chambers, *Witness: 50th Anniversary Editon*, (Washington D.C.: Regnery Publishing, 2002), 493.
26. Ibid.
27. Ibid., 504.
28. Nathalie Robins, Alien Ink, (New Brunswick, NJ: Rutgers University Press, 1993), 305.
29. Allen Weinstein, *Perjury: The Hiss-Chambers Case*, (New York: Random House, 1997), 308.
30. T. S. Matthews, *Angels Unawares*, 177
31. Sam Tanenhaus, *Whittaker Chambers: A Biography*, (New York: The Modern Library, 1998), 446.
32. Ibid., 447.
33. *Letters of James Agee to Father Flye*, George Braziller, New York, 1962, p. 201.

34. John Huston, *An Open Book*, (New York: Da Capo Press, 1994), 188.
35. Ibid.
36. Agee to Huston, John Huston papers, Academy of Motion Picture Arts and Sciences Library.
37. Ibid.
38. Arthur Miller, *Timebends: A Life*, (New York : Grove Press, 1987), 461.
39. Agee to Chaplin, collection of Association Chaplin, Paris, France.
40. Agee to Chaplin, unpublished letter, courtesy of the Chaplin Estate and the James Agee Trust.
41. Agee, unpublished notes to *Life* editors, James Agee papers, Harry Ransom Center, University of Texas, Austin.
42. Ibid.
43. For this quotation and for Taylor's letter on the same page: Frank Taylor papers, Lilly Library, Indiana University, Bloomington Indiana.
44. Promotional videotape produced by the Westland School.
45. Chaplin's FBI file.
46. Ibid.
47. Ibid.
48. *New York Times*, January 9, 1949.
49. Ibid., February 14, 1949.
50. Ibid., February 14, 1949.
51. Interview with the author.
52. *The Quiet O*ne, press book, Film Documents, collection of the author.
53. Interview with author.
54. *The Quiet One* press book, collection of the author.
55. "A Conversation with Helen Levitt," *DoubleTake* 28 (Spring 2002), 46.
56. *In the Street* (1948)
57. Videotape provided by San Francisco Film Festival.
58. Farber, *Negative Space*, p. 45–46.
59. Ibid.
60. Ibid.
61. *A Love Story*, unpublished manuscript, University of Tennessee, Knoxville.

CHAPTER 5

1. John Huston, *An Open Book*, (New York: Da Capo Press, 1994), 188.
2. Ibid., p. 153.
3. Agee to Huston, John Huston papers, Academy of Motion Picture Arts and Sciences Library.
4. Ibid.
5. Frank Taylor to Agee, April 26, 1949, Frank Taylor Papers, Lilly Library, University of Indiana.
6. Ibid.
7. Buster Keaton, *My Wonderful World of Slapstick*, (Da Capo Press, 1982), 11.
8. Agee to MacDonald, April 24, 1929, Dwight MacDonald papers, Yale University Library.
9. Ibid.
10. List of proposed *Life* articles, James Agee papers, Harry Ransom Humanities Research Center, The University of Texas at Austin.

11. James Agee, "Comedy's Greatest Era," *Agee on Film*, (reprint from *Life*, September 3, 1949), 393–412.
12. Ibid.
13. Ibid.
14. Ibid.
15. Ibid.
16. Huston to Agee, John Huston papers, Academy of Motion Picture Arts and Sciences Library.
17. Agee to Huston, September 14, 1950, John Huston papers, Academy of Motion Picture Arts and Sciences Library, Beverly Hills, CA.
18. Ibid.
19. Ibid.
20. *Agee: His Life Remembered*, ed. Ross Spears and Jude Cassidy, (New York: Holt Rinehart Winston, 1985), 158.
21. Interview with author.
22. Letter from Agee to Frank E. Taylor, January 30, 1950, Lilly Library, University of Indiana.
23. *Agee: His Life Remembered*, ed. Ross Spears and Jude Cassidy, 157.
24. Letter from Agee to John Huston, June 21, 1950, John Huston papers, Academy of Motion Picture Arts and Sciences Library.
25. Ibid.
26. Ibid.
27. Ibid.
28. John Huston, *An Open Book*, (New York: Da Capo Press, 1994), 17–19.
29. Ibid.
30. Ibid.
31. Ibid.
32. Ibid.
33. James Agee, "Undirectable Director," *Agee on Film*, (New York: Modern Library, 2000, reprint of *Life*, September 9, 1950), 415–427.
34. Ibid.
35. Ibid.
36. Ibid.
37. John Huston to James Agee, September 14, 1950, John Huston papers, Academy of Motion Picture Arts and Sciences Library.
38. Ibid.
39. Agee to Huston, September 13, 1950, John Huston papers, Academy of Motion Picture Arts and Sciences Library.
40. Huston, *An Open Book*, 188.
41. Agee to Huston, September 14, John Huston papers, Academy of Motion Picture Arts and Sciences Library.
42. Agee to Huston, September 19, ibid.
43. Chaplin, *My Autobiography*, (London: Readers Union, 1966), 494.
44. *Letters of James Agee to Father Flye*, Tuesday night, early December,'50, (New York: George Braziller, 1962), 185–186.
45. Lillian Ross, *Moments with Chaplin*, (New York: Dodd, Mead & Company, 1980), 8.
46. John Huston, *An Open Book*, (New York: Da Capo Press, 1994), 136.

47. Salka Viertel, *The Kindness of Strangers*, (New York: Holt, Rinehart & Wilson, 1969), 315–316.
48. Chaplin, *My Autobiography*, p. 471.
49. Ibid.
50. Peter Manso, *Mailer: His Life and Times*, (New York: Penguin Books,1985), 139–140.
51. Ibid.
52. Ibid.
53. Salka Viertel, *The Kindness of Strangers*, 152.
54. Ibid., 107.
55. Florence Homolka, *Focus on Art*, (New York: Ivan Obolensky, 1962), 109.
56. Victor S. Navasky, *Naming Names*, (New York: Hill and Wang, 2003), 169.
57. Lillian Ross, *Picture*, (New York: Da Capo Press, 2002), 157.
58. *Santa Barbara News-Press*, January 9, 1951. Reprinted with permission from the *Santa Barbara News-Press*.
59. Huston, *An Open Book*, 189.
60. Peter Viertel, *Dangerous Friends*, (New York: Nan A. Talese, Doubleday, 1992), 125.
61. *Agee: His Life Remembered*, ed. Ross Spears and Jude Cassidy, 149.
62. Huston, *An Open Book*, 189.
63. Agee to Evans, January 22, 1951, James Agee papers, Harry Ransom Humanities Research Center, The University of Texas at Austin.
64. Peter Viertel, *White Hunter, Black Heart*, (New York: Dell, 1987), 9.
65. Ibid., 10.
66. Peter Viertel, *Dangerous Friends*, 125, 131.
67. Bosley Crowther, *New York Times*, February 21, 1952.
68. Bergreen, *James Agee: A Life*, 355.
69. Peter Viertel, *Dangerous Friends*, 131.
70. Ibid.
71. Agee to his Aunt Mossie, *Agee: His Life Remembered*, ed. Ross Spears and Jude Cassidy, 155.

CHAPTER 6

1. James Agee, "Mr. Lincoln," unpublished screenplay for *Omnibus*, courtesy of the James Agee Trust. Agee quotations that follow are all from this screenplay.
2. Norman Lloyd, *Stages* (New York: Limelight Editions, 1993), 141.
3. James Agee to Ilse Lahn, Agee, June 1, 1951, Archiv der Stiftung Deutsche Kinemathek, Berlin, Germany.
4. Marion Meade, *Dorothy Parker: What Fresh Hell is This?* (New York: Villard Books, 1988), 345–346.
5. Frank E. Taylor, unpublished memoir, courtesy Curtice Taylor.
6. Ibid.
7. Winthrop Sargeant, *In Spite of Myself: a Personal Memoir* (Garden City, New York: Doubleday, 1970), 233.
8. Ibid.
9. James Agee, *Bloodline* treatment, Frank Taylor papers, The Lilly Library, Indiana University, Bloomington, Indiana.

10. Agee to Kohner, Paul Kohner papers, Archiv der Stiftung Deutsche Kine-mathek, Berlin, Germany.

11. Agustin V. Sotto, "The Celluloid Route of 'Genghis Khan,'" *Readings in Philippine Cinema*, ed. Rafael Ma. Guerrero (Manila: Experimental Cinema of the Philippines, 1983), 55–66.

12. Ibid.

13. Ibid.

14. Ibid.

15. *Letters to Father Flye* (New York: George Braziller, 1962) November 23, 1951, 197.

16. Agustin V. Sotto, *Readings in Philippine Cinema*, 55–66.

17. Hanns Eisler, *Composing for the Films* (Freeport, New York: Books for Libraries Press, 1971) 1947, 167.

18. Theodor W. Adorno, "Chaplin Times Two," *The Yale Journal of Criticism*, Spring 1996, Volume 9, Number 1, translated by John MacKay, 58–59.

19. *Agee: His Life Remembered*, ed. Ross Spears and Jude Cassidy, 157.

20. David Robinson, *Chaplin: His Life and Art* (New York: Da Capo Press, 1994), 569.

21. Unpublished comments on *Limelight*, James Agee papers, Harry Ransom Center, University of Texas, Austin.

22. Jeffrey Vance, *Chaplin: Genius of the Cinema* (New York: Henry A. Abrams, 2003), 302.

23. Belinda Rathbone, *Walker Evans: A Biography* (London: Thames and Hudson, 1995), 215.

24. Charles Chaplin Jr. with N. and M. Rau, *My Father, Charlie Chaplin* (New York: Random House, 1960), 341.

25. Chaplin, *My Autobiography*, 500.

26. *Agee: His Life Remembered*, ed. Ross Spears and Jude Cassidy, 159–160.

27. Harry Crocker, unpublished memoir, Harry Crocker papers, Academy of Motion Picture Arts and Sciences Library, Beverly Hills, California.

28. Ibid.

29. *New York Times*, September 23, 1952.

30. *Los Angeles Times*, October 3. 1952.

31. *New York Times*, October 4, 1952.

32. Crocker, unpublished memoir.

33. *Life*, December 22, 1952.

34. Feuchtwanger to Chaplin, August 8, 1952, Lion Feuchtwanger papers, Lion Feuchtwanger Memorial Library, University of Southern California.

35. Feuchtwanger to Oona Chaplin, June 9, 1953, ibid.

CHAPTER 7

1. Judith Malina, *The Diaries of Judith Malina: 1947–1957* (New York: Grove Press, 1984), 280.

2. Agee, "Noa-Noa," *Agee on Film, Volume II* (New York: A Wideview/Perigree Book, 1960) 17–18.

3. Ibid.

4. Whittaker Chambers, *Cold Friday* (New York: Random House, 1964), 271.

5. Agee, *Noa-Noa, Agee on Film Volume Two*, 138–139.

6. Judith Malina, *The Diaries of Judith Malina: 1947–1957* (New York: Grove Press, 1984), 281.
7. Ibid., 289.
8. Charles Chaplin to Lion Feuchtwanger, September 2, 1953, Collection of the Lion Feuchtwanger Memorial Library, University of Southern California.
9. Lion Feuchtwanger to Charles Chaplin, October 20, 1952, ibid.
10. Ibid., 302.
11. Carol Matthau, *Among the Porcupines: A Memoir* (London: Orion Press, 1992) 88–97.
12. David Robinson, *Chaplin: His Life and Art,* (New York: Da Capo, 1994), 275.
13. Charles Chaplin Jr., *My Father,* 308.
14. Chaplin to Agee, December 16, 1953, collection of the Chaplin estate.
15. For whatever reason, it has been widely claimed that Agee was paid $30,000 for his work on *The Night of the Hunter,* more than Laughton himself was paid. These recently discovered payment documents indicate that Agee was in fact paid only $15,000 plus living expenses of $300 per week.
16. Agee to Ilse Lahn, between April 9 and April 16, 1954, Paul Kohner papers, Stiftung Deutsche Kinemathek, Berlin, Germany.
17. Agee to Huston, John Huston papers, Academy of Motion Picture Arts and Sciences Library.
18. Interview with the author.
19. Agustin V. Sotto, "The Celluloid Route of 'Genghis Khan,'" *Readings in Philippine Cinema,* ed. Rafael Ma. Guerrero (Manila: Experimental Cinema of the Philippines, 1983). 55–66.
20. Ibid.
21. Ibid.
22. Ibid.
23. Agee, "Noa-Noa," *Agee on Film, Volume II,* 126.
24. Ibid.
25. *New York Times,* May 17, 1955.
26. Interview with the author.
27. *Letters of James Agee to Father Flye,* Saturday night, January 24, 1955, 221.
28. Helen Gee, *Limelight* (Albuquerque: University of New Mexico Press, 1997), 115–116.

CHAPTER 8

1. *Film Comment 5* (Winter 1969), 33–43.
2. Ibid.
3. Ibid.
4. *New York Times,* September 28, 1952.
5. *A King in New York,* (1957).
6. Ibid.
7. Chaplin, *My Autobiography,* 495.
8. *A King in New York,* (1957).
9. *A Countess From Hong Kong,* (1967).
10. Agee, *A Death in the Family,* (New York: McDowell, Obolensky, 1957), 11.
11. Ibid., 11–14.
12. Ibid., 14–15.

13. T. S. Matthews, *Angels Unawares*, (New York: Ticknor & Fields, 1985), 238.
14. *Agee: His Life Remembered*, ed. Ross Spears and Jude Cassidy. (New York: Holt Rinehart Winston, 1985), 130.
15. Paul Ashdown, "Prophet from Highland Avenue: Agee's Visionary Journalism," *James Agee: Reconsiderations*, ed. Michael A. Lofaro, Tennessee Studies in Literature, Volume 33, (Knoxville: University of Tennessee Press, 1994), 76.
16. *Time*, August 26, 1946, 28.
17. Unpublished notes on *Life* article, James Agee papers, Harry Ransom Center, University of Texas, Austin.

INDEX